Breaking Eighty

HYPERION
NEW YORK

A Journey Through the

Lee Eisenberg

Breaking Eighty

Nine Fairways of Hell

LIBRARY OF CONGRESS CATALOGING-IN-PUBLICATION DATA

Eisenberg, Lee.
    Breaking eighty : a journey through the nine fairways of hell /
    Lee Eisenberg.—1st ed.
        p.   cm.
    Includes bibliographical references (p.   ).
    ISBN 0-7868-6199-1
    1. Golf. 2. Eisenberg, Lee. I. Title.
  GV965.E36   1997
  796.352'02—dc21   96-48379
                CIP

Design by BTD/Robin Bentz

FIRST EDITION

10 9 8 7 6 5 4 3 2 1

To Linda with love,
for everything

Contents

The whole body must turn on the pivot of the head of the right thigh-bone working in the cotyloidal cavity of the os innominatum or pelvic bone, the head, right knee, and right foot remaining fixed with the eyes riveted on the ball. In the upward swing, the vertebral column rotates upon the head of the right femur, the right knee being fixed; and as the club-head nears the ball, the fulcrum is rapidly changed from right to the left hip, the spine now rotating on the left thigh-bone, the left knee being fixed; and the velocity is accelerated by the arms and wrists, in order to add the force of the muscles to the weight of the body, thus gaining the greatest impetus possible.
—**Arnold Haultain,** *The Mystery of Golf,* **1910**

The golfer must be made aware that analyzing what happens in the golf swing and learning the golf swing are two entirely different things.
—**Vivien Saunders,** *The Golfing Mind,* **1988**

Breaking Eighty

Introduction

This book began the way a round of golf begins—with much excitement, good intentions, and aspirations that were, frankly, grandly delusive.

The idea was to devote eighteen months of resolute, back-bending effort to the mastery of golf.

There would be a beginning, which would introduce the old me, a long-suffering hacker who occasionally got lucky and broke 100; a middle, which would feature the emerging me, a golfer moving inexorably from bad to better; and an end, which would star the born-again me, a sweet swinging ace with a relaxed and elegant demeanor.

The main action of the book, as I figured it, would unfold on multiple fronts. The main piece of business would involve my taking a slew of private lessons from a diverse faculty of teaching pros, some of whom would be considered masters in their field, others just guys from down the road. With their help I would elbow my way to the front line of the 24 million American golfers who spend untold billions in their resolute efforts to knock strokes off their sorry scorecards. I would also enroll in whatever golf schools were deemed to be appropriate to the mission. I would surround myself with how-to books, videos, and magazines. I would become a denizen of the driving range, bashing bucket after bucket of balls until my hands were as tough as tack leather. And I would embrace whatever inane and questionable methods seemed like a good idea at the time. Golf is busy with such drills, exercises, and practice routines. If it meant turning the bedroom carpet into a mock putting green, I would move the furniture to do so. If I was inspired to chip golf balls across my yard after dark (Yo, O.J.!), I would straightaway sacrifice my lawn to the havoc of footprints and divots.

While I regarded my plan as a laudable, even heroic, gesture toward radical self-improvement, others reacted to it with varying degrees of skepticism. Some people, notably my mother, were not especially generous of spirit and viewed the project as little more than a transparent attempt to play a lot of golf, as opposed to working a lot of work. As for my golfing friends, they were alternately skeptical, resentful, jealous, and vaguely curious about how it would turn out—though mostly, of course, they not so secretly hoped I would fall on my face. Yet even the most competitive of these buddies had to admit that the idea was pretty alluring. Like no other game, golf drives us, dares us, to seek redemption in the guise of self-improvement. What hacker *wouldn't* want to steal away for eighteen months to repair, once and for all, his game? Mindful of this, I disingenuously tried to convince my pals that there could be something in it for them, too; something for any golfer who has ever tried to gain a better grip on his or her abiding mediocrity. My own journey of discovery, I suggested, would offer benefit to those who (like me) almost never hit a golf ball long and true; who regard even the most commonplace sand bunker as a godless hell pit; who never practice chipping or putting (boring!) even though, as we are told ad nauseam, these shots account for upwards of half the strokes we make in a round. If all went according to plan, I said (pushing my luck and everyone else's tolerance), I just might stumble onto golf's holy grail: a flawless and repeatable golf swing. Having discovered its secret, I'd lead others to it—not so much by providing step-by-step driving directions, but by helping my fellow hackers avoid the detours, wrong turns, and broken bridges of learning that invariably hinder our progress. As the great golf course architect Alister MacKenzie once wrote, "The average golfer would gain more assistance in learning the game . . . from someone who has suffered all the agonies of the dub and had finally conquered his troubles, than from one [who was born] with a natural swing."

Not many of my friends saw it this way, though.

"Where do *you* get off writing a book about how to play golf?" said one guy who had seen me play golf all too often and whose cynicism was thus firmly rooted in reason.

"Hey, this isn't a book about how to play golf," I replied. "This is a book about how to *learn* to play golf, which is different."

He rattled the ice cubes in his glass and looked out at the heavy black clouds gathering over the ocean. We were seated at a bar, having just walked off a seaside golf course, where each of us had shot in the low triple-digits.

I called for another round, then changed the subject.

• • •

Right from the beginning, an obvious question hovered in the air: Assuming I did all that I said I would do—the lessons, the schools, the hacked-to-death lawn—just *how good* could I get?

To be perfectly honest—and I'm embarrassed to admit this now—getting *better* didn't strike me as enough of a goal back then. I wanted to get better-than-better. Not Bobby Jones better-than-better, I wasn't that deluded. Not even club-champion better-than-better. I wanted to get so that I could, at least on occasion, go out and play somewhere between par-golf and bogey-golf.

The goal would be to break eighty, I announced to all associates, friends, and family. Breaking eighty would be the glorious, trumpet-blaring payoff to the narrative. The book would unfold as a kind of Rocky in Polo by Ralph Lauren, the story of how an average, no longer young, but highly motivated hacker manages to knock a dozen brutal strokes from his handicap—without relying on dangerous pills, diets, rigorous exercise, illegal golf clubs, or divine intervention.

Breaking Eighty.

Nice ring, no?

But let me be clear. It's not that I thought the task would be easy. Long before this project occurred to me, I'd done what I could to improve my game—lessons, books, schools, all of it. But nothing ever worked. If anything, my game only got worse with time, the more my brain danced with images left behind by a variety of well-meaning teachers. These years of unrequited striving weren't altogether wasted, however. They raised a lot of questions in my jumbled mind about how we learn and why we frequently don't—and not just how we learn golf, but how we go about trying to master all the other skills adults elect to take up, then typically abandon: playing the piano, foreign languages, tap dancing.

Why is it that we often don't get very far, despite the enthusiasm that marks our early stages? Maybe, I figured back then, it had something to do with how we age, with how our ability to adapt atrophies with time.

Or maybe it had to do with our disposable culture, I reasoned, with how we have grown so accustomed to the idea of the quick fix that we are unable to commit to anything that requires serious time and effort.

Maybe, I reckoned, we Americans are just bad learners—spoiled, impatient, harried, lazy.

On the other hand, though, maybe the teaching was at fault.

Do enough teachers know, or even try, to find ways to break through to us as individuals—or are too many of them content to pass on the conventional wisdom and methods, oblivious to our age, body type, physical conditioning, temperament, coordination?

What makes a good teacher, anyway?

The good ones I remember from my school days, the teachers whose lessons stayed with me, were variously irascible, nurturing, sly, hammy, hilarious. They were characters—colorful, and even a little bit mad. They loved to perform, so much so that I have often thought since that all teachers should be required to take acting courses. They were people who knew when and how to goad and when to step back. They had the instinct, curiosity, and energy, and most amazingly could find the *time* to teach every kid as an individual.

How many golf instructors have you met like that? How many of them are inclined to think hard about what it takes to teach a given person a physical skill as elusive as the golf swing?

One who did was the Silver Scot, Tommy Armour, who believed so much in the need to respect his pupils that he insisted that only new golf balls be used in the lessons he gave—so that his charges might be "subconsciously reminded" that "nothing was too good for the job at hand." Unlike many of his fraternity, Armour ruminated endlessly about lesson plans and procedures. "[Everything] I teach is pointed toward inculcating beneficial habits," he wrote. Armour never allowed students to work with irons and the driver on the same day, out of concern that they clearly understand that irons do their hitting on the downswing, while striking a ball off a tee is accomplished with the clubhead moving upward.

Bookstore shelves sag under the weight of books that purport to teach us to play *winning* golf. These books fall into one of two categories. By far the greater number of them do what golf books have mainly done for 100 years: They presume to tell us how to configure, then precisely set into motion, our various body parts so that we might transform ourselves miraculously from squeaking wheels into smooth-turning and reliably consistent strikers of the ball. They attempt to accomplish this by guiding us through the Classic Golf Swing (that is, a Tour player's or Tour player's teacher's idea of one) in its infinite, warp-speed complexity. They carry out a precise analysis, as they jauntily roll along, of the proper interaction of each of our major and minor muscle groups, joints, and nervous system.

The other kind of golf book, fewer in number but increasingly popular since the 1960s, is the kind that deals with golf as it is played from ear to ear, from the base of the chin to the top of the dome. These head-game books are to golf what Deepak Chopra's meditations are to life: shrewdly affecting inspirationals about how to play through the knots of fear, doubt, and insecurity that produce the physical tension that wrecks our swings. While these books never quite come out and ridicule us for it, they assume—with good reason—that when we step onto the course we collapse into emotional nut cases, terrified of failure, supremely unconfident. These books care less about whether we properly shift our weight than whether we maintain the optimum balance between the left side of our brain and the right. They urge us to chill out and take things nice 'n' easy. The most popular recent example of this genre, Dr. Bob Rotella's *Golf Is Not a Game of Perfect*, preaches a sermon of acceptance: *Hit the shot you know you can hit, not the shot Arnold Palmer would hit, nor even the shot you think you ought to be able to hit.*

Advice such as this, while reasonable and soothing, offers meager practical reward. It certainly won't transform a plow horse who shoots in the hundreds into a thoroughbred who breaks four-score. No, a change such as that calls for much, much stronger medicine. Electroshock therapy? A frontal lobotomy? Prozac through an IV?

Rotella and company will figure prominently in the saga that follows. This golf book is built in large measure on theirs, for they have helped to persuade us, as our own performance hardly ever does, that weekend hackers can soar with the eagles; that the holy grail is indeed somewhere out there; that it *is* possible to induce our legs, torso, hands, arms, and shoulders to make music like the Cleveland Symphony.

But *Breaking Eighty* was meant to be different. How could it not be? Those books are by world-renowned players and teachers possessed of a magic that most of us can only dream of, sorcerers who can put some chew on it, who can make a golf ball curve and spin to a screeching stop, at will. This book is by somebody who has spent a lifetime fitfully trying to master just a touch of any of those skills.

Those books are all from the teacher's point of view. This one is from the learner's.

Ambition

I see no reason, truly, why the average golfer, if he goes about it intelligently, shouldn't play in the 70s. . . .
—**Ben Hogan,** *Five Lessons: The Modern Fundamentals of Golf,* 1957

DEEP IN THE SHED

Golf is a game that stirs the spirit and stokes the fires of the heart. So it would be sweet if this story could begin on a dewy morning, when the azaleas are in bloom and the earth is enveloped in the perfume of freshly mowed grass.

But it doesn't. It begins instead on a crappy, blustery afternoon in midwinter, when the ground is semifrozen and crunches under foot, when the Bermuda grass is dormant, the color of buff.

It's a shame, it really is, that this story's curtain doesn't rise to reveal seaside links at dusk. Or the flagstone verandah of a leafy country club, where rich men with florid faces and slender women with tanned legs sip Mount Gay-and-tonic and chat about each other's scandals, or worse, the putts they missed that afternoon.

But this tale doesn't begin in Cheever country or anywhere close to it. It begins in East Tennessee, in a cavernous, soulless metal shed, a building that had once been used to store tractors and other earth-movers. The shed sits on the edge of a public golf course, a more or less natural place, but on this freezing day, no chorus of songbirds fills the air, there is no busy buzzing of bees. Inside the shed the only sound, the *only* sound, is the roar of a torpedo-shaped kerosene heater, the kind of blaster you see parked along the sidelines at Green Bay Packer games.

The shed, grim and foreboding, is something out of Fleming or LeCarré. It smacks of forces dark and unknowable, where half-mad men pursue experiments of emotional inquisition and physical manip-ulation; and, indeed, such practices will prove to be central to the saga that begins on this cold-assed day.

The shed is of no discernible hue. Like the sleeping grass that sur-rounds it, it's kind of buff-colored. It is devoid of even the slightest architectural or cosmetic nicety. This joint means business. Once you're inside there is nowhere to hide, not even in the bathroom. There is no bathroom.

The shed holds little by way of amenities or furnishings: a few mis-matched chairs, a television set, a VCR, and a couple of video cameras set up on tripods. Scattered across the concrete floor are remnants of old carpeting. The shed's long back wall is draped with nylon netting.

And, oh yes, there's a man in the shed, short, graying, bookish. That man is me. To judge from my cotton golf slacks, white Foot Joys, turtleneck, wool sweater knitted in the Hebrides, and a new, skin-soft, white leather golf glove on my left hand, you might think I was a seasoned artist at this pastime. The sorry truth is, I'm about to take my first golf swings in about a year. I am apprehensive, disoriented. The shed has unsettled me. There's something cruel and banal about it—a place outfitted for the purpose of taking and holding hostages. Apparently, I am merely but the latest in a long line of these.

The shed is bizarre. The fluorescent lighting makes everything look bluish. I take it all in with wary eyes.

This is Day One.

To be fussy about it, the saga at hand doesn't start in the shed at all. It starts in a garage. It was the garage in the house I grew up in, and it was there that my father, who died too young, left his golf clubs behind.

My father was a scientist, a professor at a medical school. He was brilliant, funny, caustic, domineering. He was not physically imposing: about five-foot-six, and rather portly. He wore steel-rimmed glasses and chain-smoked Benson & Hedges. Athletic he was not. When we played catch he threw stiffly. He made little attempt to move sharply in any direction to snare my wild throws. Unlike some dads in the neighborhood, he was never one to reminisce about a bygone exploit, some indelible season in the sun, an eighty-yard run. He carried with him no real or imagined glories of this sort.

My father was sedentary. He lived the life of the mind. He never set aside a bowling night for himself, or a standing golf date with the guys. About the only thing sporting he ever did was to fish, and here his best and most reliable companion was me. We didn't do anything fancy, no fly fishing, no boats. We were content to amble out onto a decrepit pier at the Jersey shore. With live minnows or frozen squid at the end of our lines, we leaned over a splintered railing and angled for rock bass, bluefish, flounder ("doormats," as my father called them). My father dragged deeply on a Benson & Hedges, reflecting silently on God-knows-what, smiling approvingly whenever I hauled something in, however trashy it might have been, a blowfish or a sea robin.

I was a puppy at my father's heels. I walked like him (feet turned out), cracked jokes like him, even dressed like him. On weekends we both wore plain white T-shirts with left-side breast pockets (where he kept his box of smokes and I my Pez dispenser). We wore "hobby jeans," baggy, cotton-wash pants with elasticized waistbands.

My father died of a heart attack in 1959. He was forty-seven. I was thirteen.

It was a little while before my mother could bring herself to get rid of my father's clothes. Then one day I noticed that his suits and shirts and shoes had been removed from my parents' bedroom. A few of my father's things—his Longines-Wittnauer watch, wedding band, high-school ring, Phi Beta Kappa key—were passed on to me. My mother kept them in a secure place until I was old enough to take reliable possession of them. Ever since then they have resided in numerous safe-deposit boxes that have come and gone with my wanderings as a grown-up.

My father's golf clubs, however, remained untouched. They were neither formally bequeathed to his surviving son nor consigned to the Goodwill dumpster. They were simply abandoned, right where my father had last propped them up in a shadowy corner of the garage. My mother didn't choose to retain them for any sentimental purpose, certainly not as a memorial, the way Tom Carvel's golf bag remains enshrined in a glass case in a pro shop ninety miles north of New York City. Carvel was the man who invented the machine that dispenses soft ice cream. He was also a fanatic golfer. His widow decreed that in honor of his memory Carvel's clubs were to be placed on permanent exhibition.

My father's golf clubs were not so consecrated. Their existence was simply and understandably overlooked. The clubs had zero meaning or significance; they were entirely incidental to my father's life. I have no recollection of his ever swinging them on our little lawn, let alone toting them off to a course. He never walked around the house with a wedge in his hand, checking his grip in the mirror. He never grooved his putting stroke across the living-room Bigelow.

That my father even owned a set of clubs is a mystery to me. A reasonable guess is that, toying once with the idea of taking up the game, he must have gone out and bought himself a bag and some used clubs that, while battered and obviously well pounded by a previous hacker, were more than serviceable enough for his needs. He then permanently stashed—had he learned something I wouldn't about our mutual golfing genes?—the bag in the corner of the garage, where it stood year after year, gathering dust and offering itself up as nothing more useful than a dark, cozy sanctuary for spiders.

The look, feel, and fragrance of that golf bag remain with me to this day. It was a golf bag for the ages, pre-Naugahyde, pre-polyester, con-structed of sturdy canvas and trimmed with leather. It was of its time, redolent of Abercrombie and Fitch. You could imagine Gene Kelly slinging such a bag across his square shoulders and strolling out for a late-afternoon nine at Riviera. My father's monogram, GME, was sten-ciled on the side of the bag, which contained a smattering of un-matched irons and a couple of persimmon woods. Some of the clubs, including the putter, had hickory shafts, so they probably dated from the thirties. Several of the irons carried the signature of Bobby Jones, an extremely popular trademark of that era. Jones's name was etched on the back of the blades in a script that was both precise and boyish. My father's putter was a reproduction of Jones's famed Calamity Jane, the magic wand with which the great player dominated competitive golf in the 1920s.

In the first years after my father's death, I occasionally hauled the canvas bag out onto the driveway, lifted out the spoon or the brassie, and made a few wild swings. I gripped and swung the club as if it were a baseball bat—and in so doing probably made a fuller, more natural turn than at any time since. As far as my golfing ambitions were concerned, that was about it. Never did I daydream about coming from behind to win the British Open, or whipping the young Jack Nicklaus with a birdie putt on the first hole of sudden death. My fantasy life was already too crowded with ninth-inning grand slams off Don Newcombe, diving catches of bullets thrown by Norm Van Brocklin, behind-the-back passes to Paul Arazin. Golf was of a place far removed from the neighborhood of row houses where I grew up. The contests we engaged in—touch football and an endless variety of stickball games—took place on concrete and asphalt. Golf was exotic, a game from another planet. Thanks to the sports page I was aware of names such as Jones, Snead, and Nelson, though I had no idea about what made them masters of their craft. Unlike boys who grow up around golf and gain an early and lasting proficiency at it, I never caddied. I never emulated the swing of a local hero. I knew nothing from country clubs.

HOGAN AS HERO

A desk, old and scarred, is jammed up against one of the walls of the shed. It is piled with books about golf. Around it are photographs of famous golfers with their glorious swings, seamless and loose-jointed. Ben Hogan is on prominent display, and his name is emblazoned on a number of golf bags that are lying about the shed.

Hogan's presence here is fitting. He was the first of many who had the temerity to think they could teach me to play golf.

At the not so tender age of fifteen, on a dog-day afternoon in August, I set foot on a golf course for the first time. I'd shlepped my father's clubs to a municipal course several miles from my house. I was one-quarter of a motley foursome made up of scruffy friends from the neighborhood, boys with whom I by now sneaked beers, listened to doo-wop, and exchanged lies about the girls we said we'd had.

What I remember mainly about my first day on the links is dust. The fairways were a sorry quilt of dirt patches, crabgrass, and clover. The greens looked as if some ferocious god of golf had chewed on them, then spit them out. Tee boxes consisted of rubber mats flung willy-nilly on the scorched earth. The balls we used were cracked, all smiles. We each shot in the low 200s, despite the fact that we cheated like crazy—partly because we didn't know many of the rules, and partly because we had never experienced a game in which breaking the rules was so inviting. We kicked and tossed our balls out of bunkers and out from behind trees. We regarded whiffs as precisely what they were: nothing. We teed up on the fairways. We flat-out lied about our stroke count.

This golf outing was fun for a while, but it soon turned into a bummer. We returned home parched, covered in a brown film, with hot and blistered feet. None of us expressed the slightest desire to do it ever again. Dragging our old, beat-up bags back to our garages, we reached a unanimous consensus that golf was a pain in the ass.

But since when has that enduring truth ever gotten in the way of golf's appeal? In no time I was out hacking again.

Like a weed, a fungus, a tumor, a neurosis, a liking for golf simply took root. One day it wasn't there at all, the next day it had spread like kudzu.

I relished—who doesn't?—the crisp click the ball made, that rarest of clicks, on those occasions when I got lucky and really lit into one. I craved the smell of grass, what little there was, at our local shitheel course. I enjoyed just putting my hands on the clubs, those strange weapons that were so defiantly difficult to use.

It wasn't long before I wanted to play again and again. And I wanted to get better, *fast*—which is how I came to take the first wrong turn of many on the cart path to damnation: I picked up a book. My initial golf lesson occurred not on a grassy practice tee but at a long oak table at the local branch of the public library. It was there that I began to try to find straightforward answers to what I thought was a simple question: What do you have to do to make a golf ball fly long and straight? There had to be a trick. What was it?

I'd already learned one thing from my sorry performances at Dogpatch National: You couldn't just walk up to the ball and whack it. You couldn't just hold the club in both fists and cut loose, the way you could bang out hits on the sandlot. It wasn't enough just to do what felt most comfortable, most natural, most right. There was some secret to uncover, a veil to lift, a knot to unravel. Why else would the goddamn ball squirt off in so many different directions, and almost *never* fly long and straight the way you wanted it to?

Ben Hogan's *The Modern Fundamentals of Golf* was first published in the spring of 1957, as a five-part series in *Sports Illustrated*. The magazine grandly staged these pieces as "a revolution in teaching." I was only ten at the time, but I remember how captivated I was by those pages. Not that I stopped to pay much attention to the text, for as I said, golf was nowhere on my radar at that point; all I cared about were the Big Four—baseball, football, basketball, and hockey. What caught my attention, rather, were the drawings that accompanied Hogan's lessons. From its inception in the fifties, *Sports Illustrated* complemented its terrific color photography with illustrations of athletes in action, rendered mostly in black-and-white. The best-known artist of this era was Robert Rieger, whose depictions of Unitas, Mays, and Chamberlain are still fixed vividly in my memory.

The drawings for the Hogan series were by another of *SI*'s stalwarts, Anthony Ravielli, whose pen-and-ink drawings had the quality of etchings. In this case, they brilliantly conveyed the physical strengths that made Hogan such a powerful and compelling athlete: his strong hands wrapped gently on the grip, the muscular forearms, the steely concentration in his eyes. Ravielli's Hogan had an apparitional quality. Part of the golfer was rendered with precise shadings of black ink, part of him simply faded to white. He was earthly and he wasn't. He was a man, he was a ghost. He was real, he was godly.

Three drawings in particular stood out—they endure in the mind of every golfer who ever turned to them for guidance.

There is the one showing Hogan at address, his driver poised just behind the ball. Hogan's body is encased in a huge sheet of glass. His head (he's wearing the signature cap) sticks out from a circular hole in the glass. The drawing is meant to convey that anything other than a proper inside-out swing plane will cause the plate to shatter (and with it the golfer's heart).

There is the one—a frontal view of Hogan's torso and head—that depicts his forearms wrapped in heavy rubber bands. The caption here admonishes us to keep our elbows and arms as close together as possible through the entire swing. I still get tense thinking about that instruction.

And then there is the one showing Hogan at the very top of his backswing. His shoulders and back are turned *well* past ninety degrees of his target, a feat that in no way has prevented his left arm from being almost perfectly straight. His hips, which have turned some but not a lot, seem relaxed and loose. His knees remain gently flexed. And his feet are solidly affixed to the ground, as if gripping the turf with five-inch spikes protruding from the bottom of his golf shoes. Here is golf's answer to Michelangelo's David, an awesome conjunction of suppleness and strength.

Not long after *Sports Illustrated* published Hogan's articles, they appeared again in book form, in an appealingly designed edition that included Ravielli's portfolio. This was the book that practically leaped into my hands that day at the local library. The manual's brevity and Ravielli's illustrations made it irresistible. Thumbing through it, I was seduced by Ben Hogan's implicit assurances that golf was a fairly simple, teachable, and learnable game. He came right out and said as much, right at the beginning: To play good golf all you had to do was master a handful of fundamentals. The golf swing could be imparted in just four concise lessons: "the grip," "stance and posture," "the first part of the swing," and "the second part of the swing." For an eager beaver like me, who didn't have the patience to read the instructions before mangling the assembly of a model airplane, Hogan's *Modern Fundamentals* was more intoxicating than a deep whiff of Duco Cement.

Hunched over the library table, I stared for an eternity at Ravielli's drawings. Unsated, I took the book home and read it over and over again. Hogan's text (ghosted by Herbert Warren Wind) was a revelation. To play decently, he said from his tee-box on the mount, a golfer had to build a swing that is "CORRECT, POWERFUL, REPEATING." Hogan, while gruff-sounding, nonetheless came across as a stand-up guy. To save a lot of time and trouble, he declared, he had already done the dirty work for us. In a long, meandering, par-five of a sentence, Hogan laid it right on the line:

> What I have learned I have learned by laborious trial and error, watching a good player do something that looked right to me, stumbling across something that felt right to me, experimenting with that something to see if it helped or hindered, adopting it if it helped, refining it sometimes, discarding it if it didn't help, sometimes discarding it later if it proved undependable in competition, experimenting continually with new ideas and old ideas and all manner of variations until I arrived at a set of fundamentals that appeared to me to be right. . . .

I probably should have quit right there, right there at that sentence. Even a kid should have been smart enough to pick up on the inconsistencies and contradictions buried in those words, the pain and suffering concealed therein.

If all we tyros needed to get a grip on the game was a handful of fundamentals, then how come his niblicks had to give over so much time to "laborious trial and error," to watching and stumbling, to refining and discarding?

Might it be because golf was just a tad more difficult than Ben made out?

Hogan stonewalled here. He no more gave on this issue than he would sway his hips on the backswing.

"Up to a considerable point, as I see it, there's nothing difficult about golf, nothing," he said (just a page or two after he has told us how hard *he* had to work to figure it out).

So golf is teachable, and learnable, is that the deal?

I can imagine Ben nodding at this. I can hear him grunting through those small, even choppers of his. I can imagine him saying *yes* in a hoarse whisper, then dragging deeply on one of his beloved cigarettes as we walk side by side down a verdant fairway, just him and me, a grizzled goat and an attentive greenhorn. Then he offers me a smoke of my own, without the slightest warning of its consequences. And I take it. All of a sudden, I feel dizzy. I am hooked for life. Ben flashes a grin with his sharp grinders.

The heater blasts away. The shed sounds like a ship's engine room, not a golf academy. I'm getting restless and annoyed, waiting for Brad Redding.

I know next to nothing about the man. But it's obvious he's the lord and master of this place. A giant banner that hangs the length of one wall announces: BRAD REDDING GOLF INSTRUC-TION. The banner also features the image Redding has selected as his professional logo: a line drawing of a nineteenth-century golfer lifted from a vintage book of instruction. Nice, literate touch,

I think. That Redding chose the little guy gives me reason to hope that a productive relationship of teacher and learner might be in the cards.

Suddenly the metal door clangs open, and in he walks. Redding has on a spiffy new golf cap with HOGAN embroidered across the front. He looks a little like Jerry Seinfeld; he's in his early thirties and physically unremarkable. He's neither short nor tall, but wiry as befits his calling, with a narrow, friendly face. Born and raised here in Knoxville, he is unadulterated white bread. If you didn't know he was a golf instructor you'd probably think from his appearance that he was a junior VP at a bank, or a branch manager at Kinko's. But more likely you'd guess he was a golf instructor.

Redding is a semicelebrity in these parts, having been named several times the state's golf teacher of the year. And while this certainly doesn't put him in a class with Penick, Leadbetter, or Harmon, it does make him the best-known instructor in East Tennessee.

I first heard about Redding from a local oral surgeon, bombastic and golf-crazed, the kind of man who isn't content to hold court just on canker sores and gum recession, but on you-name-it: Alsatian wines, selling short, how to hit low draws into the wind. Now and then I ran into him at parties, and he was nice enough to ask me to join him at his club for a round of golf. I always declined, mostly because I'd grown so unsure about my game and didn't want to be humiliated by this character who—is there no justice?—plays to a single digit.

"Haven't touched a club in a couple of years," I told him. "I really need to take a few lessons."

"Well, listen. Around here you have exactly three choices," he replied, setting down his Chardonnay and clearing his throat. "Brad Redding. Brad Redding. And Brad Redding." The dentist then talked a blue streak about how Redding had fixed a nagging hook he'd developed with his Big Bertha War Bird. Although I zoned out, Redding's name lodged in my head.

But I didn't pick up the phone, not for a year or so. Then, toward the end of 1994, my wife Linda and I and a group of friends made plans for a late-winter vacation in Barbados. We'd booked a house there that happened to sit on the fairway of a golf course. So as not to ruin entirely this tropical sojourn with my usual rotten play, I called Redding and booked a couple of sessions—which is how and why I find myself in the cold, cold shed, this place that looks like a golf school in Chechnya, this place of dreams, dread, and lies.

MY SO-CALLED LIFE IN GOLF

Right off the bat Redding sits you down and asks in a soft voice what the story is. He doesn't ask to see your swing, not just yet; he merely wants to establish a rapport. This face time is meant to relax the student, and no doubt to give Redding some preliminary fix on whatever psychological and physical conditions may be afflicting the pitiable duffer who sits before him. The introductory phase also provides students a chance to throw around some clichés—"over the top," "my shots are mostly too fat," "everything leaks right"—phrases that are meant to signal that even though they can't walk the walk, they can at least talk the talk.

I recount for Redding my own sordid relationship with the game. I tell him about how I tried golf out when I was a teenager, going so far as to read a golf book now and then but never taking lessons or playing with any regularity. After that, I told him, I gave the game up for— what?—some twenty-five years.

But in the early eighties, along with a couple of friends (also returning from decades of voluntary exile), I concluded that the time was ripe for a comeback. Together we reintroduced ourselves to golf with the equanimity of hyperactive brats. For the next five years the game obsessed us. New Yorkers all, we had no convenient place to practice, and none of us belonged to a club. So we flew off for long weekends to places like Pinehurst, Grand Cypress, or the Boulders, where we played golf in unquenchable, frenetic bursts. We were, to borrow writer David Owen's insightful phrase, "Golf-Dependent Personalities," crazies who "go to bed early, play thirty-six holes a day, and lose sleep worrying about frost delays." Upon arriving at one of these Valhallas we asked the bellhop to take our suitcases to our rooms while we headed straight to the practice tee. There we pounded range balls until our hands were hamburger. Then we hacked, flailed, skulled, gouged our way across the premier fairways of America. After a few years of such violent marauding we were mostly shooting in the high nineties and low hundreds, not counting mulligans and other charitable scoring arrangements adopted by unanimous consent (though sometimes we just cheated the old-fashioned way, that is, when none of the others was looking). As a typical weekend wore on, our mood swings corresponded to the number of strokes on our scorecards. One of us, invariably me, would frequently break down and seek a lesson from whichever Tom, Scott, Nick, or Andy happened to be available. None of these golf professionals ever suggested that an impromptu session with a stranger I'd never see again was, in fact, a major waste of money and time. Nor did any point out that these lessons might even be *dangerous*—each added yet another arbitrary voice to that most loathsome of all choruses, the choir that wails in our ears whenever we walk onto a tee box, or contemplate a sand shot, or stand over a routine putt. The guys in this chorus, call it the PGA Tabernacle, sing a hundred different lyrics simultaneously, consisting of fragments of lessons, random bits of conventional wisdom, adages, axioms, whatever. The voices grow louder and louder, even as our hands take hold of the club and proceed through the swing.

Having established sufficient rapport, at least for the moment, Redding stands up and switches on a computer that's hooked up to a television monitor and a couple of video cameras. He tells me to take my five-iron and stand on a swatch of Astro Turf. One of the video cameras is directly behind me, the other faces me as I address the ball, taking the so-called "caddie view." Redding now says earnestly, "What we are going to do from here on out is work on the *cause* of your problems, not on the results of them."

It isn't exactly, "Now vee may perhaps to begin. Yes?" but it's a start.

LIVING THE NOW

There are certain secrets I choose not to share with Redding, not on this first day, and probably not ever.

For instance, there exists in my deeper past a single, glorious round of golf, a remarkable eighty-three that I shot nearly a decade ago. The reason I keep it to myself is because while I know it really happened, I'm all too aware that it doesn't count for much. It was just a one-time thing, a delirious blip. This triumph occurred on Sunday, June 8, 1986, at a pleasant, if hilly, nine-hole course in Worthington, Massachusetts, a small town in the central Berkshires. (The eighty-three was indeed for *twice* around the course, not once, a score marred only ever so slightly by a mulligan taken on the first nine, in accord with the established policy of our foursome that day.)

The round took place the morning after Linda and I were married, which is why, in the annals of my golfing life, it is remembered simply as the Wedding Round. The Wedding Round was played on a gray and sultry morning, when the mountains were shrouded in mist and so, I suppose, was my head. The warm-up event of the weekend, that is, the wedding itself, was held late Saturday afternoon at the home of Dan and Becky Okrent (whose idea it was, by the way, to rent the fairway villa in Barbados)—just a handful of friends in a comfortable house for the weekend. The ceremony was charming and brief, and followed by several rounds of champagne, a spectacular dinner served up by Becky, then by a vast amount of additional drinking and dancing.

Early the next morning the men in the wedding party—felicitous, how the guest list had worked itself out to be a tidy foursome of male golfers—drove over to the Worthington town course. There, the Wedding Round just kind of plopped out of me. That it happened on *this* weekend, just hours after my marriage, may simply have been a matter of coincidence. Or, it might well have been a result of how happy and relaxed I felt in the afterglow of the event. Or, not to be crass or unromantic, it could just as well have been due to the post–alcoholic fog I was in, whereby my gin-soaked cognitive synapses were temporarily on the fritz. Or none of the above. Or all of the above. Who knows? A round of golf, like marriage itself, does not lend itself to definitive deconstruction.

The point is, I don't reveal any of this to Redding.

Nor do I share any speculation as to the reasons I am *really* here, what I might be secretly seeking in this shed. For it has occurred to me that this quest to self-improve might just be the sort of grand, if dumb, impulse that visits a man in his forties, like climbing Everest, or sailing solo across the Atlantic, only vastly, *infinitely* less scary and demanding. In other words, it may be a Gail Sheehy–type thing, an attempt to affirm my vigor, potency, and manhood as the shadow of the Big 5-0 looms closer and closer. It may be a game of beat-the-clock, in which I might be able to delude myself into thinking that I can stave off ever-slackening muscles, creakier joints, hips, and shoulders that grow harder to turn, and at the same time reconstitute myself into a paragon of physical grace. For it is precisely at the age I find myself, according to Sheehy, that we begin to perceive that our bodies, careers, sex lives, wealth, and athletic abilities are (or were) about as good as they are going to get. It is now, they say, that we start to hear voices: "Time is running out. Time must be beaten. Can I accomplish all that I'd hoped before it's too late?"

Others are less charitable about this passage, this obsession with living the now. The late historian Christopher Lasch viewed all such palaver as rampant "immortalism" awash in a culture of pervasive narcissism. He ridiculed Sheehy and her ilk for their persistence in urging us fledgling graybeards to "defeat the entropy that says slow down, give it up, watch TV, and to open up another pathway that can enliven all the senses, including the sense that one is not just an old dog."

But, as I say, I don't choose to bring any of this up in the shed.

ME CHEETAH, YOU COREY PAVIN

Redding tells me to take my customary stance and hit a half-dozen balls into the net. Two cameras rolling, he captures these swings on videotape. It is hard for me to know with much certainty how well or badly I hit these balls—they just clunk into the net. Redding then motions me to a chair in front of the TV, where, using a slow-motion replay, he analyzes my performance.

As many hackers know, video is now routinely employed in golf instruction. Video came into vogue a decade or more ago, and since then cameras have pitilessly revealed millions of ill-begotten golf swings. Rare is the golf-school package that doesn't include a tape to take home and play repeatedly in the family room, a form of home entertainment that can drive even the most loyal wife into the arms of the UPS man. Before this day in the shed, I myself have been video-taped on at least six different occasions, my swing micro-analyzed by specialists from Monterey to Palm Beach Gardens. I have by now spent thousands of dollars to obtain these cassettes, and all I've got to show for it is the ultimate golf video library from hell. It isn't that they haven't shown me anything. Sadly, the recordings have enabled me to perceive, through terror-stricken eyes, the adverse physics, the plundered laws of motion and velocity that are the root causes of my lousy shots.

These transgressions are once again plainly apparent the instant Brad Redding punches the Play button on his VCR.

As I watch the screen I observe that I have taken my accustomed, tortured stance over the ball. My shoulders are scrunched up tightly. My head hangs deep down into my chest. Physiologists tell us that the neck is where the body's tension tends to gather, which is vividly illustrated by what I see on this monitor. My neck has entirely contracted; it is missing from my body. My skull appears to be directly attached to my shoulders. Also, my knees are tightly locked. My forearms are turned inward. I choke the iron's Golf Pride grip as if to squeeze juice from it.

From toes to golf cap, the look is classic simian, as my friend Okrent likes to point out whenever we're on a golf course together. Frozen and framed on Redding's video screen, I see myself as Okrent sees me. I stand here tensely, loathe to set this collection of old bones into motion. For many seconds, I stand here, staring blankly at the yellow range ball at my feet. The inside of my head, though, is anything but still. A thousand ideas ricochet around my gray matter. They form a duffer's epic *haiku*:

> *Keep your head down,*
> *Right elbow tucked in,*
> *As if holding a towel under there.*
> *Left arm stiff—*
> *Well, not stiff stiff,*
> *But stiff enough.*
> *Weight shift is everything—*

And so is shoulder turn.
Don't sway.
It's about tempo, tempo is everything.
Tempo is key.
Tempo is God.
Tempo is your mantra.
Say it as you swing.
Tem . . . po. Tem . . . po. Tem . . . po.

These snippets are remnants of tips gleaned from magazines and books, wisdom imparted by an army of teachers. They race through my consciousness with much the same sound a modem makes when it is connecting to a distant server: *Ccccchhhhhhhhh* . . . The infernal static grows even louder as I finally begin my backswing.

Remember, follow through.
Turn!
Back to the target at the top,
Belt buckle to the flag at finish.
Grasp the club with no greater pressure than if
you were holding a live bird.
(Whatever the hell that feels like as I have
never held one, thank God.)
Don't lunge!
Swing through *the ball, not at it.*
Golf is not a hit game, it's a swing game.
Let the clubhead do the work.
Visualize where you want the ball to go.
Relax!
Relax your hands!
Relax your shoulders.
Relax, you dick!
You're strangling the bird!

With these words shooting through my being like a hail of bullets, I let loose the overwound, Gouge-O-Matic machine that has for so long passed for my golfing self.

Let's go to the videotape for a closer look:

No-neck, dwarfish, danger-sensing primate in golf togs yanks the club severely skyward, far too vertically to achieve a proper path. He then takes it back further with a scant turn of the body. At the top of this sad phase of the performance there flashes an unconscious warning in the creature's brain, obviously not visible on the videotape but plain to any practiced observer: a tiny residue of athletic instinct buried God-knows-where tells the anthropoid that if he wants to strike ball *at all* he must—*in the next instant!*—execute a drastic, midswing adjustment, even though the club is hurtling on a crash course toward the object of its boundless fury.

The videotape is very revealing here. It clearly shows how I transmit an urgent order to my hands, which dutifully obey by redirecting the clubhead along a dreaded outside-in route to the pellet, which just sits there oblivious to the confusion high above, content on its spongy bed of Astro Turf. My arms are by now on a suicide mission. At point of contact, and in spite of the forgiving soft artificial surface, my tightly gripped hands clearly register the sorry result of the pathetic swing. On a golf course this action would result in a thick, deep slash in the earth, a scar that betrays the extreme right-to-left direction of a wayward clubhead. The shot would swoop sickeningly to the left or right, or just dribble feebly along the ground, a pathetic worm burner. It would be followed by a medley of primitive expletives.

Redding runs this horrendous swing back and forth a few times in mortifying slow motion. He then picks up a felt-tipped marker and proceeds to the Winky Dink phase of the analysis.

Over a frozen frame showing my initial "takeaway," Redding traces the angle of my club shaft to get me to envision the ideal swing plane along which one's club shaft should travel up and down. Anyone who's had any golf instruction knows what I'm talking about. Good players swing *along* this plane as if their bodies were encased in a large barrel; or, as the Hogan book illustrates, as if in a sheet of glass. Good players start and finish their swings without ever breaking the barrel, or shattering the glass. I *would* shatter the glass. The videotape reveals that I'd pulverize it, chopping down and through it as if my intention is to tee off and loot an appliance store at the same time.

"So, tell me." I say to Redding at the end of this first session. "Let's assume that I really, *really* applied myself and worked hard at this. Let's say I took lessons once or twice a week and hit a ton of balls in between. Is it possible that I could, eventually, break eighty?"

"Absolutely," he replies, rather too promptly.

"Within a year? Maybe sooner?"

"Oh, sooner," he says. "Maybe six months. Maybe a little longer, it depends. But can you, *will* you, do it? Absolutely."

We walk out to my car. "You know," Redding says, as I load my clubs into the trunk, "Hogan writes in his book that just about *anyone* can learn to shoot in the seventies, that golf really isn't all that hard. We just make it hard."

"I read that book about a million years ago," I tell him. "It was the first golf book I ever studied. I liked the stuff about the sheet of glass, and the rubber bands stretched across the forearms, and the drawing that showed where the calluses ought to form on your hands."

"Yeah, those drawings are great," Redding agrees. "But you can take some of the stuff he says a little too far. Remember, just because something worked for Hogan doesn't mean it's going to work for you."

"And why not?" I ask.

There's a long pause.

Then Redding says, "For one thing, you may not have the same size fingers."

Impatience

As long as a man doesn't take a death grip and lurch off balance, it's not bad practice for him to haul back and swing with most of what he has. . . .

—**Sam Snead,** *The Education of a Golfer,* **1961**

MR. CHIPS

Brad Redding presents himself as a pretty confident guy. Like most teaching pros, he's got that certain swagger, a cool, a cultivated cockiness. But unlike most of them, he doesn't numb you with a lot of clichés. Quite the contrary. Redding is exceedingly careful about the words and images he uses to convey the mechanics of the golf swing. He cautions you over and over that what a swing feels like to him is not at all what it feels like to you. He is a teacher who insists that his students struggle to find their own way of describing what it is they ought to be doing, what things feel like when they "feel right."

With Barbados drawing closer, I book a couple of more lessons with him. I want big-time results and I want them to arrive on schedule. I want to Jiffy Lube my golf muscles so that I might amaze my golfing pals with a newfound dexterity. The thought is exhilarating. I feel the stirring of the addiction I'd thought I'd kicked. The Fever is on the rise, that coursing, pulsing, superheated lava flow of lust, fear, and intense pleasure that overwhelms me whenever I get near a golf course. It enflames the mind and constricts the muscles. It's what a thirteen-year-old feels in his loins. In a grown-up golfer it's everywhere: hands, arms, neck, back, shoulders, legs.

"Look at the screen. Look at your shoulders and neck," Redding says. We're at lesson two. Redding and I are again on the mat in the shed, the bazooka heater blasting away.

"Relax the muscles in your shoulders. Lift up your chin and stretch your neck out. Look, look over there."

He points to a poster on the wall: Johnny Miller, circa mid-seventies. To be honest, I *think* it's Johnny Miller, though it could easily be some other rubber-jointed, sun-bleached Adonis of the fairway. Whoever he is, tan and tall and blond and lanky, he is poised, relaxed, and athletic at his address position. He bends at the hips, his knees are flexed, his spine and neck are as straight as a broomstick.

Redding tells me to lean out, *way* out, over the balls of my feet. This isn't any fun. I feel as if I am about to topple forward, drive my nose into the Astro Turf.

"You won't fall, I promise you," Redding says.

He tells me to stick out my butt. I feel like a ski-jumper having a bad hemorrhoid day. There's an uncomfortable burning in my too-tight hamstrings. There's an ache in the small of my back. But Redding isn't satisfied. He taps the backs of my knees and tells me to flex even more. Then he takes me by the hips and pulls my buttocks yet higher into the air.

I no longer feel like a ski-jumper with hemorrhoids. Now I feel like a pug in heat.

Redding orders me to take a good look at myself on the video monitor.

Must I?

"Now, fix that image in your mind," he tells me.

MUST I?

"We are going to work on this until it becomes second nature to you. Chin out, head up, back straight, bend at the hips, knees flexed, weight on the balls of your feet. Now, take a couple of swings."

He's got to be kidding.

HOLD IT RIGHT HERE

Redding now goes to work on my grip. Gripwise, I am a disaster. It turns out I have always held the club too much in the *palm* of my left hand, instead of the three last fingers of the hand, which most teachers say is the only good way to hold it. If you hold the club too much in the palm, they'll tell you, there's no way you can achieve the hand action and the wrist-cocking necessary to hit a golf ball properly. Taking my left wrist into his hands Redding pushes in against it, kneading it. He firmly holds the heel pad of my left hand securely *over* the Victory Pride grip, noting that this placement is essential to keep the club from slipping in the course of the swing.

"It's no different than holding a hammer or a fishing rod," he explains.

"Then why does it feel so unbelievably awkward?" I ask him.

"Because you're not used to fishing with your left hand," he says.

Oh.

When Redding is satisfied that my left hand is properly situated—

with the heel pad on top of the club and the grip nestled in the so-called roots of the last three fingers—he turns his attention to my right hand, which, it turns out, has been much too *on top* of the club. He wedges the lifeline of the right hand securely against the side of my left thumb. Instinctively, I apply a powerful death grip to the shaft. Imagine a glow of white ash radiating off the knuckles. Redding tells me to relax. This is like telling me to wiggle my ears.

"Okay, great!" Redding says. "Now you've got it. Hold it there. Feel it."

I do. It feels weird. Waggling the club back and forth is so loosey-goosey that I am convinced I couldn't possibly strike a ball with my hands arranged like this.

"Take a couple of swings," Redding commands.

Instantly, my brain sends a code-red alert to my hands, which once again promptly lock onto the club with the force of an industrial vise. I couldn't hit a nail or cast a worm with this grip, though I most assuredly could squeeze the life out of a bird with it. Even a very large and uncooperative bird. I could kill a bird faster with this grip than Ozzy Osbourne could with his teeth. Redding again tells me to cool it.

"Now, take a couple of swings," he orders again.

I believe that a lot of casual players tend to think of the grip (if they think about the grip at all) as the most achievable of golf's fundamentals. What's the big deal? You put your left hand on the club, then your right. You place the pinkie of your right hand around or over the top of the index finger of your left, and you're in business.

That's certainly all the attention *I* ever gave it. I was of course aware that there was a relationship between the position of the hands on the club and the direction of the club face. I knew if you kept your hands in a so-called strong position (turned to the right), the club would be more closed at impact. Conversely, if you placed them in a "weak" position, the opposite would occur: The club head would be left open at impact. But I didn't much worry about such fine-tunings when confronted with more pressing priorities, such as the need to get the ball into the air. (As if that, too, wasn't a function of the grip.)

I knew from looking at a lot of golf books that the grip is universally deemed to be one of the crucial building blocks of a good swing. Almost every instructional book tees off with a chapter on the right way to hold the club. This is a chapter I invariably skipped. The information always struck me as simple-minded, self-evident. (Imagine if every cookbook began with a chapter on how to hold the whisk.)

But now that Redding has started to work on the correct placement of my hands, I realize that taking the grip for granted is one of the dumbest things a hacker can do. This insight dawns on me only after he tries to pry loose my stiff, unyielding mitts and resituate them in a more or less proper manner. My crablike claws resist his labor, intent on clamping themselves around the handle the way they've always clamped. I just can't help reverting to my usual form—Redding's technique feels ridiculously wrong.

But in fact a grip that feels wrong, according to Arnold Palmer, is just the grip you want. I happen to know Arnie's view on this matter because an acquaintance of mine once told me about how he tried to learn golf from Palmer's book *My Game and Yours* (1983). When this friend learned about my sessions with Redding, he strongly suggested that I, too, get acquainted with the title. So the next day I went down to the Knoxville public library and found a copy on the shelves.

Like the man himself, Arnie's manual is infectious and exuberant, filled with unrestrained outbursts of love for just about every grand (even absurd) aspect of the game: "[I] even enjoy the mingled pleasure and discomfort of breaking in a new pair of golf shoes," Arnie effuses.

Palmer attributes his grip obsession to the preachings of his dad, who for many years was head pro at the Latrobe Country Club. Palmer *père* held that a good grip is a "virtue that can compensate for dozens of golfing sins." Only about one in fifty golfers can be said to have a good grip, Arnie explains, because most of us hold onto our clubs in whatever way feels "natural." To Arnie, the "natural" way is wrong— the club, he tells us, is "neither a baseball bat, a suitcase, a broom, nor a frying pan."

There isn't a golf teacher on earth who doesn't immediately check out the grip when eyeballing a new student. The oracle of Austin, Mahatma Penick, liked to say that nine out of ten problems with the swing begin at this point (actually, with the grip or with the stance, which is itself often a function of the grip). Rather than fix the grip, Penick asserts, we erringly spend a lot of time trying to cure the symptoms caused by its misapplication, which under Redding's patient guidance I am just beginning to understand. As he pries and pulls and pushes my fingers, I am becoming aware that a good grip does a whole lot more than help you square the clubhead at impact. A good grip allows you to keep your forearms relaxed, for the obvious reason that you can now hold the club firmly with just the hands. You don't need further assistance from muscles further up along the arm. Relaxed arms allow you to make a more relaxed and a fuller shoulder turn. This in turn produces a smoother swing. A smoother swing means better balance. Better balance spells b-r-e-a-k-i-n-g e-i-g-h-t-y.

Am I the last dimwit with white-hot knuckles to figure this out?

I go home and pick up the pitching wedge I keep around the house. Lots of golf teachers suggest we keep a club at hand as much as possible. They want us to get familiar with it so that we come to regard it as an everyday utensil, like a fork or spoon, and not as a piece of weekend sporting equipment. They want us to be perfectly comfortable with it. A too-tight grip is a restless grip. It slips and slides and wanders about. When left to its devices, it creeps back to the warm, cozy womb of the dreaded palm. It isn't easy to keep a good grip. Patty Berg once said that the most important thing she could teach anyone was that the grip was forever losing itself—day to day, shot to shot—and for this reason it was necessary to check it incessantly. When you place your hands around the club, you want to caress it, not strangle it. As a former British amateur champion once advised, "Don't look for a feeling of power in the grip. Search for elegance, sensitivity, and freedom . . ."

Others, less eloquent, offer their own two cents. Sam Snead held that the wrists should feel "oily" when we make our waggles, and recommended that we grip the club no more tightly than we would a billiard cue. Seve Ballesteros said we should grasp it "as tightly as you need to squeeze a tube of toothpaste." Someone else, I forget who, suggested that we use no greater pressure than we would use to hold a child's hand.

Redding asks me to swing the club a few more times. There's no question I can hinge and cock my wrists more easily. The club feels lighter; there's more whip to it.

He tells me to hit a few balls into the net. I clank a number of thin shots with my six-iron. The strain down the backs of my legs has become most unpleasant, the tension in my back unbearable.

If Redding reads exasperation in my face he chooses to ignore it. Like most in his profession, he has a remarkable ability to disregard the all too evident miseries and frustrations of his pupil. Undaunted, he continues to lay on hands. He takes me by my waistband and again yanks my butt higher. He presses my left wrist hard in against the club, massaging it, coaxing it to do what it plainly doesn't want to.

"You've got to *feel* it," Redding says again and again. "*Feel* the right way. You can't read what it feels like in a golf book. You can't see what it feels like in a video. And you can't feel it just by having a teacher stand behind you and tell you what to feel. This is why I will move you, move you hundreds of times before we're finished."

He stands in front of my face. He reaches out and takes hold of my arms. He tells me to keep my eyes on the ball, my head still. He pushes down slightly on my left arm as he takes my shoulders and torso back and around to the top of the backswing. "*This* is what it's supposed to feel like."

Hmm.

He does it again.

"I'll do it over and over and over, hundreds of times, until you feel it."

He's for sure going to have to, because what all this feels like is unlike any feeling I have ever felt before. For my entire life I have begun my swing by lifting my hands, taking the club back too high, too fast, outside the desired swing plane. Even today, my hands are a couple of rabbits set loose on a mad dash toward some calamitous rendezvous with the golf ball. Other body parts are entered in this race as well. My shoulders and my head, for example, vie to see which can get through the swing fastest. The result is an anatomical frenzy of muscles and joints hell-bent on getting to the golf ball first. To nail, crush, atomize it. What Redding is trying to get me to feel is something very different: a slower takeaway, with the left shoulder lower on the backswing, my left hand kind of pushing *down* on the club as it guides it back around my body. That's what it feels like to me, anyhow. The club feels more like a cricket *paddle* as it moves back and around. Strange.

"Is it supposed to feel, well, like a paddle?" I ask Redding.

The reply comes in the form of the familiar shrug.

"Don't fight me," Redding says, moving me again and again. "Just let your muscles go where I'm trying to take them."

But I resist.

Why?

What accounts for this stubbornness?

Why can't I simply will my shoulders to let go, allow Redding to move my arms from point A to point B?

Why does the body obstruct?

"*Feel* it," Redding says, moving me over and over again. "*Feel* it." Even though I am expending little energy—it's Redding who's getting the workout, shlepping my arms around and around my body—I find myself growing tired. The mental concentration required to make this simple movement—the slight pushing down with my left hand as I take the club around—is intense. I can't wait to get the hell out of the shed, into the winter afternoon.

What I don't realize is that, for the last few minutes I have actually held the golf swing in my grasp. *I've held it in my grasp by pushing slightly down, which, for me anyhow, felt like some sort of paddle, something like a cricket bat.*

But it's a sensation that vanishes as I step outside and into the bracing air. The feeling is gone.

HIT A BRICK!

While golf may be played out in obeisance to good fellowship and exquisite manners, it is much more a game of self-indulgence than a game of empathy. No player wants to listen to the boring details of another golfer's ineptitude. We'd much rather slobber on about our own. A golfer who laments to others about the details of his personal swing faults hits his listeners like a syringe full of horse tranquilizer.

That said, just how bad a golfer was I?

Average-bad, I suppose. In that I've never had much reason to record my scores in a systematic way, my handicap existed as little other than an unofficial estimate: 25. Depending on how often I was playing at any given point, my scores ranged from 95 to 110. More often than not, I was over 100.

My game was a classic version of its kind, a melange of dumb luck and disaster. A typical round played itself out as a discordant, five-hour symphony. As featured soloist, I worked my clubs with the mellifluousness of a beginning violinist.

Off the tee: *Exceedingly erratic.*

Now and then I had the good fortune to smack the ball 200-plus yards down the middle of a fairway. But far more often I sliced my drives into rough or woods or ponds or the crabgrass yards of the condos that line America's fairways. Two or three times a round (at least) I'd hit a tee shot so mortifyingly ugly that I would have liked to crawl into my golf bag and plunge a spike wrench through my heart. These drives were utterly bizarre and unfathomable. They were no less impressive than those in a repertoire of trick shots you might expect of a master shotmaker at an exhibition: drives that flew *straight up*, then hung suspended in the sky for what seemed the better part of a lazy afternoon, only to plotz back to earth no more than twenty or thirty yards out from where they were launched, often well short of the ladies' tee. In a foursome of strangers, these moon shots were greeted with complete and utter silence, though I knew, of course, what everyone was thinking: that I'd have to play the rest of the hole with my little Willie peeking out of my khaki shorts.

There were other kinds of mishits that rivaled the moon shot on the well-worn Humil-O-Meter: topped drives, muffled and squirrelly, that never deigned to leave the ground ("worm burners" to most duffers, "Warren Burgers" to my circle of erudite friends). Then there were shots that careened violently to the right, at a ninety-degree angle ("perps," as we called them). A perp triggered an instant swoon of suicidal dejection and the desire to fire off a fax to Dr. Kevorkian.

Long game: *Erratic.*

My success rate with fairway woods was somewhat better than my record with drivers or three-woods off the tee. After all, I had had a lot of practice in this phase of the game. Given my anemic drives, the five-wood became a predictable companion on most par-fours, since I generally needed 180-plus yards to reach the green in—dare I use the word?—regulation.

While I've kept no official statistics, I'd say that the following represents a pretty good accounting of my successes and failures as a fairway-wood player:

Shot result	Frequency rate
Longish and accurate	15%
Hideous slice	25%
Screaming pull/hook	25%
Warren Burger	15%
Dipshit pop-up	15%
Wussy whiff/dribbler	5%

As for my luck with long irons, there are no reliable data whatsoever, because I almost never had the guts to take these clubs out of the bag. I owned a two-iron some years ago, but trying to a hit a golf ball with it was like trying to hit a golf ball with a fireplace poker. My "touch" with three-and four-irons was somewhat better, though these clubs routinely produced deep gashes in such fairways unlucky enough to be caught beneath their violent swipes. Again, the usual result was slices, pulls, or chief-justices, more or less in equal proportion.

Middle game: *Erratic.*

The most reliable weapon in my "arsenal" was the seven-wood, which was fitting and proper, seeing that the seven-wood (or utility wood) is as close to idiot-proof as a golf club gets. It is also one of the most versatile. This utility is a function of its high degree of loft coupled with the fact that its clubhead (1) is heavier than that of a mid-iron and thus capable of producing more oomph; and (2) offers a much more generous sweet spot than a blade of comparable loft. I rarely flubbed a seven-wood, whether hitting it off the fairway or from short fairway rough (which was far more often the case). Typically, a seven-wood strike flew high and straight but carried only about 165 yards.

As for my mid-irons, who knew from one shot to the next? Despite my misbegotten grip, excessive body tension, and over-the-top swing, these clubs occasionally rewarded me with reasons to come back for another day of punishment. Seldom did they propel the ball with such precision that a shot wound up sitting prettily in the center of a green. No, a good shot from the middle distance generally ended up on the fringe to the left or right, or just as likely in a greenside bunker. Such was the nature of my petty triumphs.

Short game: *Erratic.*

It is axiomatic that a halfway decent short game, like a proper grip, can compensate for a multitude of sins. It is a fact that hackers can save ten to twenty strokes a round by the acquisition of a halfway decent short game. And it is unarguable that a halfway decent short game requires minimal athletic coordination—and that through work, practice, and concentration, a halfway decent short game can actually be learned by all male and female misfits, young or old, who have the temerity to think of themselves as golfers.

So much for conventional wisdom, rational analysis, and good intentions.

My short game was, to get to the point, pretty lame. From one frustrating season to the next, I never bothered to remember whether you were supposed to hit sand shots off your front foot or your back. My chip shots routinely left in their wake putts of twenty feet or more. My pitch shots sailed long, skittered short, skulled right, chili-dipped nowhere. My putting stroke from round to round, from hole to hole, was a function of whim and mood swing: elbows in, elbows out, open stance, square stance, overlapping grip, baseball grip, index-finger-down-the-shaft, index-finger-wrapped-around, lots of wrist, no wrist. My trademark putt was (1) short of the hole; (2) below the hole; and (3) hardly ever struck with that sparkling *ping* that comes with hitting the ball off the sweet spot. (More commonly, mine was a muffled *glunk.*) Because life on a putting green was boring beyond words, I spent as little time as humanly possible on or around one.

Such was my sorrowful game. And to make matters even worse, I could be hotly intemperate, given to bellowed cries of self-detestation whenever I shanked a shot or blew a putt, screaming foul epithets and curses at my despicable being: "I HATE YOUR GODDAMN HEART!," meaning my own.

Très élégant, n'est-ce pas?

As was fitting, I paid dearly for this unsavory flaw. Not only did it reflect miserably on my character, casting grave doubt on my maturity, it was a trait that cost me plenty of money.

Consider the case of the legendary O-fer.

This episode occurred back in the early eighties, when I had just started playing golf again after the long hiatus. This was the time, as I mentioned, that a small circle of us rediscovered the game of golf with a lunatic vengeance. We played in the mud and the rain, and once or twice in blinding snow. We passed our lunch hours scouring golf shops in Manhattan, spending way too much on a never-ending quest for the latest clubs, shoes, and bags, and even idiotic accessories such as a cheap plastic "range finder" that purported to gauge the exact distance between one's lie and the flag stick.

It was on a golf weekend during this manic period that I found myself paired with a stranger on the Magnolia course at Disney World. The man was a plastic-sign mogul from Racine (or something like that, from somewhere like that, I don't honestly remember). The fellow was a high-handicapper who played unremarkably except for the fact that his drives—his drives!—were unfailingly impressive: lovely, soaring fades of about 225 yards, one right after the next. After marveling silently for about nine holes, I broke down and complimented him on this part of his game. On the next hole, a par-four, he asked whether I'd like to try his driver.

The club was called the O-fer. The sign king confided that you could only get it by mail. He explained that it was manufactured by a pro-verbial mom and pop, presumably in their garage or basement work-shop, someplace in Ohio. (Ah, the *O*-fer, get it?) What made the O-fer so deadly was the fact that it was, literally, a bastard. Its head was the size and weight of a driver; in fact, it was even a bit larger and heavier than most drivers were back then. But the O-fer's *loft* was that of a three-wood.

The sign king handed it over. I waggled the O-fer back and forth, remarking nonchalantly that the club had a really good feel and bal-ance. (Having made well over fifty for the front nine, I qualified as a maven.) I planted a tee in the ground and set a new Titleist on top of it. Taking my best simian stance, I suddenly panicked, fearful that I might hit one of my moon shots, which I knew from prior experience could very easily deface the top of this poor guy's club-head. *Swing easy and smoothly through the ball,* I told myself. And that's precisely what I did. The O-fer and the Titleist made crushing contact, after which the ball just scoffed in the face of gravity. It valiantly strained for every last yard before it finally succumbed to the earth's pull and rolled to a rest about 230 yards from where it had begun its majestic journey.

My response was immediate.

"I gotta have this club!" I shpritzed, ostensibly to the plastic-sign titan, though the exclamation was as much a supplication to God, a plea for deliverance, a cry for redemption.

The man told me that he had seen the O-fer advertised in a golf magazine, and provided me with enough information that I was able to track down Mom and Pop's number when I got back to my hotel room. It was Mom who answered the phone. I told her I wanted to order an O-fer, and she was very pleased. She told me what the club cost—about $200, though I wasn't really paying at-tention—*Just give it to me, mama.* After taking down my credit card number, she said she would mail it to me in New York within the next few days, and that I should allow a couple of weeks for delivery.

There was no way I could wait two weeks for that club. I had already made plans to play golf with the Wedding Round boys in the Berkshires on the coming weekend. It was unthinkable that I could do so without benefit of this miraculous new piece of heavy artillery.

"Could you send it overnight?" I asked Mom plaintively. I could feel my heart beating in my throat. "Could you send it by Federal Express? I'll be more than happy to pay for the extra shipping, whatever that comes to."

Mom, who was obviously of solid, Midwestern stock, was stunned by this reckless request. Imagine anyone crazy enough to shell out another—what? Twenty bucks? To hell with what she thought. *I just wanted that club!*

When I arrived home the next day I found a long cardboard box waiting for me. I tore it open and lovingly removed the O-fer, my very own O-fer, the secret weapon, the miracle cure, the talisman. I took a few half-swings right there in the living room. Again, wonderful feeling, great balance. I admired its shiny head, its fine ebony finish, as yet unmarred by dimples or nicks. Maybe I should order another one, I thought. What if Mom and Pop go belly up? Or get interred in a nursing home? Maybe I should order *two* more O-fers, maybe *three*? How many O-fers would I need to last the rest of my life? I carefully folded Mom and Pop's shipping invoice and put it safely away in the small wooden box in which I kept my father's Phi Beta Kappa key.

The week stretched on forever. Saturday dawned hot and humid, the day of the great Unveiling. I slipped the O-fer into my golf bag, gently closed the trunk lid, then headed up toward western Mass. Our foursome had reserved a starting time at a hilly track built on the grounds of an old private school, just down the road from where Edith Wharton once lived.

There was no practice range at the course, so I decided not to bring the O-fer out of the bag until I was loose and relaxed. By the fourth hole I was ready. Saying nothing to my partners about the new club, I teed up a ball, trying to keep my excitement under control. *Swing easy. Let the O-fer do its thing.* I didn't, and it didn't. The O-fer's maiden effort was a sickening squirt to the right. The ball just kind of skipped and hopped and disappeared into thick underbrush not far from the side of the tee box. In its world premiere, the O-fer had produced a dreaded perp.

On the next hole, the O-fer and I collaborated on another dramatic mishit, this time a sky-ball that left a tattoo of white dimple marks on the top of the club. The shot traveled about thirty yards high and, oh, maybe forty yards long.

And on the hole after that, the O-fer completed its dazzling display of versatility when it unceremoniously topped a ball, a half-cooked chief justice that rolled about 100 yards along the sun-baked ground before it came to a merciful stop.

My high expectations now thoroughly dashed, I felt the surge of hot blood behind my eyes. Enraged, I tried to hurl the club as far as I could down the fairway. But this, too, I screwed up. The O-fer flew far *left*, whooshing into dense woods. I had banana-hooked it into oblivion. The club had cost $200, plus shipping. I had hit it all of three times. Now it was gone.

"Aren't you even going to look for it?" one of my playing partners asked, after he had stopped laughing.

I turned and began to stomp down the fairway.

"It's a brand-new club, how can you throw away a couple of hundred bucks just like that?"

He was right. To leave it and walk away would make me an even bigger horse's ass.

As I approached the woods I spied the densest growth of poison ivy I had ever encountered in my life. Hairy vines as thick as my wrist wound around every tree. The ground was completely covered with the stuff. Even though the day was now sweltering, I took the plastic rain suit out of my golf bag and put it on, covering my head with the hood of the jacket. For ten minutes I searched without luck, completely soaked in sweat. An elderly couple who were playing behind me stared in disbelief as I emerged from the woods in my blue plastic suit on this, the hottest, stickiest dog day of summer.

The O-fer was gone. Today, some ten years later, it probably still lies there, its ebony head rotted out and bug-chewed to a fine powder, its once gleaming shaft turned to rust.

THE SILENT, STATIONARY BALL

If there's a moral to the tale of the O-fer, it's this:

Clubs don't make the man, the swing makes the man.

And to accomplish that swing, you've got to be relaxed, not tense; loose, not tight; measured, not fast. It's better to premeditate a shot than to hope for the best, better to "see" the path of a shot before hitting it than to be hell-bent on knowing where the shot actually goes. To smack a golf ball right on its shnozzola, deliberate is better than impulsive, shrewd is better than reckless, patient is better than everything.

But who has the time to be patient?

A stationary ball is irresistible; not a sitting duck, exactly, which might imply that it's hapless, hopeless, a victim. No, a golf ball isn't a victim—it's proud, alluring, unafraid. It dares us to mug it, stoic to the end. It gives us all the time we need to worry, to get worked up, to succumb to the Fever. That's its edge. That's how the ball evens the match. It's how it plays us off against ourselves. It derails our balance, induces us to lunge and flail. How much easier to return a volley, short-hop a grounder, sink a jump shot. When you're on the move your balance is important but not always crucial to the result. But when you're swinging at a golf ball, balance is everything. Larry Miller, a

Tour player briefly in the 1970s, now a teacher and author, maintains that "there is no such thing as a good golfer with poor balance, but there are poor athletes with good balance who are good golfers."

You hear this all the time about golf: The reason it's different from the other orb sports is that the ball isn't moving when you go to strike it. This is why nongolfers think golf is easy, the least physically demanding of games. How could hitting something that's dead on the ground be more difficult than hitting something that's whizzing, curving, rising, or falling?

What fools these cynics be.

With golf, the ball's fixation is *our* fixation. It's the *non*movement that kills us: how the ball cries out to be hit, smoked, smashed with that delirious *kccck*, the sound that sends golf scribes to their graves without having spelled it. You can't possibly write that sound. The only way to hear it is to make it, to hit the ball right on its button. So do it, already! Hey, the little guy's just sitting there. It isn't moving toward us or away, it isn't bouncing. It's just waiting patiently, as if for a bus. Why, then, is it so hard to hit the living daylights out of it?

ON THE ROAD TO BARBADOS

By the third lesson with Brad Redding, I am aware that the uncomfortable stance and the awkward grip are a little easier to achieve. As my muscles are relieved of old instincts, they surrender more to Redding's coaxing. Stepping up to a ball in the shed, I notice that my hands now close around the club more or less according to plan, that I make a move to straighten my back without having to be told. As I unconsciously incorporate these techniques into my repertoire, I am learning about learning itself. These lessons will become clearer and clearer to me as time goes on:

Lesson #1: When you're trying to master something, you can't accurately gauge your progress at any given moment. There are many reasons for this, but one of the most important is that our baseline—the "natural" way we feel or do something—is constantly changing. What was difficult yesterday is not quite so difficult today and might well be pretty easy tomorrow. Such progress may be extremely subtle, all but imperceptible. We may not even be aware that any progress is being made whatsoever—which can lead, as I am soon to find out, to premature and unjustified disillusionment.

Lesson #2: Because this baseline is ever-changing, there's a risk that we can overlearn. For example, say that yesterday you felt awkward sticking out your butt when you set up for a shot. Today, you feel pretty relaxed when you do so, and tomorrow you'll just do it automatically. But because your baseline of feeling has changed, from butt in to butt out, you will be tempted to move it even *further* out because you'll try to apply the same relative fix you applied yesterday when your butt was in.

In the case of my own butt, I have now begun to so tense my lower back that I have created a spanking-new swing problem, thus negating whatever fleeting progress I've made but wasn't sufficiently aware of to hang onto.

When I try to convey some of these tortured insights to Redding, he listens politely. But I can actually make out the film spreading over his corneas.

In between these first few lessons with Redding, I dutifully make the time to visit a driving range. This particular garden spot is located just off Kingston Pike, one of Knoxville's principal commercial strips. Nearly every town has thoroughfares like these, choked with strip malls, auto dealerships, and franchises of every imaginable sort: APPLEBEE'S, TED RUSSELL FORD, HARDEE'S, YOUTH WORLD, GRAYSON PONTIAC, KRISPY KREME DONUTS, WALGREEN'S, INTERNATIONAL HOUSE OF PANCAKES, THE POOL PLACE, BURGER KING, TOYS 'R' US, PIZZA HUT,

BOOKS-A-MILLION, BIG SUR HOT TUBS, BUDDY'S BBQ. Nestled just behind this mess is the Lee-Jane recreation complex. It consists of batting
cages, a disused and overgrown go-kart track, and a driving range whose
singular charm is an old, rusting pickup truck that whimsically serves as
the 100-yard marker. The words HIT ME are spray-painted on its side.

Though shabby, there's something magical about Lee-Jane. Cher-
okee burial grounds, perhaps? How else to explain the way I hit golf
balls here, as compared to how I hit them for Brad Redding over at
Willow Creek? At Lee-Jane I enjoy daily confirmation of the effects
offered by my improved grip and protruding coccyx. Yet when I show
up for a lesson with Redding, and he asks me to hit a few on the range
outside the shed, I revert to basket-case status, slicing, smothering, and
shanking.

"I don't know why this happens," I say sheepishly. "I was really
hitting them great in practice all week."

The truth is, I know precisely why it happens, and it has nothing
to do with Lee-Jane's being built on old Indian burial grounds or
anything like it. At Lee-Jane, no one's eyeballs drill into me as I swing.
At Willow Creek, they do; hence, my movements are not smooth and
loose, they're rushed and tight. At Willow Creek, fear of failure rules
the occasion. This is exactly what happens to so many hackers on the
first tee, as we attempt to perform under the scrutiny of others. The
golf manuals, true to form, have no shortage of easy solutions for this
particular distress. Relax. Breathe deeply. Take five minutes to stretch.
Imagine a giant bullseye strung across the fairway, just twenty yards
out. Now, plunk it. Don't think about the shot, think about the swing.
Think about making the most gorgeous swing in you, so when you do
louse up the shot others will take it as a fluke.

Right.

Redding looks on as I hit a half-dozen fungoes—among the worst
shots I have made all week—but he remains perky. In his chipper way,
he leads me back to the shed, where he videotapes two or three swings.

He again sits me down and plays them back in slow motion. With his black marker, he winky-dinks a diagonal line—from the ball through the shaft of the club up through my groin then out my back and skyward—along which my hands should travel on both the backswing and downswing. He points out that my back and shoulders are still too bowed, that I hunch over the ball. He indicates that my hands are too close to my body, causing them to start back too high, way over the swing plane he has marked off on the screen. This excessive lifting of arms and hands forces me to come over the top when I start my downswing, the classic "death move," as instructional guru Jim Mc-Lean calls it. This out-to-in path is my eternal damnation. It results either in a shot pulled way to the left (if impact occurs with the club-head closed) or a disheartening slice to the right (if the clubhead remains open).

Why is it so goddamn hard to get this right?

There are now two days to go before Linda, the kids, and I are to leave for Barbados. I resolve to spend a part of each of these days at Lee-Jane, gearing up for the real thing, my first encounter with a golf course since Redding and I began working together.

On the first of my range days—wouldn't you know?—a break-through occurs. (It will not be the last.) This one strikes me with such force that I ask to borrow a pen from the guy at the bucket counter so that I can scribble down the details of what I take to be a true epiphany. Here is what I write:

You've got to turn to load—shift your weight so that the left heel comes up naturally. You don't have to think to lift it. As you go to hit the ball, you kind of step into and through the shot.

I realize this is neither original nor profound, one of a million such truisms that cling to golf like barnacles to an ancient hull. But to one who has been a flat-footed lunger, this discovery is the athletic equivalent of a toddler's first step. On the drive home I stop for a light and reread what I have written, the most sagacious three sentences I believe I have ever composed.

You've got to turn to load—shift your weight so that the left heel comes up naturally. You don't have to think to lift it. As you go to hit the ball, you kind of step into and through the shot.

What this perception signifies to me is that for the first time I have an inkling of what a proper weight shift is supposed to feel like—even though the term "weight shift" is a no-no, according to Brad Redding. He is already on record as saying that he doesn't like the image of a golfer "shifting" from the back foot to the front. Instead he refers to this as a "redistribution" of weight, a distinction that strikes me as too subtle by half. But inasmuch as *he* shoots in the seventies, and I pretty much suck, who am I to quibble with his semantics?

When I get home I clean my clubs and shine my Foot Joys. The Fever throbs in my head. I can't wait to get to Barbados, rip off my clothes, yank on a pair of shorts, slip into my nails, and take dead aim.

DOWN THE TROPICAL FAIRWAY

To get from a small city like Knoxville to a small island like Barbados, you just don't jump on a plane and arrive a few hours later. To get from Knoxville to Barbados, you first have to go through Atlanta, a flight of about half an hour. Actually, you don't go *through* Atlanta, you go *to* Atlanta, where you've got to spend the night, because the first flight out—to San Juan, which will take you to a flight to Barbados—leaves at the crack of dawn. This being the case, it makes no logistical sense to drag your suitcases and golf clubs to a swanky hotel such as the Ritz in Buckhead, where you can soak in the tub and think peaceful swing thoughts. The more sensible move is to book accommodations at one of dozens of interchangeable, franchised dosshouses that are conveniently located within five minutes of the busy air hub.

You have your choice of Days Inn, Ramada Inn, Hampton Inn, Quality Inn, Holiday Inn, Comfort Inn, all with the same noxious, mildewy air heavy with the fragrance of Lestoil and old cigarettes.

Hungry? Your choice here is no less bountiful. You've got your Shoney's, your Ruby Tuesday's, your T.G.I.F.'s, your Bennigan's. So if you've got a hankering for chicken fingers and french fries—in other words, the palate of a preschooler—you'll be as happy as a pig in culinary poo-poo. No matter. You need to be up and back at the hub before sunrise, to catch the flight to San Juan, there to kill a couple of hours before you can board your jam-packed airship to Barbados. Finally, after a journey of nearly twelve hours, tired and sweaty and stinking of airplane—presto!—you are there, eager to tee off.

The house we have booked is splendorous, a vast white Moorish villa known as Dar es Salaam. Its absentee owner, we are told, is a rich Saudi doctor who lives in London. The place sits high on a hill and overlooks a fairway on the golf course at the Sandy Lane Hotel. As tenants of the house, we enjoy playing rights to this track and in short order we will take advantage of them. But first there's the business of settling in, assigning rooms, oohing over the expansive pool, aahing over the sweeping patios and decks that will serve as home for the coming six days. That is, when we are not on the golf course.

Linda and I are one of four couples here, all of whom have been friends for years. Shockingly, we find ourselves now in the full flower of middle age. But as Gail Sheehy predicted, this has turned out to be a generally good time in our lives. Careers are in reasonable enough shape, biological clocks are no longer keeping anyone awake. Everyone—knock wood—is presently healthy, and while no one among us is filthy rich, we are all doing well enough to afford this vast house, complete with a domestic staff, and a breathtaking view of the sunset.

We turn in early this first night. As Linda tucks the kids into bed, I leaf through one of the books I've brought along. A vacation in a sun-drenched place like Barbados, with its long, languid afternoons and lazy evenings, is a perfect time to get reacquainted with a half-remembered Flaubert, or knock off an overlooked Simenon or Chandler. But the book I choose to open is *Bobby Jones on Golf*. Back in the twenties and thirties, Jones turned out a couple of weekly newspaper columns, which are the basis of this admired work. In an adulatory forward, Charles Price tries to explain why Jones was different from players before and since—citing Jones's intelligence, modesty, and of course his natural talent. But "what really set him apart," writes Price, "was his insight into the game, gorgeous in its dimensions if you have waded through the treacle and sophisms [of other golf books]." It doesn't take long for me to understand what Price is talking about. Though my eyelids are drooping, I come across a passage in Jones's introduction that perfectly captures the first weeks I have spent in that shed with Brad Redding:

> It is not easy to teach golf either by personal instruction or by writing. [The] player must have the feel of the proper stroke. Being unable to view himself objectively, he has no other guide than the sensations produced by the action of his own muscles. Yet the words . . . that we must use to describe [this feeling] are necessarily vague and susceptible to varying interpretations among different persons; so that no one can describe the feel of a muscular action with assurance that he will be readily and inevitably understood by another. For this reason, I think it necessary in all forms of golf instruction to repeat over and over descriptions of the same movements, all the while altering the modes of expression and terms of reference. Often the learner will grasp the teacher's meaning when stated in one way when he has failed to understand it in any other forms.

I am pleased that Georgia's finest, Bobby Jones, and my man from Willow Creek sing from the same hymnal. I think about how Redding has so adamantly refused to put into words what *it* is supposed to feel like.

I also think about how, when Linda or I try to teach something to Ned and Katherine (who are five and three), we don't tell so much as show, setting them up to discover something on their own. That's what Redding is trying to do with me.

I think about a question that occurred to me on the practice range back in Knoxville. It just popped into my mind as I was hitting balls at Lee-Jane one afternoon.

Is it possible that the swing, that which we search for relentlessly, is already inside of us? Or is it indeed something we need to go out and find, piece by piece, and then assemble?

Before I drop off for the night, I think about how kinky this game is, how everybody's a professor, how everybody's got a gimmick. Sam Snead said that if you want pars and birdies the trick was to "get chummy with your golf ball." He confessed that sometimes when he addressed the ball he actually talked to it, murmured sweet nothings into its dimples. Sometimes, he said, he whispered to it: "This isn't going to hurt a bit," or, "I see you're sitting up fat and ready; let's have some fun."

Even weirder, the ball talked back. "O.K., Sam," the Slammer said it replied. "But treat me gentle."

Soothed, and ready to seize the morning, I fall asleep.

Frustration

If everybody could learn to hold his head still
[this] would be a really happy country. . . .
—**Arnold Palmer,** *My Game and Yours,* **1983**

LONG NIGHT'S JOURNEY INTO DAY

Golfers, the good and the bad, come in every body shape and personality. They can be brutish (Daly), fat (Stadler), fiery (Ballesteros), prickly (Hogan), puckish (Rodriguez), massive (Els), ferretlike (Pavin), phlegmatic (Nicklaus), or just plain vanilla (Kite). Given this diversity, I cannot easily plead that I am golf-challenged because of some physical and/or temperamental idiosyncrasy. Nonetheless, I do feel genetically disadvantaged. My squinty-eyed field studies suggest that, despite their variety, most good golfers fit a pattern. They are, more often than not:

Lanky   Loose   Unassuming   Affable   Laconic
Pleasant   Personable   Uncomplicated   Gentile

I'm talking about the guys with flaxen hair and cowlicks, with heads that look good in sun visors. Guys whose Dockers break exactly right at the tops of their spikes. Guys who have no trouble sleeping late. Guys who don't drink or smoke much. Guys with resting pulse rates of fifty or less. Guys who move through the day with unhurried motion, always running a couple of minutes behind, but don't seem to care. A lot of them are apparently double-jointed. Or ambidextrous. Or both. A lot of these guys, I've noticed, drive Hondas, I'm not sure why. Brad Redding, for example, drives a Honda. His is outfitted with Tennessee vanity plates: DR GOLF.

Then there are people like me:

Driven   Tense   Self-critical   Egocentric   Impatient
Harried   Grouchy   Overbearing   Type A+

Guys like me look absurd in sun visors. We look dippy in hats with PING, LYNX, or COBRA splashed across the front. We bellow on the course. We bitch and moan about the foursome in front of us. We knock back too many beers after our rounds, and too many hot dogs during. Our swings are fast and constricted.

And we wake up too early.

I was born under a curse—the fear that I might miss something were I ever to sleep in. When I was a kid, I always rose well before dawn, wolfed down some breakfast, grabbed a ball and fielder's mitt, and bolted outside. There I stood and sat and watched and twitched and scratched and picked my nose for hours, waiting for the next kid to come out. Sometimes the next kid was away for the summer, so he never came out. Eventually, I went back in the house and ate lunch.

Now, even as I contemplate the lengthening shadows of middle age, not much has changed.

I awake long before the sun comes up, pay some bills, read the papers. On those too-rare mornings when I'm scheduled to play golf, I am as jumpy as a cat on a string. Even though I try to reserve the earliest possible starting times, I still need to kill a good couple of hours before sunrise, and I tend to think that it is here, during these nervous, excited, anxious hours, that my golf game starts to unravel. Staring off to the east for the first sign of the rosy fingers of dawn, that bubbling, gurgling, overheated sap, the Fever, begins to seep, then pump, through my veins. To stay steady and calm, I've tried deep breathing and stretching, to no avail. I've foregone coffee, the deprivation of which only makes me loonier. I've popped a Valium, even quaffed a pre-dawn shot of Scotch, but no substance yet has been yet able to alleviate the Fever.

This compulsiveness is, I'm pretty sure, directly tied to my inability to play better.

Consider the first morning in Barbados. With Linda and kids asleep, I grope through the darkness for a pair of shorts and one of the new Ashworth shirts I bought for the trip. New swing, new wardrobe, fresh start. By four-thirty, I am dressed and ready to go. I step outside into the thick, wet tropical air. I feel my way across the tiled verandah to the kitchen, where I put on a pot of coffee. I am trying to think about something other than golf. It's useless.

So I reopen the Bobby Jones book.

This is a mistake of no small proportion. As the java kicks in, a host of vivid images and insights start to spring off the page, making me almost giddy in anticipation of the round ahead. Jones says that we mistakenly fixate on the *shaft* of the club as the transmitter of the force that strikes the ball. Better, he says, to *forget* about the shaft and focus instead on supplying velocity to the clubhead. He writes: "I like to think of a golf club as a weight attached to my hands by an imponderable medium, to which a string is a close approximation, and I like to feel that I am throwing it at the ball with much the same motion I should use in cracking a whip. By the simile, I mean to convey the idea of a supple and lightning-quick action of the wrists in striking—a sort of flailing action."

Yes! I think, draining the first large mug of high-octane joe, then pouring a second. *When you are out there today,* I vow silently, *try to forget that a shaft even* EXISTS *between the hands and the clubhead. Think string! Just* WHIP *that string to make the ball fly. Keep it taut— just* THROW *the clubhead at the ball and you'll be fine.*

I need a club in my hand; I need to *feel* the string, to transfuse the image from my head to my muscles, to take a few practice swings. I contemplate whether I should risk waking the rest of the house by stumbling around in search of my sticks, which are stashed somewhere in an unlighted hallway. I want to *feel* the sensation Jones writes about. To try to grasp it mentally isn't enough.

And where the hell is the Big Shooter, anyway?

The Big Shooter has been my principal playing partner for the past fifteen years. That he's called the Big Shooter has nothing to do with golf. He was once standing in a supermarket checkout line on the West Side of Manhattan when a guy turned to him and said, in a much too sweet way, "How ya doin', Big Shooter?" Shaken, the Big Shooter beat a hasty retreat, though he later made the mistake of telling the story to a couple of friends. He's been the Big Shooter ever since. This isn't to imply the Shooter isn't, in fact, very big: He's an extremely large, bearded, and for the most part genial Texan, except when he's playing lousy golf. When this is happening, his geniality gives way to earth-shuddering tremors of self-loathing.

Though he owns a Ph.D. in European history, the Big Shooter makes his living, at least in part, by traveling to resorts and writing about them for various golf magazines. Most people think this is the greatest job in the world, but while his assignments enable him to visit all the great resorts and play golf for free, they also oblige him to be resolutely cordial to the hosts. These courtesies he performs with the utmost affability—*even* when he's playing lousy golf. But once back in his room, a day's sorry round quickly chokes off any good cheer the Big Shooter may have marshaled at drinks and dinner. On these occasions, *nothing*—not a complimentary bottle of wine, nor a fancy cheese plate, nor a capacious basket of fresh fruit—can console him. During or after a round of lousy golf, the Big Shooter descends into the depths of misery, and it's best at such times to give him wide berth, bid him goodnight, seek the safety of cover. But the Big Shooter is indomitable, and any such blackness invariably passes by the following morning, when, returned to his accustomed, cheerful self, he bounds out of bed, eager to revisit and rechallenge the lush golf course that lies beyond his *casa de comped*. Happily, he peels a free banana and contemplates another lousy day in paradise.

LOST IN THE BARBADOS TRIANGLE

The Big Shooter ambles out just as the sun peeks over the horizon. I can see that his Fever, too, is on the rise, though on the surface he appears fairly calm. I tell him about the string, and how that will be my one and only swing thought for the day. He has heard this song before. For years and years we have traded swing thoughts, even though both of us know by now that they really never work. Life on a golf course gets too complicated. There are too many variables, too many kinds of mistakes to make, too many things to go wrong. One mantra, image, swing thought, does not fit all. A swing thought evaporates as quickly as the early morning dew.

We drive down the hill to the golf course. Today, the first of the rest of my golfing life, we are to play the scruffy and unassuming course at the Sandy Lane hotel. There's nothing much to the place, really. The track was carved out of rain forest about fifty years ago by some rich property owners who just wanted to knock the ball around. Built by amateurs, it was never planted with the right grasses, and because it is neither manicured nor irrigated, the course is dry and patchy. Considerable acreage, hot and hilly, must be traversed between several of the weirdly designed holes, so an old truck is now and then dispatched to trundle golfers and their weapons between selected greens and tees. But it's a golf course, a pleasant experience, especially in the company of the club's Bajan caddies, who are to a man as astute about the game as they are eagle-eyed. They don't so much tell you where to hit your putts as softly sing their suggestions in the lilting tone typical of this pretty island.

Stepping onto the first tee box, I hear a swirl of admonitions from a distant Brad Redding. I focus hard on Bobby Jones and try to imagine the shaft of my driver as a piece of string. With a final self-instruction to *swing easy*, I let loose a blast, a cannon shot. Up, up, and up it goes, then hangs suspended for an instant, then down, down, down until it makes a hard landing on the bumpy landscape some thirty yards down the fairway from where the Shooter and I, along with our caddies, stand watching in wonder.

Swinging with growing fury, I shank and skull and slice until I stagger to the eighteenth tee, where I pick up my ball and heave it nowhere in particular. Assuming a double-bogie on this one, my stroke count for the morning is approximately 105 (including a smattering of mulligans and a few other liberties taken with the cognizance of the Big Shooter, who has likewise carded a score in the low three digits). What is most impressive about the round, however, is not the colorful variety of mishits that clank off my golf clubs, but how little, if at all, my game has changed despite the lessons with Redding, the hours on the range, and all the manuals I've been reading.

"You're not turning your shoulders enough," the Shooter points out, after I invite his diagnosis. "And you're holding the club in a really funny way. I'm surprised that you're even hitting the ball at all with that grip." He tries to emulate it by twisting his wrists severely to the right.

"But that's how my teacher says I should hold the club," I protest.

"Can't believe it," the Shooter says, shaking his head. We drive back to our luxury villa in near silence, each of us humbled by the day's sorry performance, yet already calculating how we can stage miraculous comebacks by tomorrow morning.

SHIVAS ON THE ROCKS

I have brought another golf book to Barbados, a modern classic. It's Michael Murphy's beloved *Golf in the Kingdom,* generally held to be the most spiritual and profound fable ever written about the game. I know that's how I felt about it when I first read the book years ago, shortly after it was published in 1972. Since then, I've run into a lot of people who take pleasure in rereading this evergreen every few years. When they speak of it their eyes grow bright, and a calm spreads over them. Murphy continues to receive plenty of letters from people whose imaginations are fired by his tale, including one from a woman who wrote to say that for her, a golf course was like "God's negligée"— when she walked on one she could see "all the way" to the Almighty. Murphy inspires this sort of thing. He is a man of vast intellectual range and curiosity, a charismatic apostle of the New Age, and a naturally gifted athlete who, I've been told by mutual friends, plays golf only occasionally but yet has little trouble breaking eighty at Pebble Beach.

What is it about *Golf in the Kingdom?* What accounts for its perennial success (over 100,000 copies sold a year)? On one level, I suppose, the book appeals simply as a pleasurable, captivating story about the magical mysteries of the ancient game. The reader spends a single day and night on the links (a fictionalized St. Andrews) with Michael (the Murphy-like narrator), the inimitable Shivas Irons, and assorted golf-mad Scots, who range from the oracular to the bombastic. During these twenty-four hours, which is described in a hallucinogenic rush, we accompany Michael on a round that is as vivid and memorable as any we may have played personally. Then we gather 'round the MacNaughtons' burning logs for dinner and an evening of impassioned discourse about golf and the meaning of life, death, marriage, friendship, progress, and evil, all fueled by a measure of good Scotch whisky, nectar of the North Sea gods. Finally, well after midnight, we return with Shivas and Michael to the wind-lashed links to explore the relationship between mind and body, to smack featheries 200 yards with an Irish shillelagh (the fabled "baffin' spoon"), and to search the craggy ravines for a glimpse of the elusive Seamus MacDuff, who looms over this scraggy earth and conducts inquiries into the deeper structure of the universe.

This first part of the book takes up all of 124 pages, which makes it easily consumable by corporate execs on a routine flight to O'Hare, a setting where I've seen many a wee *Golf in the Kingdom* yanked from a bulging briefcase. It's also a perfect companion on a vacation such as this, when a hacker has time to contemplate the mystical underpinnings of his obsession.

Part two of *Golf in the Kingdom* purports to be a collection of passages that Michael says he copied from Shivas's journals. Tacked on as they are after the main narrative, these essays read like extended footnotes to the tale itself, remnant musings that Murphy could neither gracefully work into his story nor bear to lose. Philosophical chip shots, they attempt to divine the deep implications that lurk under the more obvious pleasures of golf.

A few examples:

Murphy likens a round of golf to a journey, and not just as in a pleasant, fat-assed, sit-on-your-butt-in-an-electric-cart kind of journey but as in some grand, central image of Western mythology. He contends that a routine Sunday morning at the club, or the day the Big Shooter and I just experienced at Sandy Lane, adds up to a lot more than just four hours of self-criticism interrupted by an occasional pussy joke. A round of golf is a way, in fact, to re-experience the Odyssey, the Exodus, the Ascension, the Crusades, Hindu's cycles, the Chinese Tao, Magellan's circumnavigation of the globe. Murphy sees Moses in every waste bunker: The patriarch's struggle to persevere, to make it to the Promised Land, is mirrored in our own dogged attempts to hack through eighteen holes and make it safely back to the beer nuts.

When Murphy (via Shivas) contemplates a golf ball he doesn't see a Top Flite Z Balata, he sees "an icon of Man the Multiple Amphibian, a smaller waffled version of the crystal ball, a mirror for the inner body. . . ." The golf ball is also a metaphor for a satellite, a planet, "a tiny universe for us to govern." It is a "reminder of our hunting past," a projectile to be launched much as we once fired arrows with stone points. It is a symbol that *we ourselves* can fly. And in its whiteness, a golf ball is "like an egg, laid by man," an icon of life itself.

But the kind of golf I played today at Sandy Lane was so lame, so dispiriting, that it conjures not so much the tales of Homer as the ineptitude of Homer Simpson.

Golf as *journey*?

How about golf as self-afflicted torture?

The ball as an *orbiting planet*?

How about the ball as a dead rock?

The ball as egg?

Now *there's* a metaphor I can relate to—at Sandy Lane today I laid 105 of them.

The Shooter, bless him, has arranged for us to play at the near-virginal Royal Westmoreland, a new and very posh residential development just a few miles from our Moroccan hideaway. The jewel in the site plan is a golf course designed by Robert Trent Jones, Jr., which will cost a staggering $14 million to finish. I say it's worth every penny: Royal Westmoreland is a knockout. Right now only the front nine are complete and even these are not yet officially open. The superintendent has limited play to a maximum of fifty golfers a day; our party is virtually alone on this beautiful course.

Royal Westmoreland represents neocolonial earth-moving at its best. Flowers and exotic tropical plantings abound, maintained by a corps of native landscapers with machetes in their belts. The sand in the bunkers is fluffy, white as snow, imported from some distant shore. The course is a monument to what a golf course architect can do with bulldozers and well-placed explosives. Royal Westmoreland has been sculpted out of an old limestone quarry. Its signature hole is the sixth, a short par-four that terminates in an expansive green surrounded by forty-foot rock walls. Hitting an approach shot into this green makes you feel as if you're hitting into the set of an Indiana Jones movie.

We arrive to find no caddies on the premises, only loathsome electric carts that, out of deference to the tender new grass, are duly sentenced to the paths. Thanks to the science of modern irrigation, plus generous dousings of herbicides and pesticides, the fairways here are the texture of sponge and the color of shamrock. Even better, they are resort-course wide (though we manage to miss more than our share), with plenty of undulation and many enormous hazards filled to the lips with that blindingly white, imported sand.

You hear a lot about how today's fairways and greens make golf easier to play, easier to score on. You hear, too, about how improvements in clubs and balls make it easier to hit shots farther and truer.

Open a golf magazine to a random page and you'll see an ad like the one for the Taylor Made Titanium Bubble driver. Its headline proclaims that EVERY FAIRWAY IN AMERICA JUST GOT 20% WIDER. The reason, it claims, is that the sweet spot on the Bubble's massive, copper-topped head is reportedly 17 percent larger than that on other big-noggin whackers. The Bubble ad abuts a lengthy article about golf balls. The piece is a survey designed to help a golfer select which one of them, in relation to the course, climate, and his or her particular game, is best.

Do you crave distance? Or, do you prefer—that'll be the day—workability? Or, not knowing what you want, or who you are, or where your next shot is likely to go, do you want a blend of distance *and* control?

Long gone are the days when the weekend foozler played just a Titleist or a Wilson. According to a chart in the article, Titleist today markets at least ten different balls, ranging from the HVC two-piece Lithium Surlyn, to the Professional three-piece Elastomer. Wilson offers even more: from the Ultra 500 Distance two-piece Trilyn, to the Ultra three-piece Tour Balata. With all these pellets to choose from, not to mention videotapes, computer-aided swing analysis, and manicured, bristly grass genetically engineered to make a golf ball sit high and hittable, you'd think we'd all be down in the sixties by now.

But the unfortunate truth is that the Big Shooter and I play as poorly on the turf at Royal Westmoreland as we did on the crabgrass at Sandy Lane. I suppose we hit a few better drives, but our touch around the greens is no better, despite the fact that the *fringe* at this course is more obsessively cared for than the putting surfaces at Sandy Lane. Stroke after stroke is lost to approach shots that fall wildly short, to chili-dips, to cued sand blasts, to twenty-foot putts that lead to a fourteen-foot putt, then a five-foot putt, then a gimme.

With help from the Caribbean heat and humidity, our wheels come off for good by the time we reach the eighteenth hole. Beautiful fairways be damned; by this point we can't even get our two-piece Surlyn 90-compression balls into the muggy air. We drill worm-burner after worm-burner across the flawless, newly laid carpet.

Angrily, we stomp off the final green and motor straight to the facility's practice range.

"What am I doing wrong?" I ask, hoping that the Shooter has enough energy left to answer.

"Your left arm is completely bent at the top of your backswing. You're still not turning enough. And both of your feet are kind of rolling left to right, which means you're not anchored to the ground when you're hitting. And that grip still really looks weird to me." A beat. "What am *I* doing wrong?"

"It looks like you're lunging at the ball," I say. "Your hands seem to be quitting—you're not accelerating through at impact. That's probably why you're losing so many shots to the right."

Whether these diagnoses are correct or not, something glorious then happens. Side by side on the range, the Shooter and I enter a *zone*, that rare and happy state of physical performance when the body, the club, and the ball are all tuned to the same frequency. With little or no conscious thought or effort, we whistle off one gorgeous shot after another. Five-irons, three-woods, it doesn't matter.

Now, granted, as zones go, this is a little trailer park of a zone, not to be confused with a seminal zone of sporting history, such as the one that happened in 1974, when Johnny Miller ran away with eight tournaments in what he described as "golfing nirvana." During this blessed period, Miller said, he knew the difference between the effort it took to hit a shot 147 yards and to hit one 149 yards, even how to take a five-iron back 100 miles an hour, as opposed to 95 or 90. He once told a golf writer, "I'd go out on the practice tee [and] hit twenty-five or thirty balls and say, 'Perfect, why am I here?'"

Nor does our zone rival a state that Tony Jacklin, a U.S. and British

Open champion, once described: "When I am in [this zone], everything is pure, vividly clear. I'm in a cocoon of concentration . . . I'm invincible."

No—what we're in is a sort of foyer that leads to a Jacklin-type cocoon. What has happened here is that we have temporarily figured out how to compensate for the flaws in our swings. We have recalibrated our timing such that our hands can make up for what our shoulders are not doing. But it nevertheless feels true and thrilling. It's Johnny Miller time, things being relative.

The following morning we return to Royal Westmoreland, and I play the worst golf of the trip.

FISHING, ANYONE?

On the penultimate day of this holiday I announce to the Big Shooter that I intend to sit out our last scheduled round. Wonder of wonders, I actually do. I spend the morning at the beach with Linda and the kids, relieved that an enormous burden has been lifted. I contemplate giving the game up for good—and I mean it this time. Why forestall the inevitable? I have proven (again!) that I am entirely incapable of mastering this game, so why extend the torture?

Yes, there will be things I'll miss.

A few years ago, a person who was thinking about starting a new golf magazine (just what we need) called and asked me to speculate on the reasons people like to play golf. I faxed him back a quick accounting:

1. It is a game of stunning beauty.
2. It is a wonderful series of idiotic bets.
3. It is a game of fine memories, which improve markedly with a world-class Scotch, or a bone-dry martini.

4. It is great to do with your wife (or husband). And it is also a great way to get away from her (or him).

5. It is assuming false identities and talking to yourself ("You gotta *hit it*, Alice!").

6. It is Arnold Palmer on a ferocious tear.

7. It is great writing (Darwin and Updike, for starters).

8. It is the serenity of dusk.

9. It is a whiff of your father.

10. It is the only good reason to retire.

Big deal, I think, walking the beach. I can readily imagine how to reap many of these rewards from other hobbies and interests. I might well be just as happy fly-fishing, at which I am much better. (There are no good reasons to keep score, and not as many people around to see you screw up.) The two sports also have a fair amount in common. Each asks that you spend long hours fully immersed in a distinct environment, a retreat, an escape from a harsh world. Each is a chess game that requires patience and strategy. Each values rhythm and grace over muscle and aggression.

Each is enchanting.

Howell Raines, who a few years ago wrote a book called *Fly-fishing Through a Midlife Crisis*, said that "people who fish do so because it seems like magic to them." Raines wasn't referring just to the hunting down, the snaring, of fish—he meant the magic of the movements we are called upon to make, the interplay of hand, arm, and body to produce the whisper-soft cast required to land a calculation of feathers above the nose of a wary trout. The body can bring this about with minimum effort, with just the right tempo and grip pressure. And when it happens, it *does* feel magical, even divine. If I can do that with a fly rod, why keep trying and failing with a three-iron?

After all, it isn't the sport, it's that *sweet spot* that we crave, be it on the links or in the water.

Hitting the sweet spot is to the performance-obsessed nineties what hitting the G-spot was to the sex-crazed seventies: extreme, repeatable pleasure.

Hitting the sweet spot, over and over again, is what a golfer must do to break eighty. And what a fly-fisher must do to put a fly just where he wants it.

About fifteen years ago, John Jerome wrote a wonderful book called *The Sweet Spot in Time.* It is a graceful and wise reflection on the subject, something of a literary sweet spot unto itself. Jerome starts off by describing what the sweet spot feels like. He says that it occurs in all forms of physical activity but is especially satisfying in games played with a stick and a ball. Jerome writes that hitting the sweet spot happens when "you swing the implement—bat, racket, golf club, whatever—as usual, but you meet the ball a little more accurately than usual, make contact more squarely. The ball simply takes off: a remarkably smooth, easy, yet forceful result." The sweet spot, Jerome says, is something you can virtually *hear.* It's the sharp *click* of the golf ball, the *crack* of the bat, the *whock* of the strings on the racket. When you hit the sweet spot, neither shock nor vibration is felt through your hands. It is, says Jerome, "finding the center of percussion." While Howell Raines finds this sensation magical, to Jerome it is mystical. The distinction is hardly worth quibbling over.

At the core of Jerome's book is what he calls the "Sweet Spot Theory of (Sports) Performance." He argues that what separates the gifted athlete from the rest of us, the scratch shooter from the dub, the fisherman who catches fish from the lunkhead who scares them off, is the ability (unconscious) to control the various trajectories of the arcs our muscles must perform to produce a critical "crack-the-whip" motion—precisely what Bobby Jones described in his own book. These requisite movements are variously described as "silken," "flowing," or just plain "relaxed." Picture the swing of Gene Littler, or of Fred Couples. Those who can move this way, Jerome says, are blessed with the ability "to damp out the assorted wobbles and wasted motions and other excursions that would otherwise screw up the true trajectories."

If I am not blessed with that ability, why not just hang up my spikes and go fishing?

Well, just as there are parallels between the two sports, there are important differences. Fly-fishing is enjoyed by people who like, *really* like, to be alone. Golf, on the other hand, is for people who *sort of* like to be alone but aren't very good at it. There are many times during a round—on the tee box, on the green—when I enjoy being a member of a tiny community. And yet there are other times—hitting second shots, trapped in a bunker—when I value being completely on my own. A round of golf alternates between intimacy and isolation. There's something awfully nice about that.

Fishing, however, will get you heaven faster, as Norman MacLean makes plain in *A River Runs Through It*. Sure, we can derive from golf a litany of spiritual rewards—stunning landscapes, whiffs of our fathers, a code of conduct—but it also comes loaded down with unfortunate baggage: exclusionary private clubs; cutesy-poo, animal-head covers; needlepoint throw pillows stitched with moronic golfing aphorisms. (Come to think of it, fly-fishing also has those pillows.)

Even though golf has been greatly democratized these last twenty years, you still hear a lot of people apologizing for their love of the sport. To be sure, these tend to be writers, not real people, pointy heads who have a hard time squaring their personal affection for the game with all of its unfortunate accouterments. Golf, they'll tell you, is like France—a great place to be except for the people you find there. An articulate expression of such Golf Shame may be found in David Owen's *My Usual Game*, an entertaining if mildly defensive golfing memoir published a few years ago. Writes Owen (who, for what it's worth, had the same first-grade teacher as Tom Watson):

One of the hardest things about becoming a golfer, for me, has been finding a way to conceive of the game as something more than just a pastime for people who have more leisure than they deserve. For an American of a certain age, cultural outlook, and political inclination, a lot of golf is more than faintly embarrassing. Is there any sound more evocative of grody Republican smugness than the sound of golf spikes on brick? [When I] exchange pleasantries with the guy who carries my bag from the storage room to the first tee, I hear myself using the same tone of condescending familiarity that my father uses with the guy who carries his.

The Shooter and I, and others of our crowd, used to share Owen's view. Years ago, in an attempt to distance ourselves from the pink-and-green froggie ashtray set, we talked about starting the CGGA—Cool Guys Golf Association. The CGGA would serve as a kind of support group for people like us, and a battle cry against people like *them*. All I can remember now about the CGGA was that we made a long list of qualities that distinguished us from them, a list that if we were to re-draft it today would read something like this:

Cool	*Uncool*
• Rural public courses	• Country clubs
• Anything cotton	• Anything polyester
• Any old golf clubs	• Callaway irons
• No keeping score	• Medal play
• Jack Lemmon	• O.J. Simpson
• Hit when you're ready	• Honors
• Playing solo at dusk	• Corporate scrambles
• Carry-bags with legs	• Electric carts
• Liberal mulligan policy	• Sandbagging
• Playing without a glove	• Sticking your glove in your back pocket with the fingers flapping when you're on the green

But why, in the end, does golf have to be *resisted*?

Despite some truly bad things about it—it takes too long, it's too difficult—golf offers sublime recompense to all who venture forth. Which is why all of us eventually drop our resistance and happily join what the great golf writer Bernard Darwin called "the bravest, stupidest race in the world."

The last twenty years have brought a torrent of tributes, anthems, elegies, and inquisitions into what makes a round of golf not only beautiful to behold but therapeutic to the body and soul. Timothy Gallwey (of *Inner Game* fame) wrote that we might look to the golf course as a splendid and rewarding place to find three of life's most meaningful rewards: the joy of successful *performance*; the lessons of *experience*; and the satisfaction of *learning*. Not to mention the fact that golf provides an excuse to take Fridays off.

FLYING HOME

How much worse can it get? At the airport in Barbados, they could be loading my corpse onto the plane in a golfer's travel bag.

I sink down into my seat to ponder next steps. Heading home, I conclude that it isn't so much the dull ache of incompetence that's bothering me about my game, it's the confusion—the usual contradictions.

Despite all the reading, watching, and taking lessons, I still get a hundred things wrong in the second-plus it takes to bring a golf club from its standing start to its fragile finish. I am proof that there is no little knowledge more dangerous than a little golf knowledge. I *know* what each of my body parts and their attendant joints are supposed to do, and when, where, and how they are supposed to get with the program. But I can't *get* them to go along. They remain adamant in their refusal to play by the book. Nagging question marks dangle up and down my body like broken ornaments on a tree:

Feet: Weight on the outside, too far back on the heels?

Knees: Shift too much on the backswing?

Hips: Tend to sway, not rotate?

Torso and shoulders: Too little turn?

Fingers: Grip club too tightly?

Wrists: Tend to cup, not cock?

Left elbow: Breaks down near top?

Right elbow: Flies open?

Head: Not still?

Brad Redding says to keep the weight up on the balls of the feet. But the gospel according to Robert Tyre Jones, whose book I pull out abjectly in the crowded airport waiting room, declares that the weight should be "more back on the heels." Jones also warns against the average golfer's tendency to place his feet too far apart, "as though he were getting set to lift a piano." We do this, he says, in a misguided effort to add distance to our shots. But with our dogs so widely spaced, Jones says, we lock the lower part of the body and impair our shoulder turn, which only diminishes our power.

What's a poor hacker to do?

Incertitude oozes from every joint, and these droplets plink and plunk into the stream of doubt that leads back to the shed in East Tennessee and further beyond that, all the way back to the scabrous public course in Philadelphia, where I so long ago came upon the headwaters of this river of endless confusion.

But all is not hopeless. I take some comfort in the fact that I have lived long enough to know how a river runs: how it twists and turns back on itself; how it is always streaming ahead; how it looks a certain way from a given spot at a bend, then suddenly changes, opens up, and eventually, despite its tumultuous journey, manages to arrive exactly where it always wanted to be.

Overanalysis

If you thought about merely walking down the street the way
you think about golf you'd wind up falling off the curb.
—John Updike, ***Rabbit Is Rich***, 1982

DIGGING DEEPER

"You're going to get there, but it's going to take time," Redding says, the next time we are back in the shed. This is one of the truly great understatements in the history of golf. But I am more heartened than put off by Redding's comment. He is forthright about the heavy lifting that lies ahead. Many teaching pros will promise you that they need only five or six half-hour lessons, plus the occasional follow-up booster, to impart everything they know about the golf swing. The rest is up to the student, wherein lies the rub. Most hackers are unwilling or unable to put in the hours of repetitive practice required to realize the potential of their lessons. And even if we were, most of us wouldn't spend the time on what we should be attending to—chipping, pitching, and putting.

All that aside, there is little consensus among golf pros about the best way to practice. Bobby Jones wasn't much enamored with the idea of hitting balls repetitively in order to "groove" a swing. His advice was to work diligently on those shots we already knew how to make in order to instill confidence and assure predictability. Ben Hogan, on the other hand, was renowned for the endless hours he spent on the practice range, hitting hundreds and hundreds of balls daily, exercising every club in his bag without mercy. "There isn't enough daylight in any one day to practice all the shots you need to practice," he once said. "Every day you miss practicing, it will take you one day longer to be good."

More than once I ask Redding what I ought to be doing between lessons. He just shrugs and tells me to hit a small bucket of balls a few times a week. I am disappointed by the answer, for I absolutely love hitting balls. The Shooter says I love hitting balls more than actually playing, and he is right. I agree with Hogan—if there's a golf swing to be learned, it will be achieved only through boundless repetition, hitting ball after ball with every club in the bag, moving from the short irons to the long irons to the woods, day after day, much as a fledgling pianist must practice scales.

So I wing it. Day after day, I hit balls at Lee-Jane. But is this getting me anywhere? Most of us who "practice" at the range aren't practicing at all, but merely hitting. We don't work diligently on a specific problem. And we certainly don't waste our buckets on short chips or pitches. What we do is flail, swing from the heels, beat balls with no particular target in mind, and thus reiterate and reinforce the very flaws we arrived with. Most hackers will tell you they're much better golfers on the range than on the course. The reasons are obvious: Nobody's aiming at much of anything, the circumstances are tension-free, and everybody's hitting off mats. Mats are among golf's greatest abominations, worse than electric carts. A teaching pro told me that mats carry "a 40 percent fudge factor." A hacker on a mat can hit inches behind the ball and still get off a decent-looking shot.

Barbados was yesterday. It's a chilly day in late March. Redding and I sit down to work out a long-term schedule for our lessons. We'll meet at least once a week for the next few months, at his usual $60 an hour. The goal is to move me from bad to better by the end of the *current* golfing season. Redding seems confident he can manage the reclamation on this timetable.

When I return home, I go right to the attic and rummage through storage boxes in search of instruction books, magazine clippings, and other golf-related stuff I've collected over the years. This archive, socked away along with meaningless old memos from work and paperbacks I've carted around since college, represents a golfer's self-directed, haphazard curriculum. Seeing it all in one place, I am surprised at how much I've accumulated, and nonplussed to realize that, like all the money I've spent on lessons, all this paper has had little or no effect on my ability to hit a golf ball.

Most of the books I haul out were published in the seventies and early eighties, in those heady days of disco, wrinkle-phobic polyester pants, and razor-cut hairstyles with luxuriant sideburns. I take a quick glance through the material as I load it into a carton to be dragged downstairs to my basement office. Nearly every book is littered with abandoned bookmarks, dog ears, and highlighted passages, an historical record of passing whims and obsessions that add up to a lifelong search for golfing wisdom and truth.

Here's *The Inside Path to Better Golf*, by Peter Kostis (talk about a helmet-cut!), a large-format, illustrated primer by one of the game's "young lions," as its publisher proclaimed. Like every contemporary golf instruction book, Kostis's did what it could to distinguish itself from its legion of competitors. Gamely, it wrapped itself in what Madison Avenue likes to call a USP, Unique Selling Proposition—or, as I call it, a GLUT, Golf's Latest Universal Theory. A GLUT is a gimmick, a shtick, a handle, a hook that sets you apart from everybody else. The GLUT gives a golfer reason to believe that the book may be the long-awaited answer to his prayers. Kostis's GLUT was pretty lame as GLUTs go: To hit the ball long and straight, a hacker needs to develop—stop me if you've heard this one—a proper inside-to-outside swing path. To achieve it we must learn the use of our "speed muscles" (the leverage system made up of the hands and arms, arms and shoulders). At the same time, we need to rid ourselves of the tendency to rely on the big, slow muscles of our shoulders and hips as a means to bully the ball forward.

A paragraph early on in *The Inside Path* well illustrates why a reasonably intelligent and otherwise sane adult can go bananas trying to learn to play golf from a book. It is a paragraph I'd once underscored on some long-ago evening of quiet desperation. It must have seemed like a good idea at the time. Yet now, as I read the sentences over and over, I am astounded that I could have ever found any value in such palaver:

> The golf swing requires the proper blending of three different actions— *lateral, vertical,* and *rotary.* The swing goes back and forth—lateral. The swing goes up and down—vertical. And the swing goes, to a certain extent, around your body—rotary. Your arms and hands are the only parts of your body that can accomplish all of these actions. Your lower body can move laterally and in a rotary fashion, but certainly not vertically. Your shoulders can rotate and can even move laterally, in a sense, but they can't move vertically if you are to have any chance of striking an

effective shot. Only the hands and arms can move in all three ways, which is why you should trust them to control your swing, providing support with the rest of your body.

That settled, what say we move on to quarks and string theory?

The next book I dust off is Tom Watson's *Getting Up and Down*, with drawings by Hogan's illustrator, Anthony Ravielli (though his work here is not nearly so compelling). *Up and Down*'s GLUT was "how to save strokes from forty yards and in," which is where, Watson sensibly pointed out, we play more than half of our shots during the course of a round.

Getting Up and Down, which often makes the list of best golf instruction books of the last few decades, is an anthology of bite-sized tips, one or two to a page. Golfers crave tips, which are to true learning what junk food is to nutrition. I remember how hooked I once was on this volume, how many times over a distant winter I picked it up, absurdly trying to memorize its counsel on how to master the short game: where to position the ball when chipping from a downhill lie, how to control the length of a blast from a greenside bunker. I remember, too, how futile this effort was, to *read* about how to do something and yet be unable to try it right then and there on a real green. This is but one of the reasons you can't learn much about golf from the printed page: A disconnect occurs between what reaches your head and what must be physically played out, then repeatedly rehearsed.

I come across Jack Nicklaus's *Golf My Way*, also routinely cited as one of the most influential of modern golf books. *My Way* manages to be detailed and technical but not abstruse or overly pedantic. Nicklaus devotes a lot of yardage to the importance of the steady head. We hear all the time that it's vital to keep our heads on straight throughout the swing. Nicklaus goes to some trouble to explain why, calling a steady head "*the* bedrock fundamental of golf." (Well, we know what he means.) There are at least four good reasons for this, Nicklaus explains:

The head is the hub of the swing and thus critical to proper coiling and leverage; move the head and you will directly alter the arc and plane of the swing; a moving head alters our vision, causing us to take our eyes off the ball; and, finally, given that the head is the heaviest part of our body relative to size, its stability is critical to our balance. Shake the coconut and everything else will wobble off-kilter. (Of course, even this contention is contradicted on occasion. Some teachers will avow that good hip movement *requires* that the head move back and down; to keep it stock still is to throw a wrench into the works.)

The best-known passage in *Golf My Way*, often quoted in books not just about golf, but about kinesiology, meditation, and sports psychology, has to do with visualization, or "going to the movies," as Nicklaus puts it. The Bear stresses that he *never* contemplates a shot or takes a swing—even in practice—for which he doesn't first form a picture in his mind of its "path, trajectory, and shape, even its behavior on landing." Some writers have implied that this technique makes Nicklaus something of a mind-over-body type, an inner-gamesman who's got a third eye concealed under his Golden Bear visor. Not so. Nicklaus goes to the movies not to *will* his ball to a given location, but to help him determine where to set his feet and whether to fade or draw the ball.

One afternoon at Lee-Jane I try an experiment. Using a nine-iron, I allow myself twenty shots to hit the old rusty pickup: ten using the visualization technique, and ten just stepping up and whacking away. Each method produces three direct hits. My conclusion is that there is a great deal of insight and intelligence in what Jack says about the value of visualization. It's also obvious that I'm not good enough yet to put it to any use.

April in Knoxville. Nothing yet in blossom. Redding's bazooka heater sits silently, shoved aside to one corner of the shed. Otherwise, not much has changed. The Bermuda grass at Willow Creek remains buff-colored, and the weekly lessons are pretty much the same. Weather permitting, which it now generally is, I meet Redding up on the out-door range.

"Hey, how ya hittin' 'em?" Redding always asks. This serves as his all-purpose greeting, a golf pro's equivalent of *shalom.*

I always take the question literally and feel obliged to reply with a detailed analysis of the week's progress at Lee-Jane. This week, for instance, was marked by a concerted effort to do little other than *extend* my arms—to keep the left arm straighter than usual on the backswing. I tried to sweep through my shots, finishing with my arms as high as possible. It seemed to work, I happily report to Redding.

"Great, now hit a few for me," Redding says.

I am by now aware of some slight improvement in my basic setup. I am better balanced. While the weight shift—check that, *redistribution*—is not as effortless as on that breakthrough day on the range, my ability to turn and load is definitely better than when I began this excellent adventure. The big problem, as it has always been, is the damnable propensity to swing from over the top, to cast the club on an outside-in path. While most golf books decry this tendency as far and away golf's worst offense, they invariably oversimplify the reasons so many of us are compelled to commit the sin. This flawed action can be caused by, or encouraged by, one of many, or *many* of many, wrong moves and misalignments: Grip, posture, foot position, knee turn, hip turn, and shoulder turn are just some of the reasons we are unable to drop the club into the desired slot. All of these in turn may be caused by, or encouraged by, our compulsion to *hit* the ball, as opposed to making a relaxed effort to swing *through* the spot where the ball happens to rest.

Though my address position has improved, I am still casting the club. It's no surprise that my shots don't go very far, and usually peter out to the right. Redding escorts me from the range to the shed, where he takes fresh video of me. I know exactly what to look for by now: that split second at the top of the backswing. This is when my hands and arms, instead of dropping *down*, attempt to throw the club forward and over—*over the top*. Each time I see this I wince.

"Set up again for me," Redding says. He moves me around, then around again, trying to get me to feel the correct swing plane.

"Set up again for me," he repeats, steps backs, and pushes the record button on the VCR. "Now, give me a nice, smooth swing."

All I can manage, even after a month, is a swing that starts out okay, then collapses near the top into an outside-in catastrophe.

Every golf teacher and every golf book promises a cure for this ailment. A respected teaching pro in Boca Raton, Martin Hall, once instructed me to imagine there was a table to the rear and to the right of me. When starting my backswing, he said, think about laying the club head down on that table. This tip had dire consequences, as I developed a horrific tendency to use my arms—he said little about how a shoulder turn might come in handy here—to effect a bizarre looping action somewhere behind my right ear.

Shortly before Hall advanced that suggestion, Jim Flick threw everything he had at me to try to get me to stop the infernal casting, also to no avail. He had me stand on the practice tee without a club in my hands, raise my arms to shoulder height, then simply drop them to my sides, over and over.

"It's called *gravity*, Mr. Lee, take advantage of it," the indomitable Flick proffered with a smile. When gravity didn't work, he tried a sterner measure. He prescribed a drill that required me to hit the ball with my back to the target so that I could feel what it was like to swing with my arms, while keeping my shoulders at bay. That didn't work, either.

"Try hitting it to right field" is a common, putative antidote numerous instructors have offered through the years. But whenever I try to do this my hands and wrists go kablooey as I attempt to line a shot to the gap.

Tips like these, however well-intentioned, are entirely capable of making your golf swing even *worse*, especially when you mush them all together into one overheated stew and let them age for a season or two. Perhaps Redding's approach, constant hands-on moving, will do the trick. He drags me around for the zillionth time. And for the zillionth time, I feel that weird paddle thing.

At this point I am neither especially encouraged nor discouraged by my progress, or lack of it. What's beginning to trouble me, though, is the fact that I don't think I'm playing enough. True, I hit a huge number of balls and dutifully show up at the shed every Tuesday or Wednesday. Most weeks, though, I don't play much more than a single round. I am wary about putting in more time on the golf course, even though I know I ought to. I don't want a measure of my improvement just yet—I'd rather not keep score for now.

There's a reason I'm so leery.

Back in 1990 I wangled a work assignment that gave Linda and me the chance to spend a year in London. Through the entire time I played golf but once, and then just for a few holes, because I was promptly blown back to the clubhouse by a blustery, torrential rainstorm. The English skies were so bleak that when we returned to the States, sun-starved, we decided to rent a house in Florida for a few months. Perfect, I thought. My golf slate has been swept clean. I'll take lessons and go to a driving range every day—and won't step foot on a golf course until I can do so completely rehabilitated.

It was then that the Big Shooter and I went off to spend a couple of days at the Nicklaus-Flick Golf School.

A golf teacher for over forty years, Jim Flick is white-haired and skinny as a one-iron. Onstage, which he always is, he is a great showman, with a full repertoire of trick shots and jock banter. He is a marvelous teacher, too, the kind we dream about for our kids. As the Shooter has observed, Flick is passionate, articulate, determined, and has the astonishing ability to make each of his students feel that he or she is getting more of the master's time and attention than anybody else.

The mantra for this particular weekend was *feel the club head*, an admonition that has been uttered by golf instructors for eons. The storied teacher Ernest Jones, who taught Alister MacKenzie how to play, based his entire approach on the words, "The club head. The head. The head."

Feel the club head and you will get a great many things right, Flick told us. You will hold the club with the proper intensity: *fingers secure, arms relaxed*, as he put it again and again. Feel the club head and you will begin to experience that golf is a swing game, not a turn game, meaning that when your arms swing freely then everything else will move naturally along with them, notably, your shoulders and your hips.

Touch and tempo, tempo and touch.

Flick tried to get us to think of a golf stick more as an *instrument* and less as a cudgel, the idea being that you hold an instrument with greater respect and sensitivity than you wield a club. Then he showed us how to determine whether we were grasping our instruments too firmly. He told us to hold one of our clubs with its club head pointing vertically to the sky. This grip was too light, he said. Then he told us to hold the club perpendicular to the ground. This grip was too tight. Finally, he told us to hold the club at about a forty-five-degree angle to the ground. This grip was just right.

Flick talked fervently about the stages we need to go through if we are to improve at a physical activity, how we need to go from being unconsciously incompetent to consciously competent to unconsciously competent, the nirvana stage at which we point we are able to play with a relaxed yet intense concentration, the way the big boys on Tour do.

Following that weekend with Flick, I worked diligently in the Florida sun. Every day after lunch, I went to a driving range to whack balls. Once a week I took a private lesson with Martin Hall. I did this for four months and had a sense that I was getting pretty good. I was ready to see what would happen on a golf course. So one fair afternoon I ventured out at the Boca Raton Resort.

It was as if I had done *nothing* to improve my game. Paired with a couple down from New York, I utterly humiliated myself, hitting popups and perps all day. My driving was pitiful, my short game was painful. In assessing the damage, I could come up with only one consolation: After four months of hard practice I'd gone from unconsciously incompetent to consciously incompetent.

That crushing Florida disappointment lurks inside, and is the principal reason I am reluctant to go out on a course, despite Redding's urging. Now and then, on a midday morning when Willow Creek is all but deserted, I play a round with some of the regulars here. On a gray and misty day in early April I walk the front nine with two old-timers, Ben and Frank. Ben is chatty, Frank taciturn. It should be the other way around, though, because Frank is a dead ringer for the loquacious Alistair Cooke, at least a working man's version of same, dressed in a long-sleeved flannel shirt and a heavy tweed cap. Ben, decked out in a Chi-Chi wide-brimmed hat with a jaunty band, is wiry and limber, dropping to his heels to line up his putts, all pretty inspiring for a gentleman in his mid-seventies. While Frank uses a standard pull cart, Ben has one of those motorized jobs, a low-tech R2-D2 with a set of Pings lashed to its back. *Boy*, I think, *that thing looks handy*! I am startled by my interest in it. I am forty-eight years old! What on earth am I thinking?

The three of us play on together. The two seniors make pars and bogies, while I card mostly doubles. Frank and Ben are decent and supportive, nice chaps who watch the seasons come and go from a public golf course. They are what's right about this game. They, not titanium drivers or stimpmeters, are its soul. On the seventh fairway, Ben points to a tree about 180 yards down the right side and wryly comments about how it is his nemesis, how it always comes into play on his second shot. He smiles and likens it to "that darned Eisenhower tree at Augusta," a reference he doesn't feel the slightest need to explain.

Playing a little better now, I par the eighth hole, and hit a couple of nice shots on the ninth. A thought hits me as I walk onto the green: *There may be no breakthrough.* Don't look for one and don't kid yourself, because that's not how learning happens. What happens is what goes on at the bottom of a stream: Layers of sediment build up, one on top of another. Learning happens by accretion, wave after wave. Sometimes the current moves through quickly, leaving measurable deposits. Sometimes, though, their production is so subtle you don't know that the waves are even at work. But it all adds up. You just have to trust in that.

HOLY GRAIL!

I am up to my ears in golf books. If one can break eighty by cramming for it, I've got it nailed.

In a *Golf Magazine* book commemorating the centennial of the sport in America, I come across an essay by John Andrisani. Entitled "The Learning Process," the piece offers a history of modern golf instruction. It says that there have been a number of contrasting schools of thought about the essence of the golf swing. After describing how technology—the advent of frame-by-frame photography and, later, video and computer-enhanced graphics—has changed (and presumably improved) the way golf is taught, the essay summarizes what has remained *constant* down through the years, "a set of time-tested fundamentals that governs the setup and swing." Andrisani's list, were it to be delivered unto us as golf's Eight Commandments, would go something like this:

1. Thou shalt hold the club with a neutral grip.
2. Thou shalt set up square to the ball, with thy weight balanced equally between the ball and heel of each foot.
3. Thou shalt employ a one-piece takeaway by sweeping the club low to the ground for a foot or two.
4. Thou shalt keep thy head still and thy left arm relatively straight. Let thy wrists cock naturally whilst turning thy hips forty-five degrees and thy shoulders ninety.
5. Thou shalt arrive at a square position at the top of the swing, club shaft parallel to the ground.
6. Thou shalt commence thy downswing with thy lower body.
7. Thou shalt swing through the ball, not at it.
8. Thou shalt finish facing slightly left of the target.

Now, while I am certainly no historian of the game, and my standing as a mere practitioner of it has been by this point established, I do know enough to assert that there is a lot of disagreement over even these precepts. In fact, I personally have received conflicting advice on at least *half* of them, namely: the first, the second, the fifth, and the eighth. Of the four remaining proscriptions, two—the third and fourth—are heavily qualified in many well-known instruction books and in lessons I've taken.

That leaves but two commandments—start the downswing with your lower body; and swing through the ball, not at it—that might be considered to be universally accepted.

In fact there is no one and only golf swing that works. As Andrisani points out, the great early golfers at St. Andrews swung fast and furiously, violating a host of modern tenets. Their swings were flat and wristy, as these legends of the misty links made no attempt whatsoever to keep their left arms straight. Verily, they looked a lot like many of the overwound bozos you see on the range today. But the technique worked for them. As Andrisani explains, a flat swing enabled the early British golfers to hit low draws into the teeth of the bitter seaside winds. There was also a sartorial factor at play here. Shackled as they were in heavy clothing, these intrepid, shivering souls *had* to use their wrists; bound in their tweeds, they couldn't move freely if they'd wanted to.

Golfologists routinely cite Harry Vardon's eponymous grip as the innovation that heralded the game's modern era. Unlike the ten-fingered (or baseball) grip, in which both hands simply wrap around the club, the Vardon (or overlapping) grip calls for the little finger of the right hand to be placed over the index finger of the left. The value of this grip is that the pinkie not only helps to neuter the right hand, which otherwise wants to overpower the left, but also serves as something of a brake against too much wrist action.

Brad Redding takes an avid interest in the history of golf instruction. He is proud of his collection of hundreds of books on the subject. One day he lets me borrow one of his prized possessions, James M. Barnes's *Picture Analysis of Golf Strokes*, published in 1919. Redding says that it is the first book to show detailed photographs of the golf swing in motion. (Barnes is the Eadweard Muybridge of golf.) As Redding admits, "I got absolutely nothing out of the text. Zero. But the pictures are *awesome*."

James Barnes was a dominant golfer of his day, winner of the PGA in 1916 and 1919. He was a tall and rangy chap with a shock of curly hair, who dressed in a white shirt with the sleeves rolled up, a narrow tie, cuffed trousers, and dark golf shoes. The pictures in the book show that he has taken off his watch and hung it on a loop on the right side of his waistband.

It is easy to imagine how compelling the *Picture Analysis* must have been to young golfers back then. Its revealing photos no doubt packed the same punch that Ravielli's drawings of Hogan held for a later generation of hopefuls. The book's implicit promise was alluring: Here, for the first time, was the golf swing captured and dissected. New technology, in this case a still camera with a fast shutter, had provided a breakthrough in teaching. One could study the golf swing as never before.

But Barnes was admirably forthright about the limitations of his book (thereby distinguishing himself from almost every other author of a modern golf instructional). He freely admitted that his pictures could not convey the movements of the hands and arms so that a tyro might easily emulate them. The photographs, Barnes said, could not get a student to *feel* what the swing was supposed to feel like. So he gave it a go in words, attempting to describe what should happen at the very top of the swing, the instant the club starts down:

> The head has remained perfectly still. The line of vision to the ball is directly over the left shoulder. The control of the club is still in the left hand, although the grip is still firm in the fingers of both hands. The face of the club is turned slightly upward. The right elbow is as close to the body without being cramped. The right leg is playing a prominent part in maintaining position, and firmly bracing the body. At this part of the stroke an even and firm balance is essential.

You'd think that by now we'd have all gotten the point.

DREAMERS

Every once in a while, when I pull into the parking lot at Lee-Jane, I sit in the car for a few minutes, drink a Dr Pepper, and watch the hackers as they go through their paces. I have begun to understand why the first American practice range—at Pinehurst—was known as Maniac Hill. These hackers have come here with the determined gazes of Touring pros, shamelessly plastered with logos on their shirts, hats, and golf bags. They keep a stiff upper lip (if not a straight left arm) when they misclobber one, which is often, and hold their pose with a proud, tight-lipped stare into the middle-distance on those precious occasions when they do nail one.

Golf lets ordinary Joes play dress-up. It provides a harmless, albeit not inexpensive, way to idealize ourselves. Through its trappings, surroundings, and etiquette, the game invites us to be cool and graceful. And since it doesn't require us to run fast (or even walk, for that matter), jump high, throw far, or ever have to hit anyone (not on purpose, anyway), golf presents itself as an athletic challenge that is well within our reach—even though so many of us may be flabby little flubadubs.

The driving range is a place of dreams. There's a poignancy to a joint like Lee-Jane. Check out the husky kid with the buzz cut, as he twists himself into knots to swing as hard as he can. Here on the mat he might as well be John Daly, shooting the lights out at the British Open. No matter that he's spraying range balls everywhere and nowhere: toppers, vicious slices, hurricane-force whiffs.

Observe the slender, supple, well-groomed Johnny with the mannered swing, with the account exec's haircut and the SkyTel pager clipped to his *faux* alligator belt. Watch how he makes like Lehman or Janzen, holding his finish with smug satisfaction after every push-hook.

Dig the Don Juan DeMarco type, wearing the Dolce & Gabbana tee-shirt and tinted *oglietti* by Armani. He reminds you of that foursome of young Eurotrash in the Bud commercial of a few years ago, *L'Homo Vogue* types in baggy whites who, pulling hand carts, no less, swaggered down the fairways with damn good-looking swings.

Check out that skinny dweeb, wearing wrinkled chinos from the Gap, a linksnerd who turns up his nose at electric carts and decries the inherent social injustice of country clubs. He's probably a Crenshaw fan, a thinking man's hacker whose passion for the game is tempered by the grave environmental consequences of its misuse of herbicides and pesticides.

With golf, it's just a short chip shot between who we are and all that we could be. Golf holds out the possibility of greatness. And while we don't achieve it often, we do now and then. It happens when the stars are aligned just right and/or when by some extraordinary act of physical compensation, or stroke of luck, we manage to *clkkkkkk* the ball squarely. We are, right at that unspellable, unpronounceable *clkkkkkk* of a split second, everything we might ever be.

The rest of the time, though, golf is cruel and unforgiving, such as when we violently smash our whistling steel into the earth, clip the top of the ball, or sideswipe it. At times like these, at dreadful times like these, golf renders us worthless.

There's a good example of golf's reductive powers in Walker Percy's novel *The Second Coming*. The narrator is a man of considerable melancholy who spends too much of his time searching for meaning, as if tracking a lost ball. The symbol of his existential angst is a persistent and incurable banana:

> The slice, which had become worrisome lately, had gotten worse. He had come to see it as an emblem of his life, a small failure at living, a minor deceit, perhaps even a sin. [But] unlike sin in life, retribution is instantaneous. The ball, one's very self launched into its little life . . . goes wrong and ever wronger, past the rough, past even the barbed-wire fence, and into the bark fens and thickets and briars of out-of-bounds. One is punished on the spot.

One is punished on the spot.

This, strange as it may sound, is one of the reasons we love golf. It isn't that we savor the punishment, wallow in the crushing despair of a thousand shots gone sour. No—we are drawn to golf because the punishment it metes out sets up our need to get golf right. To get golf right sets us on a arc of self-discovery and revelation. It sets us on a path. The path is its own reward.

Gullibility

When I ask you to take an aspirin,
please don't take the whole bottle.
—*Harvey Penick's Little Red Book,* 1992

BUCKETS FULL OF MIRACLES

In the minds of many around the globe—certainly in the minds of certain golf-mad Asians with a penchant for triple-decker driving ranges—we Americans have grown fat and lazy. We have the staying power of gnats, they say, and have become a nation of wad-shooters. And while cultural stereotypes are dangerous and cruel (you'll never hear *me* criticizing others in the family of man for their excruciatingly slow play on the course), these critics may indeed have a point. Look at the circumstantial evidence: NordicTraks and E-Z Riders clutter our attics. Lustrous new Baldwins sit in stony silence. One of every two American marriages ends in failure. We bolt when the first blush of enthusiasm fades.

Am I the proud, patriotic exception?

The more balls I fire at the rusty pickup with HIT ME painted on the side, the more I exult in my own perseverance. It is now mid-April. Spring bulbs have bullied their way to the surface. On the golf front there's good news and bad news. The bad news is that my scorecard has shown no effects of a spring thaw. As my father used to say, I have gone from Joe Stinker to Charlie Stinker.

The good news is that more and more of my shots assume a semi-respectable flight pattern as they whiz through the warmer air corridors above Lee-Jane.

But frustration and impatience, like a couple of vultures who've caught a whiff of rancid meat, have moved onto the utility wires high over the range. I sense I am tottering on a slippery slope, the one I set out to conquer just three months ago, just before Barbados, when I gave myself until the end of the summer to break eighty. Based on my rate of progress to date, the chance I will achieve this goal in the allotted time ranges from diddly to zip. I am in dire need of a growth spurt. But aside from steroids (and at my age all they would likely do is speed up the growth of ear hair), I can envision no great leap forward. So I live the day-to-day existence of a golfing tortoise, spurred on by the dreary conviction that slow and steady will win the day.

This mature and sensible view is as dicey as it is dour. It leaves me too much time to think. I second-guess everything. The obsession of the moment is that I may be grossly *overpracticing:* hitting too many balls, too weakly, too often; chasing my own tail; reinforcing flaws, not correcting them.

The issue is framed one beautiful afternoon at Lee-Jane. I have finished whacking the first half of my daily dose, which is typically two jumbo buckets containing about seventy-five balls apiece. This many balls a day doesn't even get me *close* to winning a frequent flogger award at Lee-Jane. The owner of the place has told me about an animal-science major from UT who shows up most days and forks over $16.95 for a "Big Bubba"—an astoundingly large bucket, a laundry basket really, holding over 300 range balls! By comparison, I'm just a piddler. But today I'm a piddler on a roll. I have had better than usual success with the first batch of balls. My arms are relaxed, my swing is nice and loose, and my shots are generally acceptable. (They continue to leak to the right, but not as badly as on the earliest days at Willow Creek.) Today, I've mostly hit five-irons, though I end with a dozen or so three-woods. The last three of these shots are gems, carrying 200-plus yards despite a gentle head wind. I have found my rhythm. I am tempted to call it a day, quit while I'm ahead, end on a high note, leave myself wanting more. There is no end to the clichés and arguments for why I ought to carry the clubs back to the car—now!—and go home to fertilize the lawn.

But there's a welter of counterclichés for why I should stay put. When you're hot you're hot. Catch lightning in a bottle. Seize the day. Keep swinging so that whatever it is I'm doing right will be absorbed into my deepest, delicate organs. Isn't this why the pros put in four, five, and six hours a day on the practice tee? Isn't the road to unconscious competency paved with a million repetitive thwacks?

So I stay.

And—no surprise—just a few balls into bucket number two I come unglued. I have pried open a can of worm burners, slices, shanks, perps, and sky balls. My arms are tired, so my head tries to assert control over this worsening calamity. My head is a microprocessor run amok. The good rhythm, the smooth-working swing, have once again been reduced to intellectual static.

Driving off in a cloud of smoking rubber, I feel the need to indict someone for the crash of my promising afternoon. But who can take the fall? Who is to blame for our failure to learn? Our schools—those overcrowded prisons of the spirit—which teach to the tests, not to the essence of learning? Our parents, who don't set a very good example? When was the last time they finished a book that wasn't by Harvey Penick? The culture at large—with its shrill, hard selling of cure-alls, magic bullets, and guaranteed panaceas that we can order *now*—pencils ready?—through an 800-number and a credit card?

IS SAMADHI OUT THERE?

Nearly a decade ago, when I was a full-time magazine editor, I helped conceive an *Esquire* cover story written by George Leonard. Back then, it was an annual rite for Leonard to produce a hefty treatment on some aspect of health and fitness. These features sold well on newsstands, and readers came to look forward to them for their reliable and enlightened advice. Now, as I second-guess, overthink, and worry over my faltering progress, one of Leonard's pieces has leaped back into my consciousness.

George Leonard and I don't have all that much in common. He remains—in chipper defiance of his seventy-plus years—a tall, courtly, and impossibly fit gentleman with impeccable posture. He's possessed of clear blue eyes that neither shrink from, nor blink at, direct and intimate contact. He is, I can reasonably say, an old-fashioned kind of Renaissance man (though he would never describe himself that way, given his characteristic modesty): a person of wide-ranging intellectual interests who relentlessly and joyfully bounds through life with an enormous appetite for knowledge.

Leonard's C.V. might serve as Cliff Notes for the second half of the twentieth century. He came into the world a child of the Old South, and his voice still carries the rich flavor of the Tidewater. He flew fighter planes in World War II, then made a name for himself as a journalist at *Look*, where he worked for the better part of two decades.

He covered the Civil Rights movement and other epochal events, always with compassion and ardor. He was renowned for his insistent and incisive writing about the problems of American education.

When he left *Look* in 1970, Leonard put down roots in Northern California, where he became involved in the self-actualization movement, and a crusader on behalf of a melange of personal-growth themes having to do with physical and spiritual fitness. Leonard wrote wisely about the proper role of sports in our society, most notably in a book entitled *The Ultimate Athlete*. He developed a close personal and working friendship with Michael Murphy, and was there when the hot tubs first gurgled at Esalen. His close ties with Murphy notwithstanding, Leonard had the good sense to develop little interest in golf. Instead, Leonard discovered a special passion for the martial art of aikido, which he describes as the "physical and spiritual art of self-defense and energy awareness." It is, he says, the most difficult of all martial arts to learn to do well, replete with demanding rolls and falls. It is also a sport infused with lessons about character. "On the training mat," Leonard wrote, "every attempt at circumvention or overreaching is revealed; flaws are made manifest; the quick fix is impossible."

That sentence begins to explain why Leonard is so much on my mind these days. That old *Esquire* cover story was devoted to *mastery:* what it is, how to pursue it, why we fail to attain it. It was rife with questions that I now find highly pertinent to these days at Willow Creek: How can we realize the goals we set for ourselves? Why do we quit too soon? Why can't our minds leave our bodies alone? How can we break the binds of age and habit?

Leonard used his experiences with aikido to work through many such questions. He discussed how aikido allowed him to channel his energy so that he wouldn't turn it back on himself through over-aggression or anxiety. Here's how Leonard describes life on the aikido mat:

The defender takes his stand. [He] is relaxed yet alert. He offers none of the exotic defensive poses popularized by the movie and television action thrillers. An attacker rushes at him, but he remains calm and still until the last instant. There follows a split second of unexpected intimacy in which the two figures, attacker and attacked, seem to merge. The attacker is sucked into a whirlpool of motion, then flung through the air with little or no effort on the part of the defender, who ends the maneuver in the same relaxed posture, while the attacker takes a well-practiced roll on the mat.

What does this have to do with golf?

Only everything, I conclude after a demoralizing hour at Lee-Jane. What happens on Leonard's mat is exactly what I think should be happening between me and the golf ball. Imagine the same scene just slightly recast:

A ball is placed on a wooden tee an inch above the grass. The player takes his stand on the tee, relaxed yet alert. He offers none of the exotic tics and waggles of the big boomers on TV. As the attacker begins to load his backswing, the dimpled opponent remains calm until the end. There follows a split second of unexpected intimacy in which the two participants, attacker and the attacked, seem to merge. The ball is sucked into a whirlpool of motion, then flung into the air with little or no effort on the part of the attacker, who ends the maneuver in the same relaxed posture, while the attacked takes a well-practiced roll down the fairway.

I want to make that happen. I want to achieve what Zen followers call *samadhi*, or oneness with an object—in this case, an object that comes three to a sleeve and costs about two bucks apiece. I want to find my golfing bliss the way Leonard has found his through aikido. I want to *be* the golf swing, not think the golf swing.

The lesson of Leonard's *mise-en-mat* is that process takes precedence over outcome. For him, the pursuit of excellence means an excursion, a grand tour of the spirit. The ritual of aikido is the arc of the rainbow. What's at the end of it isn't important. The real reward, the beauty, is the arc itself. The idea of taking a shortcut, of rushing mastery, is self-defeating. Why cut short the journey when the journey is the prize? This is why Leonard wrote his piece in the first place, to "warn against the bottom-line mentality that puts quick, easy results ahead of long-term dedication . . ."

OVERTIPPING

We seek improvement through a tangle of tips, panaceas, and pipe dreams. We scurry through golf magazines like birds in a barnyard, pecking at kernels of information scattered hither and yon. We tear out pages full of promising bits and pieces and stash them in manila folders for future reference.

One day I'm on an airplane, armed as is my custom with the latest issues of *Golf* and *Golf Digest*. The latter has enlisted the pedagogic talents of Jeff Maggert. Jeff's day job, of course, is decidedly not devoted to opening our minds to the deeper mysteries of linkscraft. It is dedicated to making it as a young and promising Tour player.

The headline of Maggert's tutorial is SWING YOUR DRIVER LIKE A 6-IRON.

My seatmate may well feel the energy as each of my bodily systems springs into hyperfixation mode. Pupils dilate with excitement, pulse notches upward a tick or two. I don't read the accompanying paragraphs, I *ingest* them:

A reason for my success with the driver is that I treat it like any other club. I'm not afraid of it the way many high-handicappers seem to be. Most of their bad drives stem from fear, which makes them swing too quickly.

Don't make that mistake. Don't be intimidated. Try to swing your driver as if it is a middle iron. Key on control and good tempo. Get those correct, and distance will take care of itself.

If you can swing your driver like a 6-iron, you'll soon be hitting longer and straighter drives.

Scowling, I stare into the seat back in front of me. I fire off a silent reply to Maggert: Jeff, bubeleh, if I could swing my driver—with its long shaft and low degree of loft—like a six-iron I wouldn't in the first place be flapping through *Golf Digest* like a chicken without a head cover. If I could swing my six-iron like a six-iron, meaning, with "control" and "good tempo," I wouldn't be all that worried about my driver in the first place. Besides, the problems average players have with their drivers are a lot more basic than just matters of control and tempo. Tommy Armour often observed that most average players don't even know how to tee up their balls when they whip out their bashers. They push their pegs too far into the ground rather than place them so that there is a half a ball above the top of the driver when it's soled behind the tee.

Bottom-line mentality. Quick, easy results.

What better examples of this predilection exist than those itty-bitty anthologies of fixer-upper tips designed as first-aid manuals to be used in ticklish spots when you're out on the course?

I actually own one of these mini-volumes, though I've never had the nerve to pull it out on the course, nor is it stored amidst the inventory of tools, unguents, notions, and patent medicines that turn my golf bag into a traveling Rite-Aid. The book is called *The Golf Doctor*, and it's about the size of a billfold, with a water-resistant cover made of "genuine leather" that can be chocked closed with a sturdy strip of Velcro. Calling all bibliophiles!

Inside these highly secure covers is a compendium of potentially life-saving hints. Imagine it's February and you're golf-starved, so you've talked your wife into letting you go off for a long weekend to the sandhills of North Carolina. You're playing Pinehurst No. 2. Having moronically forgotten to swing your driver like a six-iron, you hit an ugly slice into a stand of pines. While you have no trouble finding your ball on a brown bed of pine needles, how the hell do you hit off this stuff? Frantically, you rummage through the large zippered pocket on your Hot-Z, casting aside some old Hav-A-Tampas, a tube of sunscreen, Vaseline, bug spray, and a half-dozen old gloves you can't bear to part with, until you locate your copy of *The Golf Doctor*. Aware that your playing partners are getting restless and the foursome behind you is breathing down your neck, you thumb madly through the book until you come to Situational Play No. 9—"Out of Pine Needles":

> Brush away the pine needles where you intend to take your stance . . . Make a long takeaway away [*sic*] from the ball with the clubhead moving straight back along the target line. Swing up to the three-quarter position. Make a sweeping-type downswing so that the club comes into the ball—not the needles—squarely.

You wave happily to your playing partners. "Found it!" you shout. Then you tuck *The Golf Doctor* back into the Hot-Z, take out your four-iron, assume a gentle grip, and proceed to make that long takeaway away from the ball with the club head moving straight back along the target line, swinging up to the three-quarter position, finishing with a sweeping-type downswing so that—yesss!—the club comes into the *ball* (not the *needles*) squarely.

The Golf Doctor has saved your keester once again.

SWEET MASTERY OF LIFE

It was George Leonard's intention to unmask how "we're continually bombarded with promises of immediate gratification, instant success, and fast, temporary relief, all of which lead in exactly the wrong direction." Leonard was keen to get us going in the right direction, which for him meant getting our butts up on that arc of discovery and true learning. This is what he meant by mastery, that "mysterious process during which what is at first difficult becomes progressively easier and more pleasurable through practice."

To Leonard, the essence of the learning process is the student's acknowledgment that the acquisition of "any new skill involves relatively brief spurts of progress, each of which is followed by a slight decline." These declines, he says, frequently leave us stranded on a plateau where no apparent progress takes place, often for a period of time that tests our patience and mettle.

Leonard uses tennis to illustrate this point. Say you're a rank beginner and you've just learned how to hold the racket but still can't hit the ball very well. After a few weeks of frustration, Leonard writes, something changes:

[A] light goes on. The various components of the tennis stroke begin to come together, almost as if your muscles know what they should do; you don't have to think about every little thing. In your conscious awareness, there's more room to see the ball, to meet it cleanly in a stroke that starts low and ends high. You feel the itch to hit the ball harder, to start playing competitively.

No chance. Until now your teacher has been feeding balls to you. You haven't had to move. But now you're going to have to learn to move side to side, back and forth, and on the diagonal, and then set up and swing. Again you feel clumsy, disjointed . . . Days and weeks pass with no apparent progress. There you are on that damned plateau.

You can say that again.

I have been stuck on a plateau for weeks now. Redding's videotapes show me standing up better over the ball, and my swing is smoother and closer to the right plane, but my shots remain weak. Someone or something has to kick me to the next plateau. Daily treks to Lee-Jane haven't done it, nor has anything Redding has tried in the shed.

Why can't I just move onward and upward?

Leonard's take is that we can't expect to execute a skill with easy grace until we can perform it without consciously thinking about it. This goes for everything from playing a musical instrument, to hitting a golf ball. It is a given that when you tell yourself in midswing that you shouldn't hit your drive into the pond, you will hit your drive into the pond. Tell yourself to relax your shoulders and you will tighten them. Leonard says that masterful moves need to be coded into our brains—which is what plateaus are all about. They are programming interludes.

Back when we plotted Leonard's piece, it occurred to us that we could better convey his ideas if we could induce readers to identify personally with what others go through when they seek to acquire a skill. Leonard came up with three basic species of learners, each with a specific pattern of behavior:

- **Dabblers:** These are people for whom new skills and interests are an endless series of one-night stands. Leonard described dabblers as men or women (they're usually men) who, while they like to think of themselves as adventurers, are similar to what Jung referred to as *puer eternis,* a person who lives his life as an eternal kid. Dabblers are forever taking up with new interests, their first step (and often the last) being to deck themselves out in the coolest, newest gear. Dabblers will talk your ear off about their latest, truest newfound love. Then, kaboom! They hit the first plateau and the new interest is history. The dabblers' learning curve equals a pathetic little squiggle that scoots northward quickly, then peters out. Premature ejaculation would not be an inappropriate metaphor.
- **Obsessives:** This is where I come in. According to Leonard, these are people with an almost bottomless and very stubborn desire to advance or acquire a skill. Obsessives are marked by a manic intensity; their m.o. is to try to steamroll the world into submission. They are always

setting goals and deadlines for themselves, and quite frequently meet or exceed them—at least for a while. Unlike dabblers, who wheeze out on the first plateau, obsessives have the drive to sail across a number of plateaus, *then* give out from mental and/or physical exhaustion. Their learning pattern is a series of jagged lurches forward, then a mighty crash.

- *Hackers:* We see a lot of these on the golf course. They are people who pitch a tent on a plateau and live there for the rest of their lives. Hackers just keep keeping on. They don't give up. They don't get worse. They don't get better. They rarely if ever take lessons. They settle for what they are. You can imagine what their learning curve looks like: the EKG of a dead heart.

LEFT-HANDED COMPLEMENT

Marooned on a plateau, I am all ears. I am a sucker for any and all advice, however bizarre. Any day now I expect to answer a rap on my door and find two men in white jackets who have been dispatched to strap me to the back of a golf cart and take me away.

Consider this: For the past two weeks I have been testing the hypothesis that the key to my advancement is a strong and more dexterous left hand. In every way imaginable, I am trying to apply my hitherto underemployed and pathetically ineffective southpaw to just about every mundane activity of daily life. These efforts include using my left hand to brush my teeth, comb my hair, open car doors, drive nails, turn out lights, eat soup, pour milk into a bowl.

This practice is recommended in quite a few books about learning to play golf, where it is almost always cast as an idea original to the author. The first time I came across it was in Al Barlow's oral history of the game, *Getting to the Dance Floor*, in which a celebrated old pro named Frank Walsh proposed it as a training exercise. Years after I read it there, I heard the same advice from a former touring pro, who claimed to have thought of it by himself, then later allowed as he had received it from Tommy Bolt.

In any case, this timeless tip is the reason I'm sporting a bruised left thumb and minestrone stains on my new Valentino tie. A strong left hand (on a right-hander) is adjudged to be a key asset when it comes to hitting a golf ball. The theory took hold long before Bobby Jones proclaimed back in the twenties that "golf is a left-handed game for a right-handed man." In the early 1930s, legendary teacher Alex Morrisson endorsed the view, stressing that the proper golf swing was a function not just of a strong left hand but of a properly effective left side, meaning that everything on a golfer's port side—especially his hip, shoulder, and arm—should be deployed as counterbalance to the more dominant right side. From this notion grew the idea that to make a good golf swing you want to feel as if you're *pulling* the club down and through the ball, not pushing it. Proponents of the left-hand school point out that a good number of history's premier golfers, including Snead and Hogan, were natural lefties who, mostly because the first set of clubs they happened to acquire were right-hand models, switched over to the other side. It is generally accepted that their naturally strong left hands kept their right hands from overpowering their swings.

The left-hand school had it all to themselves until the 1950s, when Tommy Armour trashed the concept in his influential *How to Play Your Best Golf All the Time*. Armour believed it was absurd to think one's stronger side wasn't critical to the ability to hit a ball long and straight. "Any time you hear any argument advanced against the right hand whipping into the shot," Armour thundered, "you may be sure that objection is fallacious." Not only was the right hand important, Armour said, the right *index finger* was *crucial* as a key determinant of a player's "hitting action."

But the Silver Scot was whistling in the wind. His contrarian argument did not ultimately shake the consensus that, for most hackers, the right side is usually the brute bully that pillages the swing, while the left side imbues it with balance and power. This is why I spend my evenings watching television with one of those metal grippers in my left hand. On light training nights I switch over to a little rubber ball filled with rice. It is also why I crawl into bed with streaks of dried toothpaste around my lips.

HOLES IN MY BALLS

There are two good ways to tell when you're high and dry on a plateau.

The first is that you feel hope draining from your spirit like a dripping faucet.

The second is that you start doing brain-sick things on the lawn, even though you know the neighbors are making fun of you from behind their balloon shades.

This latter symptom announced itself just last Saturday, and in a rather peculiar way.

As if in a trance, compelled by invading alien duffers from outer space, I drove over to Knoxville's Nevada Bob's and promptly bought four cellophane bags of plastic golf balls, the perforated kind, six to a bag, twenty-four balls in all. I immediately returned home, ripped open the bags, dumped the balls on the front lawn, and began hitting them back and forth, using an old Tom Watson pitching wedge. I now do this six or seven times a day, rain or shine, for ten or so minutes each session. On many occasions I have spied neighbors gazing at me from adjacent houses, or checking me out as they zoom by in their SUV's. "And when did the Yankee get religion?" these golf-loving East Tennesseans no doubt ask one another over coffee and Krispy Kremes. Who cares what they think? My perf ball routine is immensely pleasurable and calming. It might even be advancing my game.

The official perfing grounds, my front yard, is circumscribed by a semicircular driveway. This elliptical portion of my suburban property amounts to maybe 1,500 square feet. It isn't just any old, crabgrass-ridden, brown-spotted, grub-infested ellipse, however, but an ellipse blanketed by a thick, I mean *thick*, comforter of Kentucky fescue. I employ no greenskeeper to tend this spot of heaven. Its meticulous condition is testament to the inordinate amount of care and feeding I myself shower on it. This is my first suburban house, and I have taken to the lifestyle with no small measure of fanatic devotion. If you were to ask me whether I'd rather spend Saturday morning on the golf course or in the lawn-and-garden department of Home Depot, I'd actually have to think about it. I like to shop for hose parts, trowels, spreaders, and pruners every bit as much as I like to browse through a pro shop.

The previous owner of our house had installed an automated Toro irrigation system beneath the ellipse, which happily refreshes my precious greensward throughout the long, hot Tennessee summer. Sustenance also comes in the form of a ton of nutrients and insect poisons with which I soak the ellipse at the first sign of need or trouble. But the *real* secret behind this perfect plot is an intoxicating lawn cocktail that I mix from scratch every several weeks and apply with a lawn sprayer. The cocktail is made up of three parts liquid soap and one part ammonia. It does for my lawn what three Tanqueray martinis do for me.

George Leonard had his aikido. I have my lawn. Here I am at one with my perf balls. Here there is no gain in trying to overpower them. Here I swing through, not at them. Here my fingers embrace the club as if cradling a toddler's hand. Here I feel not the slightest bit of tension in my arms or shoulders. Here my hips lead the downswing just right.

Hitting perf balls has brought a different perspective to my daily drill. I am reminded of that passage in the *Little Red Book*, when Penick tells us to get a weed cutter and swing it back and forth.

Perf balls and weed cutters are about *training*, the books tell us. The idea of training has just about replaced the idea of practice in our sports culture. Nobody practices, everybody trains. This has to do, I guess, with how we have come to accept the interconnectedness of skills, how mental and emotional factors influence our play, how we now recognize the importance of being relaxed, how diet affects us. Training invites us to use all of our faculties, to visualize and internalize, to play the shot out in our mind before attempting it.

The modern rules of training often recommend that we occasionally take a step back, vary the routine, take some time off. In the morning I am scheduled to fly to New York for a few days. I am spooked by the idea that I will not have a chance to swing a golf club, even at a perf ball. The thought of club deprivation sends me into a frenzy of concern. What if I lose my edge (as if I had an edge)? What if lose my *grip* (as if I had a grip)?

I go to the workbench in my garage. From my golf bag I remove the two-iron, with which I haven't attempted to hit in about ten years. I secure the club between the clenched jaws of a fearsome blue vise. With a hacksaw I cut the club in two, then wrap the jagged edge with duct tape. I then pack the implement in my garment bag so that I can put in some serious grip work in the privacy of my New York hotel room.

It is official: I am off the deep end.

I tell no one, not even my wife, about the truncated golf club concealed in my garment bag. (The O.J. trial, by the way, is now in full swing.) I also stash George Leonard's book on *Mastery*, the somewhat expanded version of the magazine feature.

I read the book on the flight to the Apple. This happens to be the week of The Masters. All the talk in the papers is about Tiger Woods, the teenage prodigy from Stanford who is playing at Augusta for the first time. The stories carry snapshots of this amazing young golfer. We see him at age four or five, when he simply picked up a golf club in his tiny hands and swung it beautifully, as if pitching a butterfly to the green.

What makes a golfer as gifted as Tiger Woods? Unusually sharp motor coordination? A superior sense of tempo and balance? Muscles and joints that turn and twist with effortless freedom? A switch—some kind of rheostat—that controls the intensity of the brain, turning up the concentration level in preparation of a shot, turning it down just before, and during, the swing itself?

Tiger Woods was probably born with this switch. All great players are, I can only reckon.

Charles Price once wrote of Harry Vardon, golf's first great champion, that he was a player "au naturel. He never asked anyone to give him a lesson and nobody had the audacity to offer him one. With all his native talent, he nevertheless knew in his mind what every muscle in his body was doing."

Vardon was in every sense what George Leonard defined as a master. Price wrote that he was "imperturbable, taciturn, seldom smiled on the course, but then he seldom scowled either. He never threw a tantrum [or, presumably, an O-fer], never gave an alibi. He just came to play." Price quotes another writer who noted, "If a dog crossed the tee in front of [Vardon] while at the top of his swing, he would be able to judge whether the dog ran in any danger of his life. If it did, he would stop his club; if it didn't, he would go through with the shot, without pulling or slicing."

Like Tiger Woods, Vardon was lean and lanky, hardly an overpowering physical machine: He weighed 155 pounds and stood a bit over five-feet-nine. His hands were unusually large, the hands of a man twice his size. "While gripping a club," Price wrote, "his fingers looked like a bunch of sausages wrapped around a baton . . . Vardon's power emanated from his hands—he performed feats of golf seldom seen before or since."

Tiger Woods also looks to have unusually large hands. Maybe that's it—maybe my hands are too small. But my hands are actually bigger than Jack Nicklaus's hands. I know this because in the Bear's book his outstretched paws are shown at actual size. I've placed my fingers down over Jack's. Mine appear to be slightly larger.

So it's not the hands.

It's something else. I will find it, damn it. Holed up in my hotel room in New York, I browse through *Mastery*, putting it down only long enough to pick up my sawed-off golf club with my unsausage-like fingers. What the hell am I doing alone in my room with this ridiculous object? Why aren't I out with friends, catching up on the buzz? Roaming through a bookstore? Scouting jazz records? Why the compulsion to stand in front of the mirror with a truncated shaft in my hand, dressed in my undershorts, back arched, butt out—good God, I am a middle-aged man!

I turn back to the pages of George Leonard's book to seek direction. To attain a level of mastery, to undertake the long-shot quest of it, we need to reprogram how we learn. Think back to when we were innocent little sponges. As babies, Leonard notes, we listened, we watched, we mimicked, we got it wrong, we got it right.

There are kids who learn golf this way. Just read the memoirs of the legends. The best players—Jones, Snead, Hogan, Armour—tell much the same story: how they learned to swing a club not from a book, nor through self-examination, but by emulating those whose bags they carried, through firsthand observation and trial-and-error. Is there anyone who has attained mastery the way I'm trying to, *thinking* as much as playing?

As grown-ups, we don't emulate well. We watch golfers on television, we play along with our betters—so why doesn't some of it stick?

Evening has descended on New York. From my window I see nothing but steel and concrete and the lights of a thousand office buildings. Golf is a million miles away. I order dinner from room service. I sit at my little table, absorbed in George Leonard's book, my sawed-off golf club sitting next to the knife and fork.

As Leonard sees it, there are five "keys" to mastery.

The first is instruction, finding the right teacher. "Why re-invent the wheel?" he asks. Why risk false starts? Begin with a firm foundation. Choose the right teacher. Look for those who themselves had great teachers, Leonard urges. Look for those who interact, who praise at least as much as they critique. Look for patience and empathy. And, oh yes, look for human beings, not tapes or books or magazine articles.

The second key to mastery is practice. The word rattles me now. I get up and walk around the room, wielding my sawed-off club. What's happening to my swing right now? Am I losing it, forgetting anything important? Or is this break actually doing some good, providing a measure of helpful distance? I worry some more, then return to the Leonard book. He suggests that we think of practice not as a chore but as a fulfilling ritual. "To practice regularly," says Leonard, "even when you seem to be getting nowhere, might at first seem onerous. But the day eventually comes when practicing becomes a treasured part of your life. [It] will still be there for you tomorrow. It will never go away." Frankly, I'm not sure how I feel about this: a lifetime spent on a plastic mat at a cheesy driving range? If we're talking *lifetime*, I ought to at least join a country club.

Leonard's third key to mastery is what he calls "surrender." Letting go. Give in to your teacher and to the requisites of whatever discipline you're trying to learn. Don't be proud, don't be afraid to look stupid. "The beginner who stands on his or her dignity," he says, "becomes rigid, armored."

The fourth key is "intentionality." By this Leonard means pretty much what Nicklaus referred to as "going to the movies" before every shot. For George, though, it's a little more complicated. Intentionality is a New Age bouillabaisse of "character, willpower, attitude, imaging, the mental game." Apply full consciousness to an activity, don't just give it the quick nod.

Leonard's fifth and final key is "the edge." A master is one who doesn't merely pursue the refinement of a skill, he pushes the edge of the envelope. The edge is the right stuff. The edge is "a balancing act. It demands the awareness to know when you're pushing yourself beyond safe limits," Leonard says.

When it comes to having the derring-do to bang a fairway three-wood across a pond 200 yards away, I don't know yet from edge. Nor do I have any right to. Before we can hope to play the edge, Leonard says, we must put in many years of instruction, practice, surrender, and intentionality.

And *then?*

And then, he says, the journey continues: more training, more time on the plateau. Then we get to stick it to the edge.

LASCHING OUT

Crenshaw wins The Masters. On the eighteenth green at Augusta he drops to his knees and cries. April showers, in the form of tears of joy, stream down Crenshaw's cheeks in tribute to the recently departed Harvey Penick, the golfer's longtime master and muse. The win is inspiring. Crenshaw's conquest underscores much of what George Leonard says about the value of a great teacher. Said Crenshaw after the tournament, "I had a fifteenth club in my bag, and it was Harvey."

I fly back to Knoxville, renewed. As the plane makes its final approach, I gaze down on a lovely golf course. It's a public track called Egwani Farms, about which I have heard nice things. I promise myself that I'll check it out in the weeks ahead. Yep, this little trip has cleared my head. Leonard's book has offered a helpful perspective on where I've been and where I'm going. But there's a nagging question about all this mastery business: Is the quest as ennobling as we like to think, or is it yet another delusion in an age of insufferable self-absorption?

Here's an intellectual aikido match for which I'd pay scalpers' prices: George Leonard versus Christopher Lasch, the late historian and the author of *The Culture of Narcissism*. Lasch would no doubt have blanched at all this prattle about inner peace, imaging, journeys, intentionality. Lasch viewed these preoccupations as symptomatic of how alienated we have become from one another. He wrote: "Having no hope of improving their lives in any of the ways that matter, people have convinced themselves that what matters is psychic self-improvement: getting in touch with their feelings, eating health food, taking lessons in ballet or belly-dancing, immersing themselves in the wisdom of the East, jogging, learning how to 'relate,' overcoming the fear of pleasure."

I have no clue as to whether Lasch ever picked up a golf club, or whether he bothered to observe the studied mannerisms of those who play the game today, how we strut and plumb-bob, how deeply self-absorbed we are when on the course. Had he done so, he probably would have interpreted all of it as further evidence of our desire to escape the growing emptiness of contemporary life. Games like golf, he argued, serve the same purpose as sex, drugs, and drink. They obliterate "awareness of everyday reality [by] raising it to a new intensity of concentration." A game such as golf satisfies "the need for free fantasy and the search for gratuitous difficulty." And while the game may indeed demand skill and intelligence, it does so in the service of an activity—putting a small ball in a four-inch hole—that has no significant consequences for our society or world. What a waste, he might have argued, that so many people of means, imagination, influence, intelligence, and authority, choose to expend their considerable wealth, time, smarts, and desire for personal glory on the golf course, and not on behalf of the planet and its humanity. Others would vehemently disagree, of course. Golf *is* character, Charles McGrath wrote just the other day in a *New York Times* tribute to Harvey Penick. "The quality of your shots depend on the quality of your soul."

All this is enough to cause terminal tension in the arms and shoulders. And who the hell needs more of *that*?

MUSCLE MEMOIR

I slide back into the accustomed routine of a weekly lesson at Willow Creek, daily tune-ups at Lee-Jane, constant at-home diddling with perf balls. I also try to get out on the course more often. Alone one early morning, I play that gently rolling course near the airport, Egwani Farms, and I develop an immediate affection for the place. It isn't that the course is especially suited to my shot making—such a course hasn't been designed yet. There's an unusual calm here, that's all.

This first round is a mixed bag. I have difficulty keeping my knees flexed and relaxed, something that now comes fairly easily on the practice tee. There's no doubt a connection between how much we actually play and how free-and-easy we can make our swings. A duffer who plays only rarely can't help but put too much pressure on each shot. Hell, he only gets about a hundred-plus tries on a given day. So rather than savor strokes, he tears into the tender flesh of each shot with jagged fangs, every muscle seized in the grip of predatory fury.

Hacking around Egwani, I make a conscious effort to minimize the damage of the bad shots. I suppose I've still got George Leonard on the brain. Think journey, not steps. Think of a flubbed shot as a pause, not a setback. A lousy shot is a blip, it's *bubkes*.

A *good* shot, now that's different.

A good shot is *not* a blip, it's a stroke of glory. Today at Egwani, I launch a few truly good shots, including a whistling four-iron that landed within ten feet of the pin on a 166-yard par-three, despite a warm breeze in the face.

A day later it's back to the shed. A hard, cold rain has driven us indoors. Redding pulls out a cassette from one of our early sessions and runs it before and after some footage he has taken today. The comparison reveals that my swing is perceptibly flatter than before, but still too vertical. I persist in bringing the club over the top. Why, after nearly three months, can't I break this pattern?

"What is it about muscle memory, anyway?" I ask Redding.

This is the sort of question most golf teachers generally respond to with a knitted brow: "Hey, like, that's a great question. You see, muscle memory is really like a superhard thing to change."

Redding, though, doesn't talk this way. He responds with a faintly intemperate look and a lengthy pause, with which he suggests a certain degree of intellectual exasperation.

"Muscles don't think, so they don't have memory," he says finally. "What people mean by 'muscle memory' is just a lot of years of doing something a certain way."

End of topic.

"Now, set up again for me, nice and straight." Then he moves me around a couple more times.

"But wait—," I step back off the Astro Turf mat. "My body just doesn't want to do what it's supposed to do. It keeps resisting, and there's got to be a reason. It's just like how we fight to keep our subconscious sealed and locked. You know how people are always fighting their shrinks when their shrinks begin to get close to some painful revelation? That's what this feels like to me. The more you get my arms to move the way they should, the more I resist the breakthrough."

Redding nods. He knows exactly what I'm trying to say. It's also clear that he has never before had a student who has tried to compare the swing plane to the dynamics of psychoanalysis.

A couple of days later I am back at Egwani. Something interesting happens on the fifteenth hole, a 400-yard par-four: my shoulders move properly. They conform to what Sam Snead has described as a "teeter-totter," meaning that the right shoulder doesn't try to outrace the left, it stays back and on the same plane. This correct movement occurs on three consecutive shots: a drive, a five-wood off the fairway, and a nine-iron to the green. These strokes are followed by a major revelation: *Golf is not as complicated as I have always made it.*

Aside from when my children were born, I have not known such unbridled happiness.

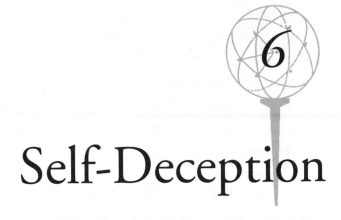

Self-Deception

"Me."

—Dave Stockton, when asked before The Masters to name the golfer in the field he was most afraid of

THE DANGEROUS BEAN

One evening I find myself seated next to a man at a business dinner. He is a successful ad exec, also a scratch amateur who one of these years hopes to qualify for the Senior Open. He listens intently as I describe the quest to break eighty. He politely asks whether I'd be interested in hearing the best piece of instruction he'd ever received in his life.

"Sure," I reply, and set aside my veal chop so that I might concentrate full bore on the insight he's about to impart.

"Not long ago I was shooting the breeze with the pro at my club," the man begins. "And I told him I was having problems hitting the driver. I said I thought I was pressing too much, and asked whether he thought a lesson might straighten things out.

"The pro, who knew my game as well as anyone, answered by asking a question, a really dumb question, I thought at the time. 'Do you know how many par-threes there are on this course?' he said, gesturing out the window of our pro shop.

" 'Of course I know how many there are. There are four,' I replied, 'two on the front, two on the back.' I was perplexed that he was treating me like such an idiot.

" 'You're wrong,' he told me. 'There are *eighteen* par-threes out there, just as there are on every golf course.'

"What he meant was that it is extremely helpful to approach every golf hole as if it were a par-three, and play it that way. He meant that we ought to let our tee shots fall where they may, then proceed to play each hole from that point forward as if we only had three shots to get the ball in the hole. If we hit our drive way left or way right, so what? Just pretend that the par-three starts there. This little trick works great for several reasons. First, it makes a little game out of every hole—adds a bit of surprise and fun to it. Second, it minimizes the importance of our drive. Knowing that we still have our 'first' shot ahead of us, we won't stew over a bad shot. We can put it behind us. Finally, knowing that all will not be lost even if we screw up our drive, we'll be more relaxed when we step onto the tee—and we probably won't hit as many bad drives to begin with.

"And guess what?" the man concludes. By now, I have resumed work on my chop—I think I know what's to come but don't want to louse up his story. "The next time out my problems with the driver all but disappeared. Not that I don't hit a bad drive now and again. I just don't let it destroy the hole."

That golf is a game played on the narrow fairway between our ears is not news. Our appreciation of how a golfer's head can wreck the best intentions of his hands and arms is about as old as links land. One day, scavenging in a used bookstore, I come across a pioneering disquisition on this theme by Kenneth Thompson. It is a book called *The Mental Side of Golf*, published in 1939. Thompson doesn't hack around the bush: The mind is the most important element in golf, he says, ramming home the point with a barrage of bold-faced declarations:

> Much—in fact, **too** much—has already been written about golf in a general way, but not very much has been said on the **psychological side** of the game. It is the **mental side** that is really difficult. By applying correct **golf psychology** and harboring a sound philosophy about the game there is no doubt that any player can better his score immediately, and that by the constant practice of the proper approach to golf problems he will on the average play more consistently in lower figures than he has been doing.

Even back then, a half-century before Bob Rotella, the psychological boilerplate was familiar to all hackers:

Golf is to be played one stroke at a time.

Dwelling on mistakes = failure.

Emotions must be bridled: "Giving way to a feeling of joy or annoyance has a direct effect on the muscles," Thompson said.

What other sport is so preoccupied with fear, anxiety, tension?

I stand before the bedroom mirror, checking spine angle and grip. This exercise, universally advised by golf teachers as a way of checking on fundamentals, is mostly useless, I have come to think. It's useless because it doesn't let us focus on the building block that matters most.

It's the head, stupid.

HACKING OFF

Before a round at Egwani Farms, I spend thirty minutes on the range without attempting a single full swing. All I do is hit half-swing pitches to a target sixty yards away, trying to effect the same easy rhythm I use to flick perf balls around the lawn. I take this disciplined exercise to be a sure sign of greater golfing maturity. These little shots are the key to golf. They are what bring us consistently close to the pin, to puttable distances where we can get down in one or two. Failing at them can leave us three, even four, strokes away from the cup. As many as twenty strokes a round might hinge on them. There's no way to break eighty without mastering these approach shots—which, in theory at least, is fortunate, in that they don't require any strength or particular athletic skill to execute. Still, I don't know a single high-handicapper who goes to the trouble to rehearse them. If most hackers practice at all, they whip out their War Birds and Bubble Shafts.

My sensible warm-up complete, I tee off with a couple of guys who are so personable and fun to be with that I don't much resent the fact that their pleasant springtime outing is underwritten by a business-expense tax deduction. The host, I discover, is a detail man for a pharmaceutical company. His guest is a local cardiologist. The two hadn't ever crossed cart paths until this balmy morning. Today's outing came about because the salesman knew that the doc liked golf and had left a standing message with the cardio's secretary: Should the physician ever have a free morning without a heart to mend, well, give a jingle. That's how it to came to pass that the two of them are out on this nearly empty golf course on a fine Monday morning, when the rest of the world is at work.

Last week, I teed off with a couple of other business deductions. These two were—how to be delicate about this?—complete and utter jerks. They were in the telephone-systems game—one sold, the other bought. As golfers they were *bad* bad, in contrast to the detail man and the doc, who were *good* bad. The distinction is that a good bad golfer knows he's bad and accepts it with humor and grace. A bad bad golfer, on the other hand, tries pathetically to give the impression that he's a really good golfer who just happens to be having a bad day. These two turkeys insisted on hitting from the blue tees, the telltale sign of a bad, bad golfer. This caused the day to be especially drawn-out and ugly. The guy who sold telephony was a loser on a couple of other fronts. He was (I admit this is petty) a highly irritating dresser, shrouded as he was in a barf-colored golf shirt. Even his swing bugged me. He took the club around his body in a huge swooping motion and wrapped it around his neck in the manner of John Daly. But here's the worst of it: No matter how wickedly he sliced balls into whatever pond, woods, or adjacent fairway happened to be within reach, he then held his finish in the form of a grossly exaggerated, inverted C, maintaining the pose so long into the shot I felt like throwing a ball at the back of his head.

These two were not exactly raconteurs, either. They had nothing of interest to say about anything, no sense of irony. My time with these palookas amounted to the most unenjoyable four hours I've had in a while, and when it was over I was eager to get home to do *anything* to help me forget about golf.

What I did was wash the car.

I scrubbed it down lovingly, using a big, fluffy mitt. I took a stiff brush to the wheel covers, wiped the windows clean with a paper towel. I accomplished all of these tasks with easy proficiency, thanks to my once useless, but now ever-strengthening, and more and more agile, left hand. I polished off that car in under eighty, with a few strokes to spare.

May has arrived.

That batch of golf instructionals I dragged down from the attic a couple of months ago has by now grown into a fair-sized archive. One wall of my basement office is piled up with old books, new books, expanding files of tearsheets and notes, a large stack of magazines, a leaning tower of videotapes. I get most uneasy whenever I look at all the stuff sitting there these days.

The reason is that Linda and I have decided to pack up and move. It is a wrenching prospect. But over the past few days we resolved to sell this house in Knoxville and head back to New York, where a couple of job opportunities have cropped up. This will require a major transplant, tough on us, hard on the kids, and especially challenging as far as golf is concerned. I doubt I will have anything up there like my beloved ellipse; the yard will probably amount to a little postage stamp of a lawn, way too small for perf golf. Most disturbing, I'll have to forsake Brad Redding. This prospect weighs heavily on my mind. Personally, I'll miss him. And I worry that the new teacher, and whatever new approach he may espouse, may undo whatever scant progress I've made under Redding's guiding hands.

I stare abjectly at the stuff stacked in the corner: thousands of pictures, millions of words, all in the service of how to swing a golf club. To the uninitiated, how inane this prattling must seem. Yet to the rest of us, they are irresistible, addictive. Every spring, new books blossom as surely as the azaleas at Augusta. And while the golf swing is the golf swing is the golf swing, from year to year it gets repackaged, re-envisioned, reworded. Golf instruction is whipped by the same crosswinds that blow through the culture at large. The way we teach golf, the way we learn it, changes along with everything else.

Once upon a time, we were expected to learn by paying attention and following orders. Not just golf, everything. We passed on knowledge not through fancy schmantzy methodology, but through an insistence on repetitive exercises and memorization. We learned, if we learned at all, exactly *what*, precisely *when*, and specifically *how* somebody told us to. Golf instruction was, according to Jack Burke Jr., "monkey see, monkey do." It works for me, it'll work for you. Don't get cute, don't get creative. Follow *my* bouncing ball.

In time, the monkeys grew restless. We became disinclined to follow orders with the same equanimity—not in the classroom, not on the golf course. Like the rest of the culture, golf instruction was transformed by at least two huge developments: a growing belief in science and technology, and an ever greater concern with our, ahem, inner selves. The game fell under the successive sway of, first, rampaging physicists, and then the touchy-feely crowd.

One afternoon in the shed I try to engage Brad Redding with my theories on the postwar dialectics of golf pedagogy. In his usual polite way, he tells me to shut up and stick my butt out. Later, however, as I'm heading out the metal door, he pipes up, rolling his eyes, "Try to find a copy of *The Golfing Machine* by Homer Kelly. Talk about a bunch of BS. It has probably confused more golfers than any book I can think of."

Redding then hands me a videotape. It is a lesson given by Ben Doyle, a well-known West Coast teacher who was Homer Kelly's staunchest disciple. The tape is curious. It's an obviously homemade production that features a single, stationary camera and spotty audio, filmed on a nondescript practice tee. There are no graphics, titles, or frills, just the gray-haired Doyle, surrounded by a collection of oddball props that include a hockey stick and a clear sheet of plastic, which Doyle uses to indicate the swing plane. It is difficult to understand some of what Doyle says. He's something of a mumbler, or at least the poor audio makes him out to be. And his presentation is full of abstruse jargon, such as "the law of the lever" and "the law of the parallels." Yet there's something seductive about the tape, an unwinding of insights I find illuminating. Among these is Doyle's softly spoken assertion that balance is a function of what we do with our hands, not what we do with our feet, legs, or head. He says that we should never consciously move our hands. It is *they* that are to be moved, by our arms and pivot. He says that we should never fix our mind on the ball, but rather on what our hands are doing (or, better yet, not doing). He also advises that we should keep focused on our right index finger, which is to be hooked firmly around the shaft and employed as a critical guide of the club path.

A day or two later I manage to track down the dissertation of Doyle's mentor, Kelly's *The Golfing Machine*. This is truly one of the most bizarre analyses of golf I have yet to encounter. Kelly's treatise, published in the late 1960s, represents nearly three decades of determined research. To Homer Kelly, the golf swing was fundamentally a set of levers governed by proven laws of physics and immutable principles of geometry. To him the word *golf* itself was an acronym—"Geometrically Oriented Linear Force."

No wonder my head throbs.

The Golfing Machine is a book that looks and sounds more like a manual for retrofitting ball-bearings in an electric motor than a book about a game, especially a game meant to be played joyfully in open air laced with the perfume of pine forest or seaside. There's nothing sensual about *The Golfing Machine*. This stuff is hard-core. The cover features mechanical drawings of bisected circles, blueprints of hinges and levers. Throughout the book, the text is arranged stiffly in numbered paragraphs. Scattered around are numerous small, smudgy, black-and-white photos of a woman with short blonde hair. She is dressed in a white blouse, dark skirt, and bobby socks. Her purpose here is to illustrate technical points ("Clubhead Lag," "Vertical Hinge," "Impact Fix"). May we presume she is Mrs. Homer Kelly, photographed in the Kelly basement *cum* golf propulsion laboratory *cum* institute for advanced golf studies?

Homer guides us through the nuts and bolts of his unified theory. I get the impression that the golf swing might be more easily mastered by an Erector Set than by a mortal with a nervous system. Consider, for instance, the author's notions on the phenomenon of "Clubface Lay-Back":

2-C-2. LINEAR FORCE—THE CUT SHOT

(SHOWN WITH IMPACT INTERVAL EXTENDED TO LOW POINT).
A "Cut Shot" is any Stroke using Vertical Hinging (10–10) through Impact regardless of Plane Line (10–5) or the preceding Wrist Action (10–18). Either the Dual Vertical or Vertical (only) Hinge Action should be used for the Cut Shot to avoid weakening the Line of Compression. It produces a higher than normal trajectory and less than normal roll—better "bite."

The 2-C-2 sketches show Dual Vertical Hinge Action (10–10).

See 2-C-1 for Vector Component Legend.

Kelly clangs and clatters through a welter of golf's other mechanical intricacies, including angular force, approach speed, axis tilt, basic planes, centrifugal force, coefficient of restitution, downstroke sequence, extensor action, gear train, in-line condition, lever assemblies, momentum transfer, power accumulators, resultant force, throwaway prevention, trajectory control, and upstroke impact . . . *Houston, we have lift-off!*

I'm just dumbfounded by all this. Why do we make golf so complicated? I ask myself, pitching perf balls across what will soon be my late, great ellipse, or on those too rare golden late afternoons when I'm alone at Willow Creek, no one in front of me, no one behind. At times like these I wonder why we have taken such a lovely and innocent game and turned it into such a head fuck.

Consider this:

In one of Bob Toski's instruction books there's a two-page chart labeled "Bob Toski's Cause-and-Effect Checklist." Listed vertically is a list of outcomes, or "Possible Effects." These include Slicing, Pulling, Hooking, Pushing, Topping, Fat Shots, Shanking, Loss of Length, Shots too High, Shots too Low, Inconsistent Shotmaking, Bad Putting. (The only fearful affliction missing here is Prostate Enlargement.)

Listed horizontally are what Toski calls "Major Causes." These include Poor Target Projection, Tense at Address, Weight Too Far Left At Address, Ball Too Far Back in Stance, Ball Too Far Forward in Stance, Ball Too Far Away At Address, Ball Too Close At Address, Mis-aiming Left, Mis-aiming Right, Alignment Too "Open" At Address, Alignment Too "Closed" At Address, "Strong" Grip, "Weak" Grip, Backswing Too Fast, Too Little Time At Back of Backswing, Right Leg Stiff At Top of Backswing, Too Little Backswing Turn, Overswinging On Backswing, Grabbing Club (Overcontrolling) On Downswing, Right Hand/Arm Shoving On Downswing, Right Hand Throwing on Downswing, Falling Back on Downswing, Swaying From And/Or To Target, Blocking Out With Hands, Blocking Out With Hips On Downswing.

In all, there are some *300* boxes in this chart, each appropriately checked when a particular effect can be said to be the sorry result of a particular cause.

Toski's chart is distressing. Not only have I suffered from every one of the listed effects at one time or another, I typically experience *every one* of the outcomes during the course of a single round! The same goes for most people I play with. Charts like these, do they really help diagnose and fix our mistakes, or do they largely add to the anxiety? If one of the keys to good golf is relaxation, what earthly purpose is there to a vast matrix that exists solely to tell us how many ways there are to screw things up?

Redding and I are back in the shed. He looks, as he always does, pressed and neat. Why *are* golf teachers always pressed and neat? Today he's got on a vivid cranberry-colored shirt (Hogan) and a bright blue-and-gold golf cap (also Hogan), tan slacks, and black spikeless shoes. He wears metallic blue Revo sunglasses.

I have just informed Redding that sometime over the next couple of months we'll be leaving for New York. I suggest that we turn up the juice, take full advantage of the time we've got left. Let's double the lessons to a couple a week, I propose, one of which might be a playing session out on the course.

"Sure thing, bud," he says. "Now give me a good setup."

So much for his lapsing into a state of disconsolation over the prospect of losing a prized student. Perhaps to sublimate the deep emotions he is fighting, he busies himself videotaping a couple of swings.

"Your posture is better, much better," he says brightly. "So is the position of your takeaway. But you still need to work on keeping your left arm much closer to your chest when you take the club back. This will cause your hands to be lower on the backswing. You want to take it back low and slow."

"Left arm close to the chest, eh? Is it better to think of it that way rather than to try to keep the right arm tucked in—you know, as with a towel tucked under our armpit?"

"Definitely," Redding replies. "Tucking in your right arm, in and of itself, does nothing for you." He runs the videotape again, stopping just at the top of my backswing. There! There it is. The awful and seemingly incurable Problem: the breakdown, the folding up, of my left arm at the top of the swing.

"Right there is where you lose all of your power," Redding says. "At this very point," he stresses, freezing the frame that shows my left arm bent upside my head—"all power is gone. Poof. You're finished."

"So does this mean I'm still not ready for new clubs?" I ask, rather too plaintively.

I have been trying for months to get Redding to fit me for a new set of irons. He has steadfastly refused, telling me that I'm not ready, that it's a waste to measure me for the irons while my swing is still in flux. The clubs, he maintains, wouldn't fit right when and if I ever corrected the plane of my swing.

Now, however, he relents. Maybe it has to do with my moving away. Maybe he sees something in my swing that I don't. It doesn't really matter why, for I am now as hyper as a kid the night before Christmas. Sure, I know that the clubs will be no panacea, absolutely, of course not, what a joke. My swing problems could hardly be the result of my golf clubs. The Big Shooter is fond of saying, "A poor craftsman shouldn't blame his tools." Point taken. But on the other hand, my present clubs—a set of steel-shafted Arnold Palmer Axioms bought in 1987, back in the Stone Age of golf technology—were never fitted professionally. I just ordered them on impulse, prompted by an ad. Maybe their length is wrong. Or the swing weight. Or the stiffness of the shaft. Or the size of the grip. Or the degree of lie.

Judging from the paraphernalia Redding is now busily hauling out, these variables are not to be underestimated.

The first thing he does is place a strip of calibrated tape on the sole of a Wilson Staff five-iron. Then he lays a sheet of hard plastic on the ground where the ball usually sits. This sheet is called an impact board. He tells me to take a few swings. What he is looking for is how the club strikes the impact board, which is observable by scrapes on the calibrated tape. Ideally, Redding says, you're supposed to hit the ground roughly around the middle of the sole, or slightly toward the heel of it. Too much toward the heel, or toward the toe, is not good. My swing leaves scrape marks between the center and the toe. Redding tells me that we can fix this by ordering clubs with a slight upright lie. The lie refers to the angle of the hosel to the ground when the club head sits properly on the turf. An upright lie of two degrees, Redding says, should be just about right. I only vaguely grasp what he's talking about, and I do not much care. What I care about is getting these pegs in my possession as quickly as possible.

Throughout this process, Redding and I chat about the vagaries of club fitting and design. "There are few if any standards with golf clubs," he says. "That's why you should never walk into a store and buy a set of clubs off the rack. Someone qualified ought to measure you. And after you pick up the set you ordered, you should go directly to another club fitter and have him check every one of the clubs for lie, length, loft, grip size, and flex of shaft, to make sure you've got exactly what you ordered."

We compare the Staff five-iron to an Axiom. My present club is a full inch shorter. Redding tells me that a shorter club makes for a slower head speed, which might have been partly responsible for my hitting the ball the way I do. "A longer club is held naturally farther from the body, which typically results in a better swing," Redding says. I am getting extremely pumped.

Redding runs a few other tests. He asks me to swing a bizarre contraption that consists of a conventional shaft with a weird-looking spring-loaded device at the end. This widget measures the degree to which I am able to "load" the shaft. My load factor varies from swing to swing—from wimpy on the low end, to average on the high. The test confirms what we already know: I am certainly not a candidate for stiff shafts. My swing lacks the speed and load factor.

"What do you think, steel or graphite?" I ask Redding. *Graph-ite! Graph-ite! Graph-ite!* I chant silently, hoping the telepathy won't be turned back by Redding's metallic blue lenses. My mind flashes to an ad I saw the other night. The headline read "SOME OF LIFE'S LITTLE MYSTERIES." Below that, the copy:

Calculus
Filling out tax forms
Your daughter dating a guy with a nose ring
Steel or graphite shafts

Redding just shrugs.

"Hey, bud, your call," he finally says. "Frankly, it won't make a huge difference. The main advantage of steel is that each club will cost you $40 less. The main advantage of graphite is that it will conduct less vibration up through your hands and arms, which some people say gives a psychological advantage. If you plan to hit a lot of balls, I mean a *lot* of balls—say, 500 or more a day—then graphite will probably save some wear and tear on your joints."

Bingo!

While I will *never*—even if I were to mount a hostile tender offer for Lee-Jane—hit 500 or more balls in a single day, the wear-and-tear argument carries the day. If only for medicinal purposes, I decide to go for graphite. After all, I owe it to my family to take good physical care of myself. How could I mow the lawn or play catch with my kids, riddled with arthritis helped along by years of swinging steel-shafted clubs?

"One more thing," Redding says, as he begins to write out the specs for me to take to the store. "Have them put on the smallest adult grip they've got, even if they are women's grips. Don't be macho about this. Your hands are slightly smaller than average, same as mine, and I've found that the smaller grip enables me to get a better wrist-cock."

Rather than make an issue out of it, I refrain from pointing out that my fingers are actually slightly larger than Jack Nicklaus's.

Besides, I'm in a hurry. I make a beeline for Nevada Bob's. It is lunch hour on a Friday, and the place is jammed with guys who are checking out the gadgets, shopping for clubs, picking up balls and gloves, buying golf favors for weekend tournaments. I spend about thirty minutes at the club racks, trying to narrow my choice. Callaways and Cobras are automatic contenders, though I tell myself (insincerely) that it's ludicrous to spend close to $1,000 for a set of irons. I tentatively reject Pings because I have never liked the way they look. I take a hard look at Hogan GCDs, Wilson Staffs (cavity-backed), Tommy Armour 855s.

But soon the plot thickens. A salesman tells me that some clubs can, and some clubs can't, be adjusted for the extra two-degree lie that Redding has specified. He says that the finish on some clubs (Wilson and Armour, for example) is such that it can tolerate the bending required to achieve the lie Redding has requested. Hogans, however, cannot be bent, though a custom set could probably be ordered. On top of all this, only the Wilson Staffs are exactly the right length—the others seem to be about a quarter-inch shorter than Redding's specs. Of course, the salesman says, any of the clubs could be ordered with slightly longer shafts. Not wanting to wait, I decide to go with the Staffs and save a lot of time and trouble. There's only one hitch. The salesman informs me that Wilson's graphite shafts, known as Firesticks, only come in black and red, which I find aesthetically unacceptable.

I leave the store empty-handed and grumpy.

UNMITIGATED GALLWEY

Without new clubs to distract me, I have more time to think. Just what I need.

Seventeen years ago, I bought a copy of *The Inner Game of Golf* by W. Timothy Gallwey. The book was published in the wake of the enormous success and notoriety Gallwey enjoyed with *The Inner Game of Tennis*, which was exquisitely timed to take advantage of a couple of cultural obsessions of the late sixties and early seventies: the huge tennis boom that swept America, and the rise of interest in self-awareness, transcendental meditation, yoga. (Gallwey dedicated *The*

Inner Game of Golf to that renowned, spiritual scratch-shooter, the Guru Maharaj Ji.)

The Inner Game of Golf turned out to be one of the sport's seminal books. There's a case to be made that it has had more influence over how golf is taught, and played, than any other over the past fifty years. It's not that Gallwey discovered something new—remember, writers like Ernest Thompson had been expounding on golf's mental side for eons. What Gallwey did was add a brilliant catch phrase, the *inner game,* and elucidate the mental side of golf with a flair and salesmanship no one had previously managed.

The essence of Gallwey—deftly drawn from such diverse philosophical thinkers as Buddha, Rousseau, Jung, and Al Geiberger—is that each of us is composed of two selves, each with his own agenda, each with his own set of clubs. Self 1, says Gallwey, is our verbalizing, thought-controlling self. Self 2 is our physical, or more "natural" self. Self 1 is a royal pain in Self 2's butt: he/she heckles, analyzes, doubts, hisses, distracts, second-guesses—*anything* to interfere with what Self 2 could otherwise accomplish with relative ease. "A single conscious thought . . . diverts the arrow from the course towards the target," as it is written in *Zen and the Art of Archery.* Gallwey proposes that we should learn to liberate Self 2 from the clutches of Self 1. If all this sounds a lot like what goes on between Michael and Shivas Irons in *Golf in the Kingdom,* it should: Gallwey and Murphy are mutual admirers who sip from the same spiritual wellspring.

The key to this process, Gallwey suggests, is to relieve ourselves of *doubt.* Doubt is what poisons our ability to perform—it tightens our muscles to the point of ultimate failure. Doubt creeps in when we try too hard. Instead of struggling in a "trying mode," as Gallwey calls it, we should cultivate an "awareness" mode, or a state of "relaxed concentration," the phrase George Leonard so favored. Gallwey lists five kinds of trying in golf, all of them lethal to success: trying to *hit* the ball, rather than swing; trying to get the ball aloft; trying to hit the ball too far; trying to hit the ball too straight; trying to hit the ball "right." Gallwey disputes the tenets of the classically grooved swing, which, he says, requires us to keep too many rules in mind.

There's not a golf instructor working today who hasn't, whether he has read Gallwey or not, incorporated some of *The Inner Game's* basic ideas into his approach, from its polite distrust of authority, to its soothing narcissism, to its fuzzy (and fussy) precepts about awareness and visualization. "What does it feel like to *you*?" Redding always answers, when I ask whether the club should feel like a paddle. The response is pure Gallwey. Jack Nicklaus, too, betrays Gallweyian tendencies. When he "goes to the movies" before every shot, the Bear seeks the relaxed concentration that lies at the heart of meditation.

There isn't a golf book published these days that isn't colored by Gallwey's philosophy. These books aren't by weird monks, but by guys with Cadillac or Nynex affixed to their breasts. Open to almost any page and you'll hear Gallwey, Murphy, and Leonard rustling through the trees.

Jim McLean: ". . . establish a game plan based on shots you are comfortable executing, as opposed to shots you can only hope to hit."

Jimmy Ballard: ". . . I spent countless hours trying to find a way to communicate . . . the natural, sequential wholeness or the unified efficiency of the actions that I could plainly see in the swings of all the great ball strikers."

Jim Flick: ". . . *feel* the clubhead."

Buzzwords, images, and training tips from *The Inner Game* are now standard equipment in most golf instructors' kit bags. Take humming, for example.

One day, Gallwey says, he was mindlessly hitting practice balls and humming at the same time. He describes how he realized that his humming was not only exerting a calming effect on his swing, but also served as an onboard biofeedback system, indicating where and when in the golf swing we unconsciously grip the club too hard. His own humming, he relates, is nice 'n' easy during the backswing, but gets squeaky and loud as he starts down, which tells him he needs to lighten up at this stage.

It's beside the point whether it was Gallwey who discovered this phenomenon or whether, like a lot of stuff in *The Inner Game*, it was adroitly repackaged by the nimble author. Not to nitpick—there goes that naughty old Self 1 again!—but Sam Snead wrote about the therapeutic effects of humming decades before Gallwey. Back when he was a young teaching pro at the Greenbriar, Snead cured the slice of some titan of industry by suggesting that the man hum "The Merry Widow Waltz."

The fact is, humming does work. I've had several lessons in which teachers—having observed how my swing was accompanied by a fiercely clenched jaw and hot, swollen knuckles—decided that I was a prime candidate for advanced humming therapy. Not one of these teachers ever gave Gallwey (and certainly not Snead) any credit for the idea. Each, rather, implied that humming was something he himself had discovered in the deep reaches of his own restless intellect. No matter. Many is the time I benefited (in the short term) from warbling through gently drawn lips. Yesterday at the range, without conscious prompting, I found myself humming my favorite song from *Guys and Dolls*—"I'll Know (When My Love Comes Along)." I promptly peeled off a series of soaring three-irons. When it comes to practice-tee humming, I am unabashedly partial to ballads. With due respect to the Slammer and his taste in music, waltzes just won't cut it for me, nor, for that matter, would light opera, klezmer, or any conceivable polka. Humming a polka while swinging a golf club would no doubt cause me to shank. Maybe even blow lunch.

Through the years I have developed a pretty good idea of which tunes work as golf hummables and which tunes don't:

Good Hummables

"Dancing on the Ceiling"

"In the Still of the Night"

"Prelude to a Kiss"

"Polka Dots and Moonbeams" (*not* a polka!)

"Stars Fell on Alabama"

"The Folks Who Live on the Hill"

Bad Hummables

"The Colonel Bogey March"

"Theme from *Mondo Cane*"

"The Monster Mash"

"How Much Is That Doggie in the Window?"

"Revolution 9"

"These Boots Were Made for Walkin' "

The Klutz Factor

What's hard is easy,
What's natural comes hard.
— **Stephen Sondheim,** *"Anyone Can Whistle"*

SHOPPING AROUND

On the eve of another trip to New York, where I'll do some business and scope out the housing market, I drop in for a quick couple of buckets at Deane Hill, once a private country club, now a daily-fee course on its last legs before a developer comes in to turn it into another Kingston Pike shopping mall. Because of its grass practice tees, I've been coming here more and more, saving Lee-Jane for rainy days when Deane Hill shuts down. Today, while paying for my balls, I spy a collection of demo clubs. I ask whether I can take a few out on the range so that I might test them. It has been five days now since Redding handed me my specs, which I am still carrying around in my billfold. Given the complex variables of lie, length, and aesthetics, I've still been unable to decide on which clubs to order. This test session will help a great deal, I figure, as I prepare to go to town with an arsenal of five-irons: a Ping Zing, a King Cobra, a Titleist DCI, an Armour 885.

I lay the clubs down on the ground and mull over an appropriate methodology. I'll hit a half-dozen balls with each club, then narrow my choice to the two with the best feel. Finally, I'll alternate one-on-one with these until a clear preference emerges.

But wonder of wonders, I hit *every one* of these clubs with greater authority and ease than I can command with my aging quiver of Axioms. Is it possible that my old clubs were so ill-fitted that they were responsible for my erratic play all these years? Is it conceivable that graphite shafts, and these newfangled larger club heads, can make such a difference to performance? Or is it all illusory? Do I hit these shots so much better because the test itself encourages me to feel the club head, which means I'm swinging with better tempo and speed?

By the end of the first round I have contracted an intense case of the Fever. I have hit each of these clubs with crisp, matter-of-fact consistency, but the two that stand out are the Cobra and the Ping Zing. In round two, the Cobra again prevails. Swing after swing, I hit silky five-irons between 150 and 165 yards, most with a slight fade. When I return the clubs to the pro shop, I ask how long it would take to get a set of Cobras to Redding's specs. Two months, the man tells me.

I race home. Credit card at the ready, I frenetically speed-dial several Knoxville golf shops. The day turns cloudier and cloudier. Here we go again. A clerk at Pro Golf tells me that a set of Cobras with two-degree upright lie would be no problem. Trouble is, he's out of stock and says that a new set will take six weeks to arrive. Someone at Knoxville's Nevada Bob's tells me he doesn't think Cobras can be ordered with the upright loft, nor can they be manually bent. A salesman at a third golf store says with the utmost confidence that the problem with making the lie more upright rests not in the finish but in the fact that "graphite can't be bent, though maybe the hosel can, though why don't you just call Cobra yourself and ask them?"

So I do.

The Cobra customer relations rep in Carlsbad, California, tells me she's not sure what the answer is but promises to have a tech person get back to me when he returns from lunch. He promptly does, and while the news is further discouraging, at least it is relayed with an air of informed assurance, which is the first time I've heard that sound all day. He explains that Cobra doesn't recommend that anyone bend its clubs to increase their lie and that all stores should know this because the company makes it a point to tell them over and over again. It shouldn't matter, though, he adds, because Cobra offers its line in three different lies: upright, standard, and two-degree flat.

"You must be pretty tall, right?" he then asks.

"No, actually I'm pretty short."

"Then you must have unusually long arms."

I tell him that, no, my arms are about normal for a pretty short guy.

"Then there's no way you want two degrees upright—they're totally wrong for somebody like you."

Oh, God.

I thank him and hang up. Five minutes later, I am back on the phone, calling various golf shops in New York.

"Do you have specific fitting instructions for Cobra irons, or a set of their demo clubs?" I ask the manager of Golf World, a vast basement shop in Manhattan that's crammed with every imaginable piece of golf equipment.

"No, we measure you according to the Ping chart," he says.

"Do you know whether Cobra's specifications are the same as Ping's?" I ask.

The question irritates him. "You come in, we take care of you."

Screw it. I stomp upstairs to pack. Just calm down and wait until you get there, I tell myself. Then you can walk over to the Richard Metz store on Madison Avenue, a golf shop with experienced sales people and indoor hitting areas. Metz has been selling clubs for decades, catering to the men in gray flannel suits and now to an ever-widening clientele of Asian businessmen and tourists. The staff there will clear up the confusion once and for all.

The next morning I catch a pre-dawn flight, visions of oversized club heads dancing in my head. I arrive in New York midmorning, take a cab to the hotel, leave my bag with the bellman, and scamper immediately to the Metz shop just a couple of blocks away. I collar a salesman and tell him I want a set of King Cobra irons but I am confused about the fitting. He hands me a Cobra five-iron and shows me to a fitting stall. He tells me to stand on a black rubber mat. He instructs me to take a few swings and to be sure to hit the mat on the downswing.

Without a warm-up, I whack a few balls into a net. Every muscle in my body is tight. I have been strapped into an airplane seat all morning, plus I am wearing a starched shirt and a tie. These must be truly ugly-looking swings, and I wonder whether the man is going to fit me on the basis of these three or four horrendous efforts. The answer is yes. He examines the sole of the club. The findings contradict what Redding observed in the shed. There it was demonstrated that I was hitting the ground toward the toe of the sole; here, the scrape marks are toward the heel.

"Ideally, you want to be sort of between the middle and the heel, right?" I say, trying to win back some of the salesman's respect after the dreadful swings I've shown him.

"No," he answers. "You want to be right in the middle. I think you ought to get clubs with a lie that is two degrees flat."

"Flat?" I gasp. "I was told to get them two degrees upright."

"Well, you were told wrong, pal."

"What about the length?" I ask. "I was told that the five-iron should be 39.5 inches long."

"39.5 inches? That's also nuts," he says. "That's at least an inch longer than most, and you're not particularly tall. To say the least."

I walk out of the store, clublessly.

Three days later, I am back on the shed, thwacking the impact board. This time I hit the ball more or less on the center of the sole. The mystery unravels: It seems that everyone is right. It's my swings that are wrong—they vary wildly from one to the next, which explains why sometimes I hit the ground with the heel, sometimes on the toe, sometimes in the middle.

"Look, what if I just get a standard lie?" I ask Redding, my exasperation all too evident.

To my relief, he agrees. So I hightail it to Nevada Bob's, whip out the plastic, and finally acquire my set of new custom-fitted King Cobras.

Length: strictly standard, off-the-shelf.

Shaft: graphite, regular flex, strictly standard, off-the-shelf.

Lie: strictly standard, off-the-shelf.

Grips: strictly standard, off-the shelf. (I do, however, intend to have smaller ones affixed ASAP.)

Cost (including tax and optional gap wedge): $885.15.

Risking life, limb, and the Tennessee State Highway Patrol, I zoom down I-40 to the Deane Hill Country Club. I crack open the long brown box nestled in the trunk and remove the shiny new Cobras.

Now, which of these babies do I fire first? I decide on the eight-iron. Tommy Armour favored the eight-iron over all other clubs as a practice and teaching tool. He said it enabled students to get the ball into the air consistently, thus circumventing embarrassment on the tee. Armour called the eight "the most constructive, as well as instructive, club in the bag."

Eight-iron at the ready, I tee up a ball, not wanting to crud up the sparkling cutlery just yet. I pause before the maiden effort. I remind myself of a swing thought I've been having in anticipation of this occasion.

Let the clubs do the work.

Let the gunmetal graphite shafts and the large, cavity-backed club heads supply the power. Swing easy and through the ball—don't try to kill it. Let the clubs do the work.

And with that—

I hit a weak slice.

I tee up the next ball.

I top it.

I tee up another.

I clank a perp.

The world goes black.

A DIAGNOSIS

I don't pretend to be digging a fresh divot with this insight, but we are what we duff.

Each of us brings a fair tonnage of emotional baggage to the golf course; over the past couple of decades, some have even attempted to quantify it. Thomas Tutko, a sports psychologist who in the 1970s helped establish the legitimacy of this flourishing discipline, wrote, "Playing a game is obviously not just a physical experience; it is a total personal experience. You don't leave your personality, habits, and attitudes behind when you walk onto the field." Tutko and others tried to objectify what it is about a player that alternately causes him to prevail, or collapse, during competition. He called his test the SERP, or Sports Emotional-Reaction Profile.

So I sit here with sharpened pencil in hand, self-administering Tutko's SERP. The fact that I am something of a basket case on the links is incontrovertible. I don't need anyone—Tutko, Rotella, Freud, Jung, Bettelheim, Pavlov, Pavlov's dog—to tell me that. I think, analyze, and futz too much. These tendencies make it impossible for me to keep my arms and shoulders as wiggly as Jell-O, to keep my mind free of dozens of negative intrusions. Still, let's see what the old SERP has to say. I am faced with forty-two statements whose applicability to myself I am asked to describe on a scale of 1 to 5. A random sample:

- Little annoyances can throw me off my game. (Often.)
- I can control my nervousness during a game. (Almost never.)
- I am a "take charge" kind of performer. (Seldom.)
- I laugh off things rather than get angry at them. (Seldom.)
- I jump from one thing to another trying to improve my game. (Almost always.)
- I worry about failures more than I enjoy my successes. (Almost always.)
- I try to avoid thinking about my mistakes. (Seldom.)

Tutko's questions are conceived to evaluate seven psychological qualities that affect us during athletic performance: Desire, Assertiveness, Sensitivity, Tension Control, Confidence, Personal Accountability, and Self-Discipline. By the time I tote up my results I'm on my second martini and feeling no pain. I'm ready for any diagnosis Dr. Tutko wants to fling my way. The results of the SERP indicate I am fairly average in all of the above categories but one: Tension Control. Tutko's tension scale classifies me as a "Nervous Wreck." This is perhaps not the most clinical of diagnoses, but I accept it. Tutko says,

"The high-strung person often lets his emotions interfere with his performance and ruin his enjoyment. . . . For instance, he might find himself feeling a great deal of pressure over a missed shot and then blow up and miss the next one, and the one after that, growing more tense with each flub."

I close the book and drain the last of my drink, then polish off the olive.

Getting golf right is driving me batty.

Earlier today I took the Cobras in for new grips. "Extra small," I said to the man behind the counter, a pudgy guy who looked just like Craig Stadler.

"Who told you that?"

"Brad Redding," I answered, confident the name would be enough to button the guy's lip. (Redding, as I have noted, is well known in these parts.)

"Let me see your hands," said the salesman.

I held them out, fingers spread wide apart.

"They look about average to me," he observed. "Put on extra-small grips, and there's no way you're gonna hold the club secure. And even if your hands *were* on the small side you'd be better off with *thicker* grips, which would give you a lot more power."

Not wanting to relive the tortured confusion that attended the purchase of these clubs, I declined his suggestion and said I'd be back in the morning to pick up the teeny tiny grips.

Everybody's a professor. Everybody's got a theory.

WORD GAMES

Golf, we are told ad nauseam, is a game of embattled sides. When we pick up a golf club we are at once conscripted into a ferocious civil war. The mind ambushes the muscles. The right side overwhelms the left. Our left brain undermines our right. Qualities that serve us well in other arenas can be our enemies on the links.

Take words. Words are what I do. But on the links they are my undoing. They confuse and distract. They can be ill-mannered and rude. They talk while I'm hitting.

Golf, everyone agrees, is a fight that is won, or lost, from within. In this corner, the intrusive, nagging, worrying, bullying, harping, doubting, second-guessing, overbearing abuser we know and despise as Self 1. In that corner, Self 2, broken, abandoned, confused, squelched, fearful, overwhelmed, battered.

Hey, guys, this is supposed to be a game!

When we were kids, when the air was fresh and the water so clean we could drink out of water hazards, playing games was simple. Self 2 was a happy little tyke. I never had to *think* about what moves to make on the field. Life was unhurried and uncomplicated: endless seasons of stickball, basketball, and two-hand touch. Who knew from the mechanics of throwing, or the physics of the jump shot? I just played. Played every day. I thought of myself as a jock first, everything else second. I hadn't the slightest clue that Self 2, my best bud, wouldn't hang in there forever; or that being an everyday jock was anything less than a permanent appointment. I threw. I caught. I shot. I passed. I tagged. I ran. I jumped. I fell. I got up. I won. I lost.

But was I any good?

Well, I *thought* I was good. I was definitely good enough. I was often the youngest kid to make a team—good enough to be picked, if not good enough to play very much. In time, though, I realized that I wasn't going to be good enough much longer, not big enough, not fast enough, not coordinated enough, to play with the shtarkers. Size—or lack of it—started to get in the way. I was a shrimp. But then again, I consoled myself, a lot of guys were shrimps. Richie Ashburn, Tommy

Macdonald, they, too, were shrimps. These pesky, agile, peppery shrimps were my heroes.

Then came puberty.

One day I was an athlete-shrimp, the next day I was a gland. I didn't give up sports exactly, but I certainly rearranged my priorities. I still played a lot of games, but by now Self 1 had started to hang out around the batting cage, smirking, second-guessing, doubting. In no time at all he had broken my confidence. He said I was too short. He said I was too slow. Once he got his hands on me I was finished as a jock. I was destined to be high-handicapper: a thinking, a glandular shrimp with a driver in his hands.

THE K FACTOR™

June is busting out all over. Big changes are in the air.

The other day Linda and I found a house to rent in a suburb just north of New York City. It's a loopy, imposing old place, a sprawling Tudor with a stone wall running across the front of the property. Stone gates frame the driveway. In one of them is etched DUNMOVIN, the name given to the house by the family that built it in 1928. I suggest to Linda that we sandblast the word *Dunmovin* and replace it with GAWNRENTIN. Gawnrentin is as sturdy and fine a house as we could expect to find. It will suit us until we find something permanent. The place has great details—leaded windows, a paneled dining room, an imposing two-story entrance. But here's the best part: The house sits on over an acre of prime pitching and chipping terrain. In the front there is even an ellipse of generous proportion, at least as large as the one in Knoxville. To the side and the back of the house are sloping lawns and hidden gardens, exceptional perfing grounds. Gawnrentin is perf golf's answer to Augusta.

Now that we know where we are going, I am prompted to take measure of where things stand. With just a couple more lessons scheduled with Redding, I continue to admire his unflagging commitment to teaching, not to mention his continuing, apparent belief in the likelihood I will improve. Overall, though, things have come to a sorry pass.

Here is the interim report card I'd give myself:

Better

- Intellectual understanding of swing mechanics.
- Appreciation of golf's difficulty.
- Hat collection.
- Respect for those who, however paunchy, loud, boorish, and badly dressed, can play a hell of a lot better than I can.

Worse

- Self-image as a jock.
- Willingness to talk to my wife about "how it's going."

No Change

- Basic ball-striking skill.
- Ability to score.
- Tendency to misalign and swing over the top.
- Persistent feeling that if God had intended me to play golf He would have made me (a) blonder; (b) lankier; and (c) more inclined to embrace Jesus.

Given the improvements still on back order, the move north gives me reason to hope that a change of scenery may do the trick. Over the past couple of weeks I've been asking every New York golfer I know to suggest a new teacher. I have weighed their recommendations and talked on the phone with at least a half-dozen candidates.

But how do you pick a teacher long distance? Haphazardly. The search comes down to who gives good phone. Is he articulate? (Aren't they all?) Is he sure of himself? (Ever met one who wasn't?) Is he honest, perceptive, capable of adapting his teaching methods to suit the individual? (Go know.)

The winner of this determined search is a man named Tom Patri, the director of instruction at the Westchester Country Club. Patri gets the nod because a friend of a friend of a friend recommended him; because he occasionally contributes tips to the national golf magazines; and because Westchester C.C. is only about fifteen minutes from Gawnrentin.

In the meantime, I hedge my bets and schedule a number of out-of-town forays whereby I'll continue my quest. I arrange to spend a weekend in New Orleans with a former Tour player who has developed intriguing new notions about the golf swing. And I reserve a spot for myself at a couple of upcoming golf schools.

All this planning masks the fact that I am growing increasingly apprehensive. What has got me uneasy is the K-Factor, a theory that I've been concocting that may well explain why some people are destined to play good golf and others are not. Details in a moment; first, some brief and necessary background.

My friends Dan and Becky Okrent—whose house served as base camp for the Wedding Round—used to keep a photograph of me on the door of their refrigerator. They had it there just for laughs, and to annoy me whenever I came to visit. The picture was taken on a winter weekend in the early 1980s and shows me bundled up in a long woolen scarf and a Philadelphia Phillies satin warm-up jacket— an *extremely* dorky look. I am standing, chilled to the bone, on a frozen pond. In one outstretched hand I am holding a hockey stick, or trying to, but that's incidental. The most revealing aspect of the picture is that every muscle in my body is ferociously knotted. My body lists severely to the left, with every joint locked in a fearsome grip. The sheer physical demand of trying to maintain my balance while on ice skates, coupled with the need to hold onto something (meaning a stick, not a railing, which I would have greatly preferred) requires a level of "relaxed concentration" far, far beyond my innate athletic ability, skatewise.

That photograph captures the essence of the K-Factor.

The K-Factor proposes that those of us who have trouble mastering the golf swing are, purely and simply, *klutzes*. Forget angles and planes and swing paths: It all comes down to simple athletic prowess. You either have the coordination to put the club on the ball, or you don't. You're either possessed of athletic ability, or you're a klutz. End of theory.

Golf detractors no doubt find the K-Factor a hilarious concept. Golf is not athletic, they snicker. Just look at how many golfers, even good golfers, are slovenly, fat, slow, and in generally rotten physical condition. As David Owen put it in *My Usual Game*, "Golf is to sports what dentistry is to medicine. . . . Golf [is] the only professional sport in which one is likely to see a competitor smoking a cigar while competing."

These golf bashers miss the point entirely.

While it's true that you can play the game, and play it well, with the stamina of a sloth and the gut of hippo, you must be able to consummate an extraordinarily demanding physical feat. You must be able to put the club face squarely on the ball at a precise millisecond, while the club head is whipping around at close to 100 miles an hour. To be able to do this requires no less "athletic" an act than the ability to defy gravity and hurl your butt over a towering, fragile bar, or run twenty-six miles in half the time it takes to watch a baseball game.

One either has this dollop of athletic ability or one doesn't, according to the K-Factor. If you can get that millisecond right, everything else—takeaway, backswing, downswing, finish—is completely irrelevant.

The K-Factor explains why so many bad players can have different swings.

It explains why some players never take a lesson and still consistently break 80.

It explains why some take lessons for their entire lives and never break 100.

It explains why some players can hit the ball with forged blades, even the one-iron.

It explains why others can't hit the side of the barn with an offset, oversized, cavity-backed pitching wedge the size of a fly swatter.

And it explains why some players deliberately shoot *for* the bunker because they know the sand blast is among the easiest shots in their bag. And it explains why others would rather share an overnight cell with Hannibal Lecter than set foot in a greenside hazard.

Lest anyone think the K-Factor is just a half-baked, self-evident, harebrained wisp of a notion plucked from the thinnest ozone, consider that the K-Factor lines up nicely with the work of eminent social scientists. Foremost among these is Professor Howard Gardner, Harvard psychologist and MacArthur Prize Fellow. Gardner's classic work, *Frames of Mind*, provides a solid theoretical foundation for the contention that golfing proficiency comes down to whether you've got natural ability or you're an incurable doofus.

Gardner's thesis, for those who were out on the links that day, is that there are multiple forms of "intelligence," and each of us has to varying degrees a measure of each of them. Gardner identifies at least five active intelligences: linguistic, musical, logical-mathematical, spatial, and the one that determines whether we're "smart enough" to hit a one-iron, namely, "bodily-kinesthetic." It is this form of intelligence that's "inherent in producing a skilled motor performance," writes Gardner. It determines whether we are blessed with "a well-honed sense of timing, wherein each bit of a sequence fits into the stream in an exquisitely placed and elegant way . . ." An accomplished golfer, therefore, is one whose gene pool has the correct chromosome sloshing around. I have this gnawing suspicion that I am devoid of that particular chromosome.

SHEDDING IT

These early summer sessions at Willow Creek hold a certain poignancy. I rerun the many days I've spent here. I remember how everything was drab and mocha-colored when I first saw this place, how green and alive it became with the passing weeks and months.

And there was the day when, just up the road, a man building a house got upset over what he claimed was a bad asphalt paving job. So he pulled out a shotgun, plugged the paver in the hips, then shot out the tires of his wife's car to prevent her from following him, only to shoot himself through the chin while driving past the entrance to Willow Creek. This prompted him to lose control of his vehicle and mow down five utility poles, though he miraculously lived through it. It is difficult to enumerate which multiple intelligences were at work in this little episode.

There was the sunny morning in April when news of the Oklahoma City bombing flashed over CNN. I was in the grill room, having a sandwich with Redding, when the terrible pictures came on. Along with a dozen decent men in colored golf shirts, I watched with disbelief and horror.

My final days with Redding pass without incident. As usual, he watches me hit a few, then we repair to the shed, where he moves me around, making sure my head and eyes stay fixed on the ball. He leaves me to hang in the address position as he steps back. He tells me to swing through. The ease of the downswing and finish are in contrast to what it feels like on the course. Here it is kind of a sideswipe. On the course it feels like a mugging. But here the club seems to slash through the ball, allowing me to finish well balanced, fully turned to the target.

Sometimes Redding has me hold my position at the top of the backswing, at which point he'll grab my left pocket and yank. He wants me to feel my hips moving first, as they lead my upper body through impact. Our final video sessions show that my posture has become pretty good: butt extended, spine held at an acceptable angle. My head and shoulders remain slightly shlumped. Redding, patient as ever, steps in and moves me again. We acknowledge how much easier it is for him to do this now. When he places my hands on the grip, my left wrist obediently folds in, doesn't push back at him. My muscles have learned to surrender.

The best part about these final lessons is that we get to spend some time out on the course. Redding slides behind the wheel of a golf cart and with the uncanny instincts of a creature utterly at home in his natural habitat, quickly finds an open run of two or three holes. Today we start on a long par-five. Redding instructs me to join him on the extreme left side of the tee box. He tells me to walk back a full ten yards behind the ball and pick out a desired landing spot. He says to select a target well to the right of where I want the ball to land. We settle on a fairway bunker some thirty degrees in that direction. I take my stance, recheck the target, then swing the three-wood. The ball, stung hard, lifts off grandly and flies down the center of the fairway. Redding applauds. I am stunned. I almost always slice the ball off the tee. Why did this one go straight? Because Redding had lined me up such that I'd be compelled to pull the shot? Reaching the drive, Redding tells me to play a five-wood. Again, he has me pick out a spot well to the right of where I want to end up. I pick out a small willow behind the green, about fifteen degrees to the right of the flag stick. I swing and hit another soaring shot, slightly to the left of the target but still comfortably on the fairway, about sixty yards from the green.

Redding now tells me to take out the sand wedge. Ordinarily, I would have selected a pitching wedge for this occasion, though I'd be confused about how hard to swing it. Redding explains that we should favor the club that yields the full distance. In this case it's the sand wedge. "The pitch shot," he says, "should generally not be made with a pitching wedge. The pitch shot requires a sand wedge, though sometimes we must shorten our swing."

This is one of those times. Redding suggests I'll need to make a three-quarters swing. Together we pick out a target, a small tree behind the green, which is about ten degrees to the right of the stick. I swing, keeping my hands low on the takeaway. The ball flies high, dead-on, and stops pin-high, about ten feet to the right of the cup. I am amazed.

After a couple more holes, we make the long ride back to the shed, during which I try out some of my thoughts about Redding's style of teaching. I tell him that I have never once caught him palming off somebody else's teaching clichés. This is a remarkable quality, I say. But Redding doesn't seem to care one way or the other. Shielded behind his Revos, he remains diffident, a trait common to those of his profession. I reckon that there's a direct correlation between diffidence and the ability to swing through, not at, a golf ball. Golf pros, with their opaque personalities, swing through. Their hapless charges, with their transparent personalities, swing at.

THE HOME COURSE

I shake hands with Redding, thank him for the valiant efforts he has made. He says if I run into problems I shouldn't hesitate to send him a videotape. We could work on my swing over the phone. I then make a final exit from Willow Creek. I will miss Redding and always remember the unnerving metal shed.

But Willow Creek, the golf course itself, will no doubt fade quickly.

Built in the last decade, it is a track without character or soul. There is nary a hole that pricks the imagination, nothing especially pretty. Redding once remarked that a golf course has an obligation to make the golfer's day as enjoyable as possible, "to worship the ground he walks on," he said, somewhat curiously. At Willow Creek, the attitude behind the counter is perfunctory. Once, when I requested Redding's appointment book, the course manager flung it across the counter at me. Another time I asked where Redding was and was told he hadn't come in "unexplainedly," which turned out to be untrue; he was over at the shed. The manager then said, "If he's not here me or Clem would give you a lesson." Neither happened to be an instructor, PGA certified or otherwise.

No—the place I will miss most around here is Egwani Farms, the course out by the airport on the southeast edge of town, in a little hamlet called Rockford. By no measure is Egwani Farms exceptional. In fact, the notorious eleventh hole at Egwani is know locally as "goofy golf," a blind drive into an impossibly narrow bottleneck, then another blind shot off a high bluff. Egwani Farms wasn't carved out of fragrant stands of evergreens, or etched into a windy bluff by an open sea. It's just one of the friendliest and calmest places on planet golf, situated on a bucolic parcel of Tennessee pasture land. The old barn on the spread is now the clubhouse, with rocking chairs set out on the porch.

Alistair MacKenzie, second only to Elohim as the greatest golf course architect of all time, said famously that "every man has an affection for the particular mud heap on which he plays." For my time in Tennessee, Egwani Farms became that mud heap. A golfer's home course is as sacred a spot as he knows. It is his hideout, a place he goes to escape the noise and pressures of everywhere else. It is where he comes to know every tree in every season, which way the breezes blow throughout the day, how the ground runs. The home course is a place the golfer cares for and looks after. Each unrepaired divot is a wound that hurts, so he fixes it whether he made it or not. He rakes the bunkers with special care. He comes to know where hidden dangers lurk, and where he can let loose and cut corners. The home course is where he has his share of triumphs, and where the occasional catastrophe is mercifully evanescent.

Assuming that our stay in Knoxville would probably not exceed a few years, I lived my golfing life as a trunk slammer, playing haphazardly at public courses in the area. Egwani Farms is the one that captured my heart. It isn't the terrain, or its layout, or the fine view of the Smokies that makes it special. It's the fact that the public face of Egwani Farms is unfailingly cheerful, smiling, and courteous. You see, almost everybody who works out in front, where the golfers are, is a woman.

You pull into the parking lot, and the person who's right there to offload your clubs and strap them onto a cart is a bright-eyed Southern belle, the first of several you'll encounter. She doesn't say "Good morning," or "Hello," or even "Hi." She gives you the local "Hey!" with a smile so huge it makes you feel like you've just holed a forty-foot chip. You step up to pay your greens fees and instead of the usual too-cool-by-half, why-am-I-working-in-the-pro-shop-when-I-can-wipe-the-course-with-these-fat-assed-suckers young stud behind the counter, there's a pleasant blonde woman who hands you your change and says, "Now y'all have a good day. Enjoy!" And when you make the turn and belly up to the counter for some refreshment, you are greeted by yet another fair and radiant lady who always remembers to ask what kind of bread you'd like on your sandwich. If you're the sort who expects the rarefied clubhouse service at the National Golf Links or Augusta, this place won't be your cup of mountain mash. In my view, though, it's golf heaven, unpretentious, pretty as a postcard.

Egwani Farms is operated by a married couple in their thirties, Lisa and Lynn Franks. Technically, the Franks lease the property from the Rockford Manufacturing Company, a textile mill that sits just over the narrow river that runs through a stretch of the back nine. But the mill is in the family, too, so it's not as if they're real tenants. The land here, originally two adjoining farms, was bought back in the thirties by Lisa's grandfather, a gentleman farmer named Ernest Koella, who grew corn at Egwani and raised Longhorns that he had shipped over from Texas. Two splendid old farmhouses still lord proudly over the land, built to last. One of these watches over the second fairway, high up on a hill. This was the seat of the old Walker Farm, and the first masonry house ever built in Blount County. The other guards the eighteenth green, also from a polite and lofty distance. That was the Russell family house, a magnificent and stately brick Federal.

One day, Lisa, her husband, and I shoot the breeze at a table in the barn-clubhouse. I've just come off the course, having played a pleasant, if inconsistent (ninety-five), round in a little under three hours. Lynn, who's burly and bushy-bearded, a Tennessee mountain man, serves as the greenskeeper here. Lisa runs the customer operation.

I am curious to know how, in a modern golf world marked by the dual pretensions of grandiloquent architecture and customer service that's nonchalant at best, insufferably pompous at worst, such a place as Egwani Farms comes to exist. I mention that I think most daily-fee courses offer abominable service to golfers, not to mention too much traffic, tee times set just six or eight minutes apart. At Egwani the range balls are free, clean, and unmarked. They are provided in unlimited quantity on a beautifully maintained range. Tee times are never less than twelve minutes apart.

"We have a pretty simple philosophy here," Lisa says. "And I'm sure it has to do with the fact that we've never had any experience at this. We just want to treat our golfers as guests, like we're havin' 'em over to dinner. We don't like to nickel and dime 'em, which is why we give out free range balls and keep them new and shiny."

"How about all the women working here? Whose idea was that?"

"The gals just kind of happened," she says. "We didn't set out to have an all-female staff in the clubhouse, but we learned that women were just a whole lot nicer, and more versatile, and frankly a whole lot better at doing all the things that need to be done to keep a place like this up to snuff.

"Most of all, though, we just want to keep a farm feel to this place. Keep it simple and pretty. That's why you don't see a lot of plantings brought in from other places, or a lot of flowers. We want things just to feel comfortable and natural. Not to be putting 'em down, I'm not sure that's something you can say about most of the new golf courses you see these days. We knew from the start that we wanted this place to look like it was always here."

Tightness

Together, the rotator cuff muscles have an essential
steadying effect on the head of the humerus. . . .
—Dr. Frank W. Jobe, *30 Exercises for Better Golf,* 1986

A BRAND NEW START OF IT

It is the end of the July, and we have been sweating it out at Gawn-rentin for five days now. Linda, the kids, and I are not happy campers. Ever since the moving trucks pulled up to our new domicile, half the nation has been in the grip of a sweltering heat wave. The thermometer has been stuck in the high nineties, with equally high humidity. The newspaper is filled with horror stories about the effects of this intense furnace blast, tales of suffering from Chicago to Boston. Linda and I spend fourteen-hour days unpacking cartons in this old and steaming house, taking frequent and wholly ineffective cold showers. Ned and Katherine are no less miserable—hot, bored, and displaced, suddenly removed from all friends, favorite toys, and their familiar rooms. Ned, who loves stories about goblins, monsters, and vampires with blood-red eyes, finds Gawnrentin unsettling in the extreme—a haunted stone castle with a massive tile roof and ancient windows, where floorboards creak and tiny clawed creatures scamper in the night across the dusty attic floor, which is directly above his little bed.

As much to escape the heat as to buy provisions, we pile into the car, turn up the air conditioner, and head off to the nearby A&P. Inside, the air is cool and bracing. This pleasant interlude, however, is quickly marred by an impatient crone whose determination to conduct her grocery shopping in less than a New York minute is momentarily frustrated by the placement of our shopping cart, which the kids have left standing askew in an aisle. The witch curses under her breath at us. Later, as we near the checkout lane, another shrew, this one pushing eighty, sizes up our pace, then accelerates her own very slightly so that she might beat us by a nose to the conveyer belt. Linda and I look at each other, stunned at the petty aggression. Was it always like this up here? Back in the car, we tarry at a green light for, oh, maybe a nano-second, when a jerk in a BMW zaps us with his horn.

Goblins, monsters, and vampires I can deal with. Uptight shoppers and sociopaths I can handle. What has gotten me truly spooked, though, is that I haven't swung the new sticks in over a week. I lie awake at night, basting in my own perspiration, contemplating the ultimate doomsday scenario: What if I am losing what little I learned from Brad Redding these last six months? What if the discoveries and breakthroughs at Lee-Jane are seeping out of my pores on the rivers of sweat that flow continuously in this wretched new existence?

On the fifth morning of this first week, I experience a flash of déjà vu. The sensation isn't triggered by a much prayed-for break in the weather, such as the onset of the kind of sudden cold front that induces nostalgia for an early autumn. No, it's yet another airless dog day, ninety degrees and sticky at sunrise. What sparks the sensation is that I find myself turning into a long driveway that leads to a golf course I've never seen before. I scan the horizon for a metal shed. Instead, there's a massive brick building up ahead, which looks like a grand hotel, a throwback to the Roaring Twenties. It's another first day of school—but this time I am not driving into just any old public golf course. This is the fabled Westchester Country Club in Harrison, New York, an American golfing landmark, home to two championship courses and 1,000 affluent members, and the site of the only annual PGA Tour stop in these parts. I pop the trunk and lift out the precious tools that have gone untouched for what seems like an age.

SEVE

Back when I was looking for a teacher up in the area, several friends had mentioned that the Westchester practice facility was one of the best in the county. Reason enough, I figured, to take lessons here. Most clubs in these suburbs are seriously pressed for practice space and have extremely small, irons-only, hitting areas. Westchester CC, in contrast, has an enormous driving range, with well-marked targets. On this day, despite the oppressive heat, some thirty or forty members are whacking shots off the well-tended turf, torrents of sweat streaming into their Dry Joys.

The teaching area is at one end of this range, adjacent to a small brick cottage, which houses the instructors' video equipment. Scattered around the teachers' stations are a variety of training devices, including a grotesquely oversized golf bag bristling with broomsticks outfitted with golf grips, ASSIST swing enhancers, and other such implements.

Video cameras on tripods stand at salute, ready to capture the swings of the golf-challenged, albeit economically privileged, men and women who are ready to shell out $100 an hour for lessons here.

I'm not sure how many PGA instructors are on the teaching faculty at Westchester but they certainly outnumber those at Willow Creek. The dean of the staff, and still active as a teacher, is the legendary Lighthorse Harry Cooper, winner of some twenty-seven pro tournaments in his time and a member of the National PGA Hall of Fame. Cooper was born in England, the son of a professional golfer who had actually apprenticed under Old Tom Morris. According to Cooper's testimony in Al Barlow's oral history of golf, *Gettin' to the Dance Floor*, it was Damon Runyon who tagged young Harry with the moniker "Lighthorse" after observing the extreme alacrity with which he attacked the game of golf. Runyon watched as Lighthorse won the L.A. Open in 1926, playing the final round in a speedy two-and-a-half hours, unimpeded by a gallery 5,000 strong. Years later, Lighthorse was asked whether there was anything he'd wished he learned earlier in his career. Lighthorse's answer was—needless to say—prompt. "I wish I hadn't been in such a hurry to play, had learned to wait, to be more patient. But that wasn't my nature."

On this particular morning, decades after his win in L.A., Lighthorse has thrown in the towel. He gives a leisurely lesson while seated on a chair at the end of the range. The thermometer has accomplished what Lighthorse's constitution never could. Lighthorse is moving no faster than an overheated snail on this insufferable day. Nor is the large golden retriever who has plopped himself down in the teaching area, lazily chewing the cover off a new Titleist balata.

"Seve, drop that ball!"

I turn to see an athletic-looking guy, brown as an acorn, walking over with an air of brusque authority. Tom Patri, who turns out to be Seve's owner, is stocky and not especially tall. His black hair is cut in a fashionable wedge, and he is wearing a pair of slick, wraparound shades that make him look as if he's about to conduct a golf clinic for the crew of the Starship Enterprise.

"Lee, right?" he asks as he strides up to me. This comes out more as a statement of fact than as a question. He presses my hand with a grip that makes sure to convey the considerable strength of his forearm.

"Let me tell you something," he says, wasting no time. "See these people?" He gestures to the long line of men and women who are bonking balls across the vast range.

"Very successful. Extremely smart. Huge egos. Which is probably what makes them so successful. Nice people, too. But they're your classic Type A's. They don't like to listen. They have no time for it. And when it comes to golf, let's put it this way: All they want to do is hit the crap out of the ball. That's all they care about. How far they can hit it. They come to me and say, 'Tom, I want to learn to play better golf.' I say, 'Fine. Every other lesson has got to be devoted to the short game.' This they don't like. All they want is to hit the crap out of the ball."

I feel Patri's intense stare through his dark windshield.

"Okay, hit a few balls for me. Let's see what we're dealing with."

Gamely, I take a six-iron and tee up a range ball. My only concern is to get the ball in the air. I manage to rattle off five or six shots—aloft, yes, but all sliced no more than 140 yards. Patri watches, then asks for a few more. He videotapes me from directly behind, after which he comes around and films me from the so-called caddie's angle. Having seen enough, he walks up to me and puts a hand on my shoulder.

"We really don't know each other, right?"

"Right," I answer.

"But you know me well enough to know that I'm not the kind of guy who beats around the bush?"

"Right." That I know. That I know in spades.

"So I'm going to give it to you straight," Patri says.

There is an interminable pause.

"Your swing really eats shit."

INTENSIVE CARE

Patri's assessment, while not necessarily unfair, hits me with the force of a runaway golf cart. *Welcome to New York.* If Brad Redding was the country pro, Patri is the city pro. During our six months together, about the most aggressively personal thing Redding ever said to me was, "Hey, how ya hittin' 'em?" His teaching was always supportive, upbeat.

Patri's method, in contrast, is your basic Big-Bertha-to-the-nuts approach.

Patri tells me that at this the first session it's more important to talk than to hit. He explains that he likes to "lay out the pieces of the puzzle so that the student knows where he's going." While this may be of sound educational value, it's a very clever way to get us both the hell out of the heat, and we repair to the air-conditioned consultation cottage.

He shows me to a chair and immediately commences what I presume is his standard stump speech.

"I have been teaching golf for a long time," he begins, "and I have had lots of experience watching people's progress or, to be perfectly honest with you, their lack of it. During these years, and even before that, golf should have gotten easier. The equipment we use is better. Turf science has vastly improved. I'd say that thirty years ago the greens at the U.S. Open were no better than you'd find today at most public courses. And we have far better teaching tools, especially video, at our disposal. But despite *all* of these changes," Patri says, "the average golfer scores no better, and maybe even worse, than before. For many years this was a great mystery to me."

I interject that if there has been a decline in average scoring, it's probably due to the vast influx of novices over the past decade. Patri gestures for me to zip it up and pay attention. I am beginning to develop a strong identification with Seve.

"Now," Patri continues, "if you're a teacher like me, and if you don't like taking people's money when you're not really helping them, which I don't, you can get really depressed in this job. And that's exactly what happened to me a few years ago. I became obsessed with why my students didn't make more progress, so much so that I took some time off and traveled around the country looking for answers. I met some physiologists who helped me see things much more clearly. We talked out there about how people have all kinds of different body types, varying degrees of muscle tone, and levels of strength and suppleness. We talked about how so many people sit in an office all week long and don't effectively stretch or work out. And I came to the conclusion that the reason amateur golfers *don't* get better is because they *can't* get better. They can't learn to execute the golf swing because their bodies just won't allow them to move in the proper way."

Patri then asks me a question I'm not prepared for.

"Who would you say are the three most important people when it comes to your getting better at golf? Start at the top. Who do you think is the *most* important person in the equation?"

"Uh, me, the student?" I venture, "because if I don't make the necessary commitment, take short-game lessons and all that, there's no way I'll ever get any better?"

"Right," Patri says. "Now, who's the second most important?"

"Well, that's got to be you, the teacher," I answer, at least in part to butter him up.

"*Wrong!*" Patri says. "I am only the *third* most important person. Who's the second most important?"

I haven't the foggiest idea what the hell Patri is talking about. Who else could it be?

Shivas Irons?

Godot?

Elijah the prophet?

I just shrug and hope that Patri doesn't respond as brutally as before.

But Patri holds back, then says calmly, "The second most important person is the physical therapist I'm going to send you to."

"Physical therapist?" I am utterly flabbergasted.

Patri nods. "His name is Skip Latella, and he's got an office just a few miles from here. You're going to see him at least three times a week, which is three times more often than you're going to see me. The deal is, unless you are willing to do what it takes to reprogram your body, I really don't think I'll be able to help you."

"I'm not sure I understand," I mumble.

Patri explains that he has sent about thirty of his students to Latella, "with very encouraging results." Under Latella's intensive program, his fat golfers have lost weight, his tight golfers have gained flexibility, and his weak golfers have gotten stronger.

"And what will he do for me?" I ask.

Patri pops in the videotape he'd taken out on the range. I am shocked by what I see. My position at address is horrifyingly bad, with many of the old problems back in force, plus a few new contortions thrown into the motley mix. My head is even more shlumped over than usual. I look like a golfer who, out on the golf course, has just gotten a call on a cell phone from his doctor. The doctor has told the golfer—this is just as the guy is getting ready to tee off—that all tests were positive and the guy has only six weeks to live. My arms are locked and held too close to my body. My left wrist has collapsed inward, contributing to an awkward and hideous grip.

On the plus side, my well-arched back and extended butt appear to be in pretty good shape. Brad Redding would have heartily approved.

Patri, however, vehemently disapproves. "Your back is far too tight and tense," he declares. Freezing the tape, he comments that he'll be curious to hear Latella's interpretation, but he would bet good money that the therapist will find that my lats, hamstrings, shoulder girdle, and hip flexors are all above-average tight. Thanks to this anatomical gridlock, my ability to execute the proper, fluid turns required of the traditional golf swing is virtually zero, he pronounces.

My mind races at this news, which, strangely enough, I take to be both good and bad.

The good news, I'm thinking, is that maybe I am not a complete and incurable motor moron after all. Maybe the root of my problem lies not so much in the Klutz Factor as with a simple lack of flexibility, a condition that can be corrected, at least in part, according to Patri, through the intensive conditioning program he has proposed.

The bad news, however, is that if there is any hope for my game, it will come only after I make a commitment to months of arduous and costly physical therapy.

Then, a light bulb goes on. *Whether he's aware of it or not,* I think, *Patri may have unlocked the secret of what we have always called "muscle memory."* Till now, the idea of muscle memory hasn't made a whole lot of sense, even though I've frequently invoked it to explain why I've had such a hard time improving my swing. But as Brad Redding declared months ago, muscles don't think, so muscles can't have memory. That much I buy. But why haven't I been able to retrain them by now? Patri's answer is that because of inherent physical constriction, our muscles can only move the way they move. It's just too damn hard or painful for them to bend otherwise. They don't *remember* to do it this way, it's just as far as they can go unless trained otherwise. So in spite of all the lessons we take, in spite of what we know to be right, our muscles must conform to the range of motion that's comfortable.

I am lying on the floor at a place called Therafit, which is a clean, modern facility located on the ground floor of a White Plains office park. The place is loaded with exercise equipment, therapy tables, and all sorts of thingamajigs to push and pull. These fun and games await me. The first step, however, is to be surveyed from head to toe by a member of Skip Latella's staff. He has already taken careful measurements of various body parts, including my not-quite-bulging biceps (10½"); less than powerful chest (37½"); hour-glass waist (33¼"); and stripling-like thighs (20¼"). He has used calipers to determine how much of this middle-aged cathedral is body fat (13.6%), and monitored my heart rate at rest (66 bps) and again during a semiserious aerobic workout (132 bps). Now he employs some sort of giant protractor to measure the degree to which various appendages can comfortably bend. He puts me through a series of tests to calculate how far muscles such as my teres minor and major, latissimus dorsi, gastrocnemius, not to mention my rotator cuffs, hip adductors, hamstrings, and gluteus maximus, can flex without risking serious rupture.

He totes up the results and gives me a preliminary assessment. My range of motion—especially in the shoulders and hips—is adjudged to be somewhat less than optimum, given the rotational requirements of the traditional golf swing. I function at more or less 85 percent of "normal" suppleness for a man of my age—presumably not good enough to break eighty.

A few days later, I return to Latella for our first therapy session. I am curious to know just how he means to turn this mass of congealing tissue into a well-oiled, par-shooting machine with friction-free, rubbery joints.

Latella is a likable guy, gentle and soft-spoken. He has been an exercise and sports physiologist for some fifteen years, servicing the tendons of professional and weekend jocks around New York. He does not claim to be much of a golfer, though he says he enjoys the game in what few opportunities he gets to play.

The main agenda ahead of us, Latella quietly explains, is to subject my old bones to numerous exercises specifically designed to increase flexibility in my upper and lower body. Over time, this regimen will enable my horizontal halves to gain some measure of independence from each other. It seems pretty clear from Patri's videotape that there's a lot of lateral sway through the hips when I try to swing. This is caused, I'm now told, by at least a double dose of muscular tightness. My hard-boiled hip flexors won't permit the free and flowing swivel of my lower half. Compounding this problem is the fact my shoulders and upper back are even more restricted. Unconsciously, then, I resort to a hip sway to facilitate rotation of my upper body—a compensation that is disastrous in terms of shot accuracy and distance.

The revelation of these arcane facts gives me reason to believe I am on the verge of a major discovery, a secret that has lay hidden deep within my shoulder cavities, long sealed by natural aging and/or inadequate conditioning. Once I pry loose the sticky doors that have kept me from moving, a giant leap forward will occur. Literally and figuratively, I am about to turn things around.

I race home and call the Big Shooter. Panting, I break the news about how we golfers have been misleading ourselves all these years. We don't execute the traditional golf swing properly because our bodies just *can't* do so. Muscle memory, in fact, might well be explained in terms of too-tight joints. I assume the Shooter is listening attentively to this breathless monologue. But all I hear on the other end of the phone is the rattle of ice cubes. I glance at my watch. It's cocktail hour.

"Sounds really interesting," he finally says. "And I'd love to hear more some time. But you'll have to excuse me—the guy with the Chinese food is downstairs."

Okay, so the Shooter isn't entirely buying in. There are still another couple of dozen golfing friends and colleagues whose ears (if not rotator cuffs) I can bend with this new theory. Everyone listens intently. When I describe some of the range of motion tests I took at Therafit, they, too, try them. Nearly everyone shows the telltale signs of limited range. And they all agree that there's probably something to all this. Most of them even say, "Maybe I should see this guy. What's involved?"

So I tell them. "You have to go three days a week, an hour a day, for about three months."

They look at me as if I've got golf balls growing out of my ears.

Jeez, they reply, if we had that kind of time we'd use it to play more golf. Even lousy golf is preferable to corporal punishment.

Resolutely, I book a string of early-morning appointments with Latella. When I show up for the first of these he casually mentions that he might want me to sign a confidentiality agreement his lawyer is drawing up. *A confidentiality agreement? To have my joints stretched?* Latella explains that he's in the process of seeking a patent for his training program, which would enable him to market it to golf schools and health clubs around the country. He says that an editor from *Golf Digest* is already interested in adding aspects of the program to the magazine's golf schools.

"But can your program work in such short doses?" I ask. "Don't you need three months, at least, to effect the necessary flexibility changes?"

"Ideally, yes," Latella says. "But the golf schools would be a great way to introduce the method. Golfers would then sign up afterwards for the full program."

As diplomatically as I can, I try to tell him that it's just not American to believe that very many time-pressed, results-*now* golf nuts are going to subject themselves to three months of hard physical labor.

I lie on my back on the training table. Latella stretches my shoulders and upper back. I close my eyes and feel the tension, the nearly five decades of it, giving way to his insistent pressure.

Now he leads me into a large mirrored room. I swing a golf shaft outfitted with fan blades, designed to create air resistance, which further loosens the muscles of the upper body.

Then the medicine balls roll out.

Latella places a giant, bright yellow ball between my knees. I feel stupid. He tells me to assume my golf address. I feel even more stupid. Now he has me take a few slow swings with a real golf club. By keeping my legs spread, the medicine ball prevents my hips from swaying. While I manage to get the club around and to the top pretty well, the task isn't easy with this obstruction between my kneecaps. Latella ratchets up the degree of difficulty by adding more balls to the procedure. What exactly does he think he's doing—rebuilding a golfer, or training a seal? He places another medicine ball (this one the size of a large grapefruit) between my forearms. Then he places a smaller one between my wrists. After checking that the giant ball between my legs is still properly braced, he tells me to try to make a golf swing. But I can't get my upper body to turn more than a foot or so. Is it any wonder that when playing golf I resort to swooping and swaying? How else can I get my body to do what the textbooks say is required to make the traditional swing?

The workout continues.

Latella has me grasp some heavy rubber tubing that's attached to a wall and then make big, slow, and difficult circles with each of my outstretched arms. Then he takes the *mother* of all medicine balls and plays a game of heavy-duty catch with me. I stand with my back to him and field his throws over one shoulder, then toss the cursed thing back to him over the other. This is intended to loosen my hips. Finally, he takes me back to the table from which we began. After a few minutes of more shoulder-kneading, I'm finally out of there.

I hightail it to the driving range before my unsuspecting muscles have a chance to snap back to their former state of rigidity. I am hell-bent on seeing what effect, if any, Latella's pushing and pulling has had on my swing.

The answer: Not much.

Well, it's early.

STRAPPED

Tom Patri is one slick dude. Today, at our second lesson, he is decked out in white Polo slacks with a sharp crease and a navy golf shirt, and is again enshrouded in those high-tech Milanese wraparounds. He is evidently pleased that I have taken his advice and started working out with Latella. Whatever the reason, he seems more patient and supportive. After watching me hit a few balls, and reiterating that I'll be a much better swinger when Latella is finished with me, he takes me back into his air-conditioned cottage to expand on his theories.

"It's pretty obvious," he says, "that when weekend golfers don't, or can't, use their lower bodies, they overuse their arms and shoulders. After all, *something* has to create club speed. So the hacker tries to throw the club as hard as he can, which makes him go over the top, which is exactly your problem and always has been."

He runs the tape of me over and over. He seems pleased at my ability to self-diagnose. I point out how much power I lose at the top of the backswing, when my left arm crumples up.

We talk some about Hogan's *Five Lessons*, about the drawing showing the rubber bands around the arms, and about how Hogan said *nothing* about how you can bring such tightly bound arms around the body only if you're blessed with a supple back and shoulders. We talk about how some other well-known pros also ignore the crucial element of flexibility. Gary Player, for example, himself a fitness fanatic, suggested that when golfers hit middle-age they should learn to "walk through" the end of their shots, as a way of compensating for their lack of suppleness.

"A terrible idea," Patri says. "Walking through a shot threatens your balance. Why not just work a little harder to stay loose?"

Patri insists that successful instruction must be based on the collaboration of one who knows how to fine-tune the mechanics of the swing (the golf pro) and one who can retrain the mechanics of the muscles (the therapist). "The bottom line," Patri says, "is that Skip will make it possible for me to teach you how to play. How your body fits together is his business. How it moves in the context of golf is mine. Each of us is useless to you without the other. For a golf pro to tell you that you can learn to play without changing your body is lying to you and to himself."

Picking up a golf club, Patri shows me in slow motion how his arms remain four to five inches apart throughout his takeaway, backswing, and finish, precisely what Hogan tried to get across with his famous rubber-band drawing. "But *you* can't possibly do this now," Patri says. "The tightness in your upper body causes your arms to fly apart. But Skip can close the gap between your arms. Once he does, I can help you find the right position for them."

Patri leaves his words hanging in the air for maximum effect.

"I also have a few tricks myself," he then says, leading me back outside. "I want to introduce you to a little something that, starting right now, will be your constant companion whenever you hold a golf club in your hand."

From an equipment bag Patri produces a strange-looking object. Made of hard plastic, it's a triangular, flangey sort of thing attached to a Velcro strap. The device, patented and copyrighted, is called the Swing Extender. As he attaches it to my right bicep in the manner of a blood pressure cuff, Patri explains that the Swing Extender is designed to give a feeling of what the right arm is supposed to do during the golf swing and also to prevent the left arm from folding prematurely. "Quite frankly," he adds, "for a while it's going to feel like shit."

Since feeling exactly like that is the prevailing theme for my golf training these days, I accept this new development with equanimity. I hit a few balls with the Swing Extender lashed to my arm. Patri is right: It feels like shit.

The Swing Extender is just one of countless dopey gadgets developed and sold to a waiting universe of impressionable hackers. Last summer, while hitting balls at a practice range, I watched as a zaftig middle-aged woman arrived on the tee and pulled an elaborate—how to describe this?—*harness* out of her golf bag. With her husband looking on, she spent some five minutes encasing her ample trunk in this device, which, as far as I could tell, was designed to keep her spine, shoulders, and arms all on some sort of acceptable swing plane.

Golf gewgaws have been sucking spare change out of golfers' pockets since the days of gutties and mashies. Decades ago they were as simple as stereo optical cards showing the swings of Vardon and J. H. Taylor, and practice balls tied to weighted wooden anchors.

Today, there is more of this junk than ever—and while the gadgets are more technically sophisticated, they are hardly of greater value. Not long ago I was flipping through the pages of *Golf Digest* when my eyes lit on a quarter-page ad in the mail-order section. It featured a picture of a sun visor with what looked to be a prosthetic device clipped onto it. The pitch ran as follows:

IT'S THE TRUTH . . . AS A 20+ HANDICAP PLAYER I NEEDED HELP!

Every golf tip I receive created a new problem. I realized if I couldn't learn to keep my head still and eyes on the ball, I was doomed. Unable to find what I need, I created the HeadFreezer™.

When I clipped it onto my cap and looked at the ball, an amazing thing happened. An optical illusion caused the ball to be framed by a double

image of my device. All I had to do was keep the ball in this "optical box"
during my swing and my game dramatically improved. It was that simple!
I'm now 74 and finished 1994 with one under par round.
AND THAT'S THE TRUTH!

—*Ray McCleery, Inventor*
$24.95

I would like to think that I am immune to such come-ons, but I am forever tempted. Just last week, while channel surfing, I ran into an infomercial hawking a dynamite little baby called a Turbo Swing. It, too, is a widget you strap onto your right arm, some kind of brace that lashes your wrist and forearm to the golf club and is guaranteed to prevent casting. Its developer is a teaching pro from L.A. who promotes himself throughout the program as "golf pro to the stars," the stars being directors of TV shows and commercials, plus a few heavyweight superstars on the order of Richard Roundtree and Frank Stallone. Anyway, the instructor was a smooth and well-groomed operator, and I came very close to whipping out my Visa card. Then I caught myself. Better to save the pennies, I concluded, so that I could piss them away on an Alien wedge.

OVERLOAD

Learning brings out the stupid in us all. Psychiatrist Thomas Szasz wrote that "Every act of learning requires the willingness to suffer an injury to one's self-esteem. That is why young children, before they are aware of their self-importance, learn so easily; and why older persons, especially if vain or important, cannot learn at all."

In *Mastery*, George Leonard echoes the point. He says that the attempt to acquire a new skill subjects the learner to a series of indignities. He might also have added that learning can also be exhausting, mentally and physically. Right now, my muscles are pooped, my neurocircuits overloaded, strained to the limit. There's just too damn much going on. I am trying to forge a relationship with a new teacher. I haul myself off to physical therapy thrice a week, to reprogram an ancient set of muscles. I hit practice ball after practice ball with a plastic doohickey wrapped tightly around my arm.

Sometimes you need to be able to tell when enough is enough. This may not be one of my strengths. Because now, on top of everything else, I am boarding a plane bound for New Orleans and a weekend of intensive study with a former Tour player.

His name is Larry Miller, and he claims to have divined the secret of golf instruction from an unlikely source: the little silver bird on his Visa card.

Even before this vision came to him, Miller believed that one could neither teach nor learn the golf swing as a sequence of moving parts. The parts moved too quickly, and the conscious mind is not remotely fast enough to coordinate them. But this has never stopped golf teachers from relying on this approach: *Point the club head to the sky waist-high on the backswing. Turn your shoulders ninety degrees, your hips forty-five. Bring the club back low and slow, about twelve inches, on the takeaway.*

Technology has further encouraged the tendency to teach fragments. Video isolates our movement in slow motion. Computers reveal the ideal angle of the swing plane. Stop-action photography graphically shows the correct position of every body part at each split second of the swing. *Move this here, move that there! Do it now!*

This is where the little bird on the credit card flew in.

One day, Miller was staring at this image, tilting it from side to side, making the little holographic bird's wings flap up and down.

Why not use holographic imagery to teach the golf swing? he asked himself. If one can't teach (or learn) the moving parts of the swing, why not focus on the swing's three *static* elements! Why not concentrate just on the position at address, the very top of the backswing, and the position at finish? If a hacker can get these three static positions more or less correct, Miller reasoned, everything in between would fall into place. The proper "interconnectedness" would occur without the golfer's having to worry about any further adjustment of his moving parts.

Miller developed this theory in a short book published in 1993, *Holographic Golf: Uniting Your Mind and Body to Improve Your Game.* It included the by-now standard New Age stuff about visualization and "implicate" reality versus "explicate" order, which I pretty much skimmed over. (Miller, it turns out, is a huge admirer of Michael Murphy and George Leonard.) Still, I was intrigued by Miller's disarming premise.

Sleuthing through PGA records, I discovered that Miller played a total of four rounds in three officially sanctioned Tour events from 1971 to 1980. He made one cut and missed two, coming away with a total of $946 in career Tour prize money. I tracked him down at his home in New Orleans and asked whether I might spend a couple of holographically intense days with him. He was entirely agreeable and quickly laid out an agenda for how we might best use our time together. We'd get together for some general golf gab on Friday night, then spend a long day on Saturday, which would include an extralong lesson and a round together.

We meet in the bar at the downtown hotel where I'm staying. I'm delighted that Larry has brought along Connie Bousquet, his fiancée. In our phone conversations, Larry cited Connie as an example of how holographic golf can enable a hacker to make astounding progress. Connie, he proudly told me, had been a twenty-six handicap just a few years ago. Now she is ladies champion at the New Orleans Country Club and regularly competes in women's national amateur events. Composed and reserved, Connie declines to be drawn into our afternoon imbibing, and instead orders a mineral water.

Miller, who's compact, teddy-bearish, speaks with a soft Louisiana lilt. He asks me to tell him about my life in golf. I am all too happy to oblige, providing a condensed version of the saga that has led me to this bar—which, incidentally, is fast filling up with Friday afternoon carousers who aren't remotely concerned about the shockingly early advent of cocktail hour. (Larry and I are now working on our second Scotch, while Connie has recognized the afternoon for what it is and has called for a beer.)

I conclude my account with an observation that brings a frown to Larry's face.

"To tell you the truth," I say, "I am starting to think that I have actually gotten a little *worse* since I began this endeavor. The more I have consciously tried to fix things, the more uptight I have become. I sometimes think that I am now overcorrecting flaws that may not have been such big deals in the first place. My grip is a good example. I think I tried so hard to fix it that I went beyond what subtle correction was called for and wound up with a major distortion of the wrist. And I tried to correct the shlump in my back by holding my spine in too rigid a position."

Larry listens with great compassion. He gestures toward Connie and says, "Well, you've got a soulmate right here. Yes, she managed to go from a twenty-six to a *two* in a very short period of time. But like a lot of people, she's an extremely visual learner, and if she gets too many images in her head, she gets really screwed up."

"It's a double whammy," I add. "You've got your old, wrong way of doing something, then suddenly, after some instruction, you've got the new, wrong way of doing it. This leaves us confused to the point of distraction. Or tears. Or worse."

"Tell me more about this physical therapy business," Larry says with a raised eyebrow.

I jump to my feet, oblivious to the dumbfounded stares of a room full of tipplers who are abruptly treated to a mimed demonstration of how three imaginary medicine balls of diminishing size, when strategically positioned in a man's crotch and forearms, can serve as an effective method for retooling one's golf anatomy.

It's clear that Larry doesn't buy into the Patri-Latella approach.

"People are too petrified of swaying," he says. "Besides, one of the most common problems a golfer has is the *failure* to shift to the right side on the backswing. The fact is, if you keep spikes of your right shoe in the ground when you take your backswing, you cannot sway. It's impossible. To properly shift and load to the right, you've got to have at least some lateral movement. Curtis Strange moves five inches to the right. And he's got a nice wide stance. Most people have too narrow a stance."

THE PRINCESS AND THE YAT

The bar is emptying, but Larry, Connie, and I are still going strong. Relaxed and more comfortable with one another, we have begun to dish some dirt about our respective personal lives. The lowdown on Larry and Connie, while not exactly tabloid stuff, is pretty juicy. Turns out they met when Larry was a teaching pro at the New Orleans Country Club and Connie was married to a member there, a golf-crazed physician (not to be redundant). Larry says he saw potential in Connie the first time he laid eyes on her, an observation that elicits a not so playful death stare from the woman with whom he now resides. Though she was at the time a mediocre golfer, she had always loved sports and was a good athlete, excelling at scuba diving, sailing, and water skiing, and was even a superb shot.

For her part, Connie considered Larry a "yat." A yat, she explains, is local parlance for a person of less than noble breeding. A commoner. A shlepper. The term "yat," she informs me, is derived from the expression "Where y'at?," which the hoi polloi down here use in lieu of a more socially acceptable greeting, such as "Hello, how do you do?"

What was especially yatlike about Larry was his golf slacks, Connie says—pastel-colored double knits that looked as if they could stand up and walk eighteen holes on their own.

Our bull session continues.

Larry believes that most weekend golfers are way too hard on themselves, and contends they don't understand that good golf can only result from an intensive process—you need to devote yourself to the game on an almost daily basis. It helps a lot if you begin when you're very young. That way, he says, you understand that the golf swing is a natural act and not something you have to "learn."

"But it isn't a natural act," I counter. "It's anything but. What's natural to me is to yank the club back with all my strength, then whack the ball from the outside in. Anything else requires massive reprogramming."

Larry can't fathom this.

"Golf *is* a natural act, but it has gotten muddled by too much emphasis on fragmentation," he says. "Hell, we know what constitutes a good golf swing. There's no mystery to it. But we need to find an accelerated, simplified way to communicate it to people, and I sincerely believe I am onto that with the holographic method."

"Which is to say that after tomorrow my problems will be over?" I ask Larry, whom I have come to regard as a man of generous spirit, a man who'd give you the bird off his credit card.

Larry just smiles.

"Why is there so much contradiction in golf teaching?" I ask, breaking the silence. "Some say it's a left-hand game, some say it's a right. Some say widen your stance, some say narrow it."

Larry answers promptly.

"The reason instructors contradict themselves week to week is that they're groping. They're trying everything they know. It isn't that they lack conviction, it's that they're dealing with a limited deck. They go to PGA seminars and are given a formula to work with—and therein lies the problem. They're given a method that can't possibly work for everyone. Every tip you read in a golf magazine is correct—for someone. But maybe not for you. In the end, most teaching degenerates into Band-Aid teaching. If I'm with you on the range and you hit six shots in a row off to the right, you'll be frustrated. As a teacher, I'll be drawn into your frustration and I'll try to do whatever I can to get you to stop hitting to the right. I'll give you a Band-Aid to cure the problem. Then I'll give you another Band-Aid for something else. Before you know it you're getting farther and farther away from a basic, balanced swing.

"Golf instruction went wrong beginning in the fifties, when the Age of Analysis began," Larry concludes. "Ben Hogan and his book had a lot to do with it. Hogan was admired for his robotlike, mechanically perfect approach, which the rest of us tried to emulate. And while there are a few really fine things in his book, I also have some big problems with it. One is that famous drawing showing the arms with the insides of the elbows facing upward, held together by the giant rubber bands. Many people look at that, try to copy it, and make themselves extremely tense. Another big problem is the relatively weak left-hand position that Hogan recommended. A weak left hand is fine if you play golf a lot and if you're strong. But for a person who plays once or twice a week and may not be particularly strong, you just can't hit the ball with a weak left-hand grip. Believe me, you just can't."

NAVEL MANEUVERS

Early the next morning, Larry and Connie swing by in their sporty little BMW, and we zoom off to Oak Harbor, a nearby public course. We scoot to the far end of the practice range, where Larry conducts his lesson. The main topic is Static Position Number One: the setup. Larry shows me how I should "step into" my address position with a relaxed pace, take a glance at the target, then fire away. Like many hackers, he says, I stand over the ball for too many seconds, adding tension to my arms. Most of us are not even aware of this delay, he says, because we are so fixated on the problems inherent in the shot we're about to make. He suggests instead that we take our "rhythm right into the swing." He demonstrates this himself by stepping up to a ball, then shifting his weight lightly from foot to foot. This is what Corey Pavin and so many other Tour players do when settling in over a shot. "What Pavin's up to," Miller explains, "is finding his *balance*. He's also finding his *rhythm*. And he's making some kind of *action* before his mind has a chance to turn to negative thoughts."

"When is the best time to grip the club?" I ask him.

He tells me to grip it before putting it down on the ground: Pick out your target by standing directly behind it, *then* put your hands on the club in a relaxed way. Walk up to the ball from an open position— which will help you to avoid aiming to the right, which is what right-handed golfers almost always do. Throughout all this, he says, leave your hands softly on the club, just where they were when you started. If you start messing with your hands you'll realign the club face and you'll probably also realign your body to match it.

I ask him about my shoulder turn, which to Patri was hopelessly inadequate, thanks to constricted muscles.

"Frankly, I think you're fine in that department," Larry says.

He points out that when we think about making a full turn, we invariably fail to. He says that when we tell ourselves to relax our shoulders, we wind up tensing them. He offers an interesting tip: Try to relax the center of the back, the place between the shoulders. This in turn will loosen the shoulders.

The most important thing of all, Larry believes, is to learn to stay "centered." Staying centered is Larry's first law of nature, a concept he says he never truly appreciated until he read George Leonard. Staying centered is crucial to the martial arts and no less so to the golf swing. Staying centered is how we maintain proper balance.

"All bad shots," Larry pronounces, "are caused by either the hands outracing the body, or the body outracing the hands. That's why it's essential that your center move along with the club head. If it doesn't, something is going to have to speed up or slow down to compensate for it."

The seat of centeredness (the source of *ki*, in George Leonard's lexicon) is the navel, or pipick, as my grandmother called it. Larry suggests that it's a good idea to keep the mind focused on your navel from the address position through the entire swing. This creates a hub around which the shoulders and arms can smoothly radiate.

Our collective belly buttons firmly fixed in our consciousness, Larry, Connie, and I take to the course. It is immediately obvious that Connie has a beautiful, swan-like swing with a huge, graceful arc. She is a joy to watch. The only apparent flaw in her game is her putting, which today is inconsistent.

Larry is truly impressive. This is the first time I have played with anyone of Tour caliber, and I marvel at his ability to control his shots—hitting draws or fades at will, making clean, crisp contact with every club in his bag. His drives routinely reach 270 yards, or more. His approach shots land softly on the sun-baked greens, as if tethered to invisible parachutes. But the coolest thing of all is Larry's advanced skill with a one-iron, or "knife" as he calls it—using it to direct well-aimed shots of over 220 yards, traversing all intervening hazards.

Throughout the day Larry proves to be a tireless teacher, walking with me to most of my shots, many of which are dreadful. I play the front nine just okay—we don't keep score, but I shoot something close to forty-eight or forty-nine. As we make the turn, though, enormous black clouds form to the east and quickly bear in on us. A ferocious thunderstorm erupts, forcing the three of us to seek refuge in the cart shed. Twenty minutes later, the rain stops, leaving the air very warm and unbearably sticky. I have lost all communication with my pipick.

"It's going to take time," Larry reassures me.

The first breath of autumn is on my neck. Shorter days, cooler nights. The summer of unrelenting steam, the season of the incurable slice, is finally giving up the ghost. I don't believe I am much closer to breaking eighty than I was in the heady days of spring. For the moment, breaking ninety will do just fine.

This morning I have back-to-back appointments with Latella and Patri. Latella is as encouraging as ever. Patri, too, is all sunshine and light, a man on happy pills. He tells me Skip's therapy is working great. My shoulder rotation has improved. My lower half, though, requires further attention. The evidence, he says, is that my left foot fails to stay in place when I finish a swing. It is yanked a bit to the left because of the tightness in my flexors. Patri suggests I keep this foot slightly splayed at setup, a position that will help keep me better balanced through the downswing and finish.

Even though I informed Patri that I was going off for a weekend tryst with Larry Miller, I feel a little sheepish reporting back to him on what happened down there. But he asks about it, so I tell him. I describe how Larry urged me to stay on the inside of my feet. Patri nods. But when I convey Larry's stated reservations about Skip's medicine ball therapy, he growls. "I never said that you should *play* with your legs held apart—just that the medicine ball was useful as a stretching device."

Today's session with Patri lasts an hour. During this time I hit only about fifteen balls, spending most of the time shooting the breeze about golf instruction. Patri says he prefers to be thought of as a coach, not a teacher. Coaching is the new paradigm, another example of how the culture of golf instruction follows the culture at large. Coaching is big these days, whether it be in the classroom or in corporate America, where "human resource" experts are rewarded for their "ability to mentor" and "guide the development" of their various charges, to "effect productive teamwork" and "foster collaboration." Nobody wants to teach, they all want to coach, which, according to the American Management Association, means establishing "an ongoing, committed partnership with a player/performer and . . . [empowering] that person [to] exceed prior levels of play/performance." Today, I watch as my coach picks out a new hat from an apparel distributor, and observe as he eats a sandwich, then fools around some with a playful Seve. I hand over a C-note and go home. I ask myself: Is this really worth it?

But a week later I'm back, hungry for more. We have the most valuable lesson to date. Patri gets me to understand how I have consistently misplayed the position of the ball: that it sits way too far back in my stance, no matter which club I have in my hands. In six months of lessons, no one has paid any real attention to this. Patri says that I should play all wedges with the ball at my sternum. As the irons get longer, the ball should move progressively from the sternum to the left breast. With woods, the ball should sit at my left armpit.

Patri says that the optics of golf are profoundly misleading for most weekend players. Sight lines are illusory—which explains why so many hackers aim too far right of their target, and why they screw up their ball position. Patri believes that a lot of this has to do with the fact that golf is about the only game we play, the only thing we *do*, standing still and erect with the object of our attention sitting at ground level. In other words, most of us don't know our sternums from our armpits.

Desperation

Have you ever felt as you talked to someone
that everything was turning unreal?
—**Shivas Irons in** *Golf in the Kingdom,* **by Michael Murphy, 1972**

AMERICA'S FUNNIEST VIDEOS

I am caught in a downdraft of discipline, losing the will to continue at Therafit, about to fall off the ergometer. With winter just around the corner, I am looking to learn in all the wrong places. Golf info-mercials command my attention more than ever. I read the golf magazines with mounting desperation. Somewhere out there is an idea, an image, a man, a woman, a book, a videotape, a putter, a wedge, a swing thought, a mantra, a pair of corrective lenses, a vitamin, a muscle relaxant, a psychiatrist, a surgeon, a rabbi, a shaman, maybe even another golf pro who can help me discover the golf swing I know is in me.

Happily, new opportunities are at hand. Some months back, I'd signed up for a weekend at the Jim McLean Golf School, which is based at Miami's Doral Hotel—yes, home of the famous Blue Monster. It might be helpful, I thought, to seek a lesson or two from McLean, one of the country's most respected and best-known teachers. Would he see something that Redding and Patri and Miller happened to miss? Could he find the switch?

I realize now I was a little naive to think that a garden-variety hacker could just give McLean a jingle and reserve a weekend with him. You can scarcely do that with Tom Patri; even Brad Redding is booked weeks in advance. Jim McLean? Forget it. Most of the time, this mild-mannered, celebrated instructor is off tending to the grips and egos of big-time moguls such as Henry Kravis, or installing a signature learning center at this or that posh resort, or endorsing Titleist golf balls. I certainly can't blame him for this—who wouldn't rather be rich and famous than sweat it out on a hot afternoon, trying to teach a common golf yat how to swing from the inside out?

In a brief phone call back in the spring, McLean considerately warned me that he probably wouldn't be around the weekend I'd be coming down to the McLean Golf School—and it turns out he isn't. However, I was lucky to be able to schedule some face time with one of his key lieutenants, Mike Lopuszynski, McLean's Director of Instruction. But this doesn't come to pass, either. Yesterday, when I arrived, Lopuszynski apparently was not feeling well, and today he seems to be otherwise and energetically engaged with an affluent-looking student whose golf bag appears to be hand-tooled of the finest Italian leather. But the McLean people are kind enough to work me into a small group of neophyte hackers, including a local woman in her sixties and three young studs who'd come down together from New York. This fivesome will spend the next couple of days in the charge of a tall (what else?), lanky (what else?), blond (what else?), and blue-eyed (what else?) staff teacher by the name of John Mills. A one-time first-team All-American, Mills attended the University of Houston with McLean, Bruce Lietzke, and Bill Rogers, as impressive a college four-some as ever studied a fairway.

Mills is hardworking and intense, but the greatest thing about him is his voice. Close your eyes and listen carefully, and you'll think you are listening to Vin Scully. Then in the next instant you'll think you are listening to Jack Benny. I never realized how much Vin Scully sounded like Jack Benny until I heard John Mills open his mouth.

Early on this first morning of school I spend a few minutes chatting privately with Mills. I describe for him the Therafit program and Patri's conviction about the importance of flexibility. Mills doesn't say much, nor does he have to. His expression says it all. The teacher reacts as if he has just swallowed a mouthful of bacterial silt from the depths of a water hazard. The next day, when we are better acquainted, Mills is rather more explicit about his opinion of the proposition that the average person needs to spend months loosening his muscles before he can hope to play decent golf.

"If you want my sincere opinion," Mills says with that great voice, "I think it's a bunch of bullshit." He adds that when he was much younger he got to spend a little time with Jimmy Demaret. It was Demaret's custom to offer to take on all comers while playing on one leg. This was evidence enough, Mills suggests, that the game of golf is eminently playable not only with stiff and recalcitrant joints, but even without the usual complement of them.

In his opening statement to our motley gang of five, Mills outlines the philosophy of the McLean center. His talk provides an interesting contrast to how Tom Patri opened his own presentation to me earlier in the summer. The most important ingredients in successful instruction, Patri had said, were (in order of importance) the student; his physical therapist; and, finally, his coach. Here at Doral, Mills ranks the facility itself, with its well-groomed practice areas and elaborate technology, and then the school's teachers, as the cornerstones of the instruction. He never once mentions a student's will to work, let alone the elasticity of one's muscles. I suppose such is the sensibility of the corporate golf school. We talk, you listen.

Another problem I have here is the degree to which the dog of instruction is wagged by the tail of its technology. Like most widely advertised schools, the McLean center boasts an impressive, multi-bay training studio (four regular stations plus a VIP section, where videotapes labeled "Stallone" and "James Woods" can be observed on the shelves). This building is wired to the max with the latest video and computer equipment, with cameras mounted strategically on the floor, walls, and ceiling. If you've gone to the expense to acquire this stuff, it's for sure you're going to flaunt it.

The first half-day here is devoted to videotaping, then analyzing in detail, five distinct, ugly-as-sin golf swings. This is done, presumably, so that we might all have a record—as if we needed or wanted one—of how bad we were on arrival, evidence that will underscore the great improvement we'll have made by Day Two, by which time we will have been molded into body doubles for Tom Kite. Watching these "before" videos can get confusing and complicated. It's numbing enough for a hacker to study the major and minor flaws embedded in his own swing. But here, before getting any basic instruction whatsoever, all five of us are asked to sit in a room (posted on the walls are numerous aphorisms, such as THE HOUSE OF SUCCESS IS BUILT BRICK BY BRICK, and THERE IS NO SUDDEN LEAP TO GREATNESS) where we suffer through the terminal overload of watching computerized, telestrated, slow-motioned, stop-actioned, split-screened dissections of the putrid swings of everybody else in class. Serving as the audience for these videos is as close to a near-death experience as golf gets. I'd rather stare at Leroy Nieman prints than participate again in the digitized deconstruction of swings of golfers who are even worse than I am.

On day two at the school, things start to look up, as Mills devotes a couple of extremely helpful hours to the basics of chipping and pitching. Not to carp, but common sense would suggest that since the mechanics of chipping and pitching are fundamental to learning a good *full* golf swing, these techniques ought to have been broached the day before. That they weren't, I reckon, is because they wouldn't have allowed the school to show off its razzle-dazzle equipment.

I come away with some serious doubts about the value of brand-name golf camps. Why spend thousands of dollars for a weekend of group instruction when the same small fortune can buy you a new set of clubs you don't deserve (and that won't make any difference to your game), plus a plentiful number of private lessons that likewise will have no discernible lasting effect on how you play?

A TALE OF TWO SAVIORS

I discontinue my sessions at Therafit after two and a half months of hard stretching. I was just getting crabbier and crabbier making the trek to Latella's place, and not at all convinced it was worth the trouble.

Are my muscles any looser?

Yes.

Is my golf game any better?

Can't say that it is.

All I know is that it's getting dark earlier and earlier.

And that Tom Patri is ready to fly south for the winter, where he plans to run a golf school in Florida. And that within a month or so golf will fold its tent here in the Northeast. I am running out of options, so I map out a two-pronged strategy.

Plan A is to seek help wherever I can find it, whatever it costs.

Plan B is to pray for the Messiah.

And wouldn't you know? Not one but *two* savior candidates drop from the heavens.

The first is an old-timer named Joe Mazziotti.

I initially spot him on a gorgeous, late fall afternoon while I'm hitting balls at the Westchester Golf Range, a public driving range not to confused with the Westchester Country Club. Even from a considerable distance—he is at the end of the range, giving a lesson to a woman—I can see that his posture is splendid, his movements graceful, almost courtly. Even at an advanced age, he has no trouble bending over to tee up ball after ball for his student to hit. But what attracts me most is that he is giving this golf lesson dressed in a starched, long-sleeved khaki shirt and red, hand-tied bow tie. Forget all the sharpies in their Oakley shades and Bobby Jones shirts and Ralph Lauren saddle shoes. This old chap is the real deal.

When his lesson is over I walk up and introduce myself, which is when I learn that his name is Joe Mazziotti, that he is in his *eighties*, and that three years ago he had a triple bypass from which he has, knock wood, fully recovered. He also tells me right off that he played professionally back in the twenties and has taught golf in the Westchester area ever since—first at some private clubs and then, for something like the last thirty-six *years*, at this very driving range.

"So you must know the secret of the golf swing," I say to him. "What would it take for you to teach it to me?"

Joe replies cryptically.

"You've heard of Tom Weiskopf?" he asks. "Well, Weiskopf had just won a tournament somewhere, and when he was asked how come he did so well, he said it was because he could feel the ribs on the club head. Do you have any idea of what he meant by that?"

"Well," I answer, "I guess he probably meant that he was in touch with the club head, even down to its grooves—that his swing wasn't overwhelmed by his large muscles, or something like that."

"Exactly," Joe replies. "Meet me at nine o'clock Sunday morning, right here." A tingle of optimism reverberates through me.

At the appointed hour I find Joe waiting on the practice tee, wearing another hand-tied bow tie. He stands directly behind me and watches as I hit a few shots.

"No wonder you're having trouble," he declares in his raspy way. "Your alignment is all wrong. That's your whole problem."

"That's it?"

"That's it."

"You mean I'm not coming over the top?"

"Nah, you're fine with that," he says.

"You mean my grip is okay?"

"Your grip is fine," he says.

"You mean my muscles don't seem overly restricted, or tight?"

Joe waves off that possibility as if swatting a mosquito.

"Like most people," he says, "you make one big mistake, and it kills you. Murders you. You line up way too right of the target. Then you try make up for it with your hands at the last minute. You can't hit a golf ball like that, it's crazy!"

Joe tells me to pick out a spot no more than five inches ahead of the ball, in line with a distant target. He tells me to square the club face to this five-inch line, then set my feet square to the club head. Remarkably, it feels as if I am now aiming way, *way* left of the target. But I'm not—it just feels that way, owing to the fact that I have been setting up to the right for about as long as Joe has been teaching at this driving range, that is, since the late Jurassic Age.

"Just line up properly and you'll be fine."

Joe makes this point over and over again. While his diagnosis is spot-on, it frankly gets a bit wearying to hear this single piece of advice for a full ninety minutes. I haven't had so much fun since the night I saw Andy Warhol's *Sleep*, which, however benumbing, was an entertainment bargain compared to this golf lesson. When I ask Joe what I owe him, he tells me that since we had the equivalent of three half-hour lessons, each at forty bucks a pop, the tab comes to $120. So I pay him, thinking that I could have realigned both family cars for the price of this lesson.

Joe walks me to the parking lot and leads me over to his flashy red Cadillac convertible. He reaches in and pulls out a framed clipping of an old newspaper story. It is an account of a day many years ago when Joe Mazziotti fired an ace in a match against the great Willie Turnesa. We chat for a while about what it was like in the good old days.

Mazziotti's a hoot, but he's no messiah.

One savior down, one to go.

DEUS EX APTAKER

It is a month later, and I fly to Florida for a business convention at the Boca Raton Resort. When I arrive my room isn't ready, so I hustle out to the course. The starter has put me into a foursome that includes a couple of nice senior ladies and one very tall, outgoing, middle-aged chap who introduces himself as Joel Aptaker. As we wait to tee off, Joel asks me whether I am down here on business. I tell him I am.

"And what do you do?" I inquire.

"Oh, I'm a golf pro," he says casually. Whereupon this tall stranger produces from his rear pocket the longest tee I have ever seen in my life—a towering five and a half inches high—and gently places a new Titleist balata on top of it. He assumes a fairly closed stance and just before swinging into action, he takes a small step back with his right foot, a dance step really. (He later reveals that he does this because he has a bum right knee and the step reduces the pressure on it.) He then makes a fantastic pivot and unleashes what might be the most awesome shot I have ever seen, a majestic and slightly fading 280-yard drive down the middle of the fairway.

"Come on, let's have some fun," Joel says with a big, toothy grin. "Maybe I can even help you a little bit."

Oh, Golf Lord, what have I done to deserve this—an eighteen-hole playing lesson with a sweet and generous pro, who hits the ball a ton, who's genial and kind, who loves to teach, and who's patient as a saint?

As we play through the first couple of holes, it is apparent that there isn't anything especially new or trendy about Joel's philosophy of instruction. He points out how one of the women we're playing with takes a picture-perfect practice swing, only to smother the ball when she actually goes to hit it, barely moving her arms and shoulders after impact. Joel is a big believer in the wheel hub-and-spokes model of the golf swing. If you picture the club head as the rim of a wheel, the arms and the club are the spokes, and our torso—from midthigh to midtrunk—is the hub. The goal, Joel says, is to assemble a smoothly turning system out of these parts, with the club head or wheel moving at an accelerated rate through impact.

Between strokes, I inquire into Joel's history. He tells me he grew up in L.A., went to the University of Florida, then spent a decade working at a bank. A few years ago he quit, went to golf pro school, and has been in the business ever since. Divorced, he travels light, with his golf clubs in the trunk and in the company of a faithful dog. He says he's down here for the winter, making ends meet by giving lessons and working at a golf shop. What he'd most like to do is land a head professional's job in New England and spend his winters in Florida, teaching. If I had a club I'd hire him in a minute. Joel is great company, articulate, a mensch.

After a couple of holes, I ask Joel about why he uses his ridiculously tall tee.

He says there are two reasons for it, one of them "off the record," he says impishly. The tall tee, he confides, is a real attention-grabber, a conversation piece, a potential trademark, something that will get him noticed when and if he makes the Senior Tour, for which he'll be eligible in a couple of years. The on-the-record reason has to do with laws of motion. (Everybody's a professor. Everybody's got a theory.) Joel says that teeing the ball extremely high allows him to draw maximum benefit from the centrifugal force of his particular swing plane. He tries to explain exactly what he means by this, but by now I've gotten myself mired in a bunker and can pay no further attention to his earnest explication.

On the last four holes of the front nine, I enter that kind of blissful zone that happens now and then, but not nearly often enough. Perhaps a passing asteroid has set me off, who knows? I string together a bunch of pars and bogies, clipping the ball cleanly on virtually every shot. This run of good fortune, I think, may well be due to Joel's constant encouragement to swing through the ball. But it may also be because it's immensely pleasurable to be out on this beautiful day, playing in the company of one who is so much better than I that I feel no pressure to compete, only the desire to please. I want to make good on this stranger's generous faith in my potential.

Then everything goes straight to hell.

I suffer through a dismal back nine, comparable in kind and misery to the disastrous back nine I displayed for Larry and Connie in New Orleans. Joel remains ebullient through my misfortune, treating each of my worsening flubs as a learning opportunity. When I top yet another fairway wood he bounds over and tells me to take the same club but this time address a leaf on the ground, pretending it is the ball. He asks me what I am looking at when I look at the leaf. I tell him I'm looking at the back end of it, where one would be expected to strike it. He then tells me to drop a ball. He asks me what I am looking at now. I tell him I am looking at the front and top of the ball. "Which is exactly why you topped it," he says. "Always imagine that you're hitting a leaf that is lying underneath the ball and you will never top a shot again."

Joel's swing is something else. As he hits down through the shot, his ability to accelerate his arms, then unlock his wrists, is wondrous. Before this explosive moment of release, his swing is measured, even slow. Throughout most of it his forearms remain remarkably close together, twin appendages traveling through space with a common purpose—to generate maximum club speed at precisely the right moment. In contrast, my forearms seem to *repel* each other, as if they can't stand being on the same torso at the same time. One is always trying to fly away from the other.

Why? Why? Why?

Patri says it's because my muscles are too tight.

Miller says it's because my pipick is out of whack.

Joel says it's because I don't sufficiently shift my weight.

Next!

Thankfully, there is yet another slender sliver of hope on the horizon. I am looking at one more chance before winter, one more shot before the year shanks into the deep woods of memory.

THE ART OF THE PUTTS

It's early December, and a sudden cold spell has hit us, the first minor assault in what reckons to be a winter to remember. No matter. I am once again snugly ensconced at the Mizner-designed pink palazzo of the Boca Raton Resort, this time to stroke my way through the Dave Pelz Short Game School. Here is an opportunity to spend three full days devoted to what everyone agrees is the most crucial part of the game of golf, as least as far as scoring (and mental health) is concerned. The DPSGS is the MIT of golf academies, perpetually sold out, shrouded in the mystique of the former space engineer who has devoted decades to relentless research into the physics of . . . the putt.

School begins early on a Friday morning, when sixteen of us (nearly everybody here looks like a Lexus owner—rich, intelligent, middle-aged) gather for coffee and bagels chez Pelz, a clapboard clubhouse just a short cart-ride down from the hotel. Everything about this place is precise and well planned: an efficiently designed micro-environment of putting greens; pitching range with movable targets, which are today set thirty yards out; and meandering bunkers for sand practice. The provost for the weekend is a gravelly voiced gent by the name of Dick Hall, a longtime Pelz crony who greets us all and turns the program over to an appealing blonde with powerful legs and a light Texas accent. Her name is Jackie Bertram, who introduces the other teachers (there's a generous one-to-four ratio here), and tantalizes the assembled group with stories of how the Pelz curriculum has worked magic on the likes of Peter Jacobsen, Steve Elkington, Lee Janzen, and Hal Sutton. All of them, Jackie effuses, went out and won the very next tournament they played after receiving the exact same Pelzification we're about to undergo. Unlike the flim-flam you often hear from golf teachers, Jackie's spiel is credible, thanks to the fact that she is evidently bright, well-spoken, vibrant, pleasant, reassuring, supportive, and immensely likable. Stockard Channing with a lights-out golf swing..

Jackie stresses that everything we're about to hear this weekend will be based on *fact*, not opinion, all of it derived from Big Dave's years of collecting data relating to the physical laws of the putting green. Jackie closes her remarks by asking the class members to introduce themselves. Among us are a couple of foreign golf teachers, a good-looking Argentine and a young German; husband-and-wife CPAs from Virginia; a near-scratch orthopedic surgeon from Baton Rouge; a forty-something plastic surgeon from Boston, who complains about the new world order of managed care and how he'd like to chuck it all so that he can just play golf; a tall gentleman named Vlasic who, yes, turns out to be the pickle king; an attractive woman named Eisenberg, who everyone assumes is my wife; and a teenager from South Carolina, Kyle Thompson, who is regarded as one of the best junior players in the country. Kyle attends the Pelz school through the grace of friends and family who kicked in the few thousand bucks so that he might soak up the most advanced short-game education available.

The first morning at DPSGS consists of personal evaluations—no instruction, no analysis—which makes much more sense than the opening-morning video festival at Doral. These assessments give the Pelzians the chance to observe us, to talk to one another about what each of us might need, to collaborate on a teaching strategy. What this amounts to is personalized instruction in the context of group teaching, something the Pelzians have figured out how to deliver in a logical and seamless way.

In one of the tests, Jackie applies pressure-sensitive tape to the faces of our putters, then instructs us to make a few rounds through a four-hole putting course. The strokes we make leave blotches on the tape that indicate where in relation to the putter's sweet spot we tend to make contact. You don't need a doctorate degree in puttology to know that if you don't hit the sweet spot, you won't make many putts, for the obvious reason that an off-center hit causes the putter blade to rotate, which in turn throws off the direction of the putt. My particular blotch, while not awful, isn't ideal. The mark left on my blade is maybe 25 percent larger than the quarter-inch circle Jackie says is an optimum sweet-spot blotch. My blotch is also somewhat off-center, too much toward the heel of the club face.

The group's next stop is a shallow sand trap. Here, I totally suck wind, hitting a series of alternating fliers and chili-dips. Mercifully, we go back inside for more putting tests, this time with the help of a little electronic gadget Dick Hall has set up. It's some sort of optical device that measures precisely how we each tend to misalign our putter blade in relation to a target. Typically, Dick explains, every hacker misaligns in a characteristic pattern, either too much to the left or to the right. Knowing this, he explains, we might eventually break the chain of errors that leads to our consistently inconsistent play on the greens.

These indoor sessions, while concise and well ordered, also serve as extended commercials for the Pelzian philosophy in general, and the company's ever-expanding catalogue of putting aids in particular. We are briefed on Pelz's credentials, too, which call to mind Ben Hogan's wonderful comment that "golf seems to bring out the scientist in a person." Pelz, we hear, is a former collegiate golfer who often competed against, but never beat, baby bear Jack Nicklaus; a former NASA hand who conducted research on the upper atmosphere; a middle-aged career-changer who launched himself into self-promotional orbit, becoming the nation's indisputable Putter-in-Chief; and golf's answer to Gyro Gearloose. Pelz's inventions are all on display at these sessions, most of them available for purchase:

- *The Pathfinder*: A clear-plastic viewing device that enables your friendly neighborhood putting consultant to judge the deviations between stroke path and ball line.
- *The TruRoller*: An eight-foot release ramp used to determine the perfect path for any given putt.
- *The Stroke Pattern Analyzer*: A device used to measure the effect of putting stroke mechanics on how putts roll.
- *The Putting Track*: A pair of parallel aluminum rails between which one makes repeated strokes with one's putter, the point being not to graze the rails. A great putter can successfully do this within a tolerance of one-eighth of an inch on either side.
- *The Teacher Alignment Computer*: The electronic optical device previously noted. It indicates in which direction the putter's face is looking.
- *The Teacher Putter*: A normal putter except for the two prongs sticking out of the face, between which is the sweet spot. These prongs have different widths depending on the skill level of the player; they may also be removed and inserted in the rear of the head when a player is out on the course.

- *Perfy*: The adjustable aluminum putting robot designed to replicate the configuration of a golfer's ankles, knees, hips, spine, and shoulders.
- *The Pelz 3-Ball Putter*: A putter made out of three regular-size golf balls affixed in a row. These help the golfer align a fourth and *real* ball, that which he intends to roll smartly and directly into the cup.

While Pelz has done much to demystify putting, he has also done more than any other person in history to remystify it. Before coming down to Florida, I read Pelz's *Putt Like the Pros* (say it fast, author and title, three times) until I landed on page 95. There I nearly fainted over a half-page chart entitled the "Putting Evaluation Matrix." This chart lists the factors that can potentially affect a putting stroke. These include the big three, or "primary," factors:

- Path of putter
- Angle of face
- Impact Point

They are joined by a long list of "secondary factors":

- Hand position
- Shoulder line
- Forearm position
- Putter alignment
- Ball position vs. apex of the stroke
- Ball position vs. the eyes
- Head motion
- Body motion
- Wrist position and motion
- Triangle motion
- Left arm swing vs. hit
- Grip position

- Grip pressure
- Stroke tempo
- Pre-shot routine
- Attitude
- Practice habits

All in all, a comprehensive accounting, I'd say. But wait, something's missing. Pelz may have actually forgotten something! He omits one variable that I have always thought to be one of the most important (and overlooked) factors of all: *eyesight.*

Dave, how to account for this blind spot?

PUTTING THINGS INTO PERSPECTIVE

The focal point of Pelz's obsession is a hole in the ground that resides inside a twelve-foot circle, a region that has come to be famously dubbed "the lumpy doughnut." This is the area around the cup where thousands of humanoid hoofs, imparting hundreds of thousands of spike marks, reduce a green into something resembling Manuel Noriega's jowls. It's a surface so bumpy that even a putt that has been stroked smoothly and true finds itself hard-pressed to reach its intended target.

Thanks to years of research and fiddling around with Perfy and the TruRoller ramp, Dave Pelz has come to a number of definite, *scientific* conclusions about the mechanics of this, the simplest-looking of all golf strokes. The best known of these conclusions, as the faculty at DPSGS points out time and again, is that most golfers—hackers *and* Tour pros—consistently misread their putts by underestimating the amount of break to be played. Then, on top of this, we misdirect our putts, which only compounds the initial misread. Then, on top of all that, we underestimate the subtle vagaries of the lumpy doughnut. The result is that we leave our putts short and on the low side of the cavity with sickening predictability. This is why one of Pelz's cardinal precepts is that we make sure to stroke our putts as if we wanted them to stop a full seventeen inches—not sixteen, not eighteen—past the cup. This principle applies to putts of every length, for such a roll will give them every opportunity to drop (or "drain," as the Big Shooter has recently taken to saying). While the seventeen-inch element is a relatively recent addition to the laws of golfing physics, the underlying rationale is hardly new. You hear it expressed all the time on greens from Orlando to Adelaide, uttered with increasingly escalating fervor and conviction as a round of golf wears on: "Never up, never in." "You gotta hit it, Alice," "*Hit* it, you useless piece of human flotsam!"

After lunch the first day, I have a pleasant chat with Jackie, who reveals that she has been a golfer since she was a little girl, being the daughter of an Austin, Texas, teaching pro named Jack Bertram. Her own promising career was cut short by knee problems, though she admits that she wasn't half the putter she needed to be to compete seriously on the LPGA Tour. Now that she has been Pelzified, however, her short game is the best part of her play.

Jackie excuses herself, as it is time to deliver her seminar on the "Four Games of Golf," a cornerstone lecture in the curriculum. According to Pelzian epistemology, these refer to the Power Game, the Finesse Game, the Putting Game, and the Mental Game. The fundamentals of each are very different, Jackie tells us, the most obvious distinction being that the Power Game depends on a coiling produced by the upper and lower parts of the body, while the Putting Game demands that our hips be totally immobile during the stroke and that wrist-cock be all but eliminated.

As for the Finesse Game, the official Pelz position is that everything—hips, torso, arms—should pretty much turn at the same rate. Unlike the full swing, the finesse swing requires that the hips stop turning when the shoulders stop. This lack of coil allows a golfer to strike the ball with greater precision. We vary the distance of our finesse shots by varying how far back we take our arms, not by increasing the coil between hips and shoulders.

By far the greatest value of the Pelz school, I am coming to realize, is how it clarifies the relatively simple techniques required by the finesse shots we are called on to play with our wedges. Jackie hauls out a big, colorful chart that demonstrates proper ball position. To hit a low-running chip, play the ball at the right ankle. To hit a high lob over a hazard, play it midway between the ankles. To escape a greenside sand hazard, take an open stance, and play the ball at the left toe. Jackie stresses that we must use our ankles as points of reference, not our feet. Otherwise, she warns, when we open or close our stance we will significantly alter the position of the ball, which will lead to dire consequences.

On day two of DPSGS, we start off making like a flock of golfing storks, as the faculty passes out putters with superlong shafts. These ungainly implements, now banned from the Tour, make it easy to effect a pure pendulum stroke. After five minutes with this big stick, I am convinced that if it weren't for the embarrassment factor—meaning, I'd look like a total bozo playing with one of these things—I'd go out and buy one immediately.

Advanced Pendulum is followed by a plenary session on Wedge Theory, in which Jackie offers data-rich proof of the correlation between short-play proficiency and money earned on the Tour. It's true: You *do* drive for show, and putt (and chip, and pitch) for dough, which is why Pelz and company advises that hackers should immediately divest their bags of redundant woods and longer irons and replace them with an extra wedge or two. They say we're nuts not to be fully equipped for the demands of the all-important finesse game. So advised, I jog over to the pro shop and in two minutes drop $100 on a Hogan sixty-degree wedge.

Throughout the weekend at the Pelz school, an expressionless figure of steely silence has been observing the proceedings, never once looking up, his head hung low as if some vital part of his Erector-Set anatomy had gone irretrievably limp. This doleful skeleton is the renowned Perfy, the macabre aluminum putting contraption Pelz invented a few years ago. His function is to simulate the bone structure of the human golfer. Early Perfy prototypes were based on the precise body measurements of real touring pros, among them Tom Kite and Jim Simons. With the aid of easily removable wing nuts, the length of Perfy's body parts can be adjusted at his ankles, knees, hips, spine, and shoulders. There are, however, no joints at all along Perfy's arms—they are "one-piece," Pelz noted, "so the swinging action Perfy performs is a pure pendulum motion."

Perfy racks up the frequent flier miles. He is crated and shlepped to just about every Pelz exhibition, seminar, and class throughout the country. Weighing just sixty-seven pounds, the metal geek can be disassembled in about four and a half minutes, then packed into an ordinary suitcase.

Spending hours and hours with Perfy, Pelz and his band of merry puttsters claim they have captured unimpeachable, *scientific* evidence of the ideal movements that determine successful putting. These principles are laid out in excruciating detail in Pelz's articles and books, and at DPSGS, where the instructors constantly urge us to practice them. We are admonished to relax our hands and arms, allowing these appendages to hang directly down from our shoulder sockets, as opposed to holding our hands either inside, or outside, the shoulders. Letting them hang straight encourages a purer pendulum, Pelz says. It's also best to position the ball no more than a couple of inches from your left instep. What you want to achieve is a stroke that allows you to make contact with the ball on a slight upswing. Your eyes should be directly over the aim line. And when you take the club back, it is critical that you maintain the all-important triangle formed by your arms, shoulders, and hands.

Having put Perfy through his pendulum paces, Pelz instructor Jim Chorniewy stashes the aluminum cipher in a corner, then strides into the center of the room to demonstrate what may be the single most invaluable golf lesson of the weekend. It is the five-part Pelzian putting process, or *ritual,* which is virtually guaranteed to prevent or cure the yips. It is guaranteed to bring a repeatable and proper tempo to one's putting stroke. And it's as simple as counting to five.

Chorniewy switches on a small electronic metronome, set to about seventy-three beats a minute (which is more or less in sync with our heart rate). The classroom falls silent as the little machine beats out a steady *tick . . . tick . . . tick . . . tick. . . .* Chorniewy drops a golf ball, which lands with a soft thud on the carpet. Pretend, he tells us, that you have by now lined up your putt, read the break, and gotten a sense of the speed. Assume your address: ball positioned inside the left instep, eyes over the aim line.

From this point on, Chorniewy says, every putt we take should be timed to a five-beat rhythm of the metronome (playing silently inside of our heads, of course):

Count one: Set the putter head down behind the ball.

Count two: Look at the target to confirm your aim.

Count three: Look down at the ball, directly below.

Count four: Take the putter back.

Count five: Make a smooth forward stroke through impact.

No yips. No rush. No fuss. Just a smooth-as-silk putting routine that does it all—except, of course, read the green for you. To help us learn how to do that, Jackie organizes yet another experiment. On a practice green she places a golf ball some twenty feet from the cup. It's obvious to all that there's a significant left-to-right break between the ball and the hole. Jackie fully extends a six-foot tape measure, running it out from the left side of the cup. She asks each of us to tell her privately how many inches we think the putt will break. The overwhelming majority of us guess that the putt will break from between twenty-two and thirty-two inches. One beanbrain guesses fifty-two inches, while another says eight inches. Using a TruRoller, the little ramp Pelz invented to send putts rolling at a controllable and consistent speed, Jackie determines that, in fact, the beanbrain was right on the money: The break in this putt is about sixty inches out from the hole.

"Here's a simple piece of advice," Jackie says. "When in doubt, *double* the amount of break you think you need. More often than not, you'll be closer to the pin than if you hadn't."

With that scrap of sage counsel, the golf year is over.

THE GHOSTS OF WINTER

I drive past a course in Westchester and find that it has been erased. The world, painted for so long a vivid green, has gone blindingly white. The blizzard of '96 has arrived and buried golf. Only the game's ghosts are active now, tending to their eternally smooth swings.

A few years ago, as a Christmas present, the Big Shooter sent me a copy of Harvey Penick's *Little Red Book*. The Shooter was smitten by it and thought I would be, too. He was right. This was an endearing work. Its message was to savor golf, not try to bring it to its knees. *The Little Red Book* had at least four qualities that helped make it the astonishing success it was:

It was gentle.

It was humble.

It was short.

It was easy.

Some time after he'd sent it to me, the Shooter began to harden a little on Penick's book (and its sequel, and the sequel after that). I think his view started to change right after he saw *Forrest Gump*, for he was intrigued by how much that blockbuster called to mind *The Little Red Book*. Here you have two gentle and humble guys, who speak in homilies and say exactly what they mean, yet millions come away inspired by their wisdom.

"What kind of times are we living in, anyway?" he groused, noting that *Gump* had smashed box-office records and Penick's book was on its way to 1.5 million copies in print.

Now, as thirty inches of snow pile up on Gawnrentin's perf course, I can't help but agree that the little red book has lost some of its charm.

A good putter is a match for anyone. A bad putter is a match for no one.

Arnold Palmer likes to grip the club tightly, but you are not Arnold Palmer.

The golf swing is one swing, but it is made up of little things all working together.

But, so what? Penick was by every account a great gentleman and wise teacher, most deserving of his permanent locker in golf's Eternal Clubhouse. As the blizzard continues, I'm spending a good amount of time reading about the Clubhouse. If a hacker's winter is good for anything, it's for keeping in touch with golf's ghosts. These are great tales, some heroic, others profane, that keep the world green through these golfless months. There are naughty-boy stories, such as the time Harry Vardon and a couple of cronies downed a fifth of Scotch just before a tournament at Whitemarsh, then went out and birdied the first hole. There are stories that put the lie to the conventional wisdom about how to play the game, such as how Ernest Jones, the great teacher who'd lost a leg in the war, held to the conviction (shades of Demaret) that making a good turn wasn't particularly necessary. "Use your upper limbs to swing the club and everything will come out okay," he said, citing hand control, good balance, and timing of the arms as the only three things that mattered.

There are the classic American boys' lives, that follow the familiar story line: country bumpkin, poor as dirt, pesky and untamable, finds old rusty club in woods, knocks rocks around fields, caddies at club where his dad cuts grass, grows up to win U.S. Open. Snead's *The Education of a Golfer* is a lively example of this genre—the story of a feisty kid who grew up in Appalachia, learned to overcome a horrible temper, stared down opponents, and turned the golf world on its ear. "Almost anybody could build a ten-or twenty-gallon still and brew mountain lightning, but our family stayed honest. . . ."

There's Sarazen, the immigrant hero; Hogan, the blacksmith's son; Hagan, the stylish rake; Jones, the elegant man-child; Palmer, the hard-charger, always with an eye for the prettiest face in the gallery.

There are ghost women, too, in this clubhouse, who are denied here no privilege, nor consigned to the course weekday mornings between ten and one. There's Didrikson, Rawls, Berg. There's Joyce Wethered, who some say was the greatest of all, not just the greatest of women but the greatest of *all*. Wethered was right up there with Bobby himself, judged Alister MacKenzie. "To see [her] play the Old Course is an eye-opener," he remarked of her. "One hole she will play with a pitch with a terrific amount of backspin, another with a pitch with topspin and run, another with a scuffle along the ground as if it were played with a putter, and yet others with a curve from left to right or from right to left. [She] has not the power of many of the men players—in fact she appears frail and fragile—but she had a greater number of shots in her bag." As the blizzard rages, I am right now staring at an old photograph of Wethered, enraptured by her serenity as she makes a regal finish, her long back gently curved, her hands held high in exultation. No ladies-keep-out house rule was forceful enough to have excluded her from this game. She is in golf's thrall.

I have been unable to hit balls for several weeks now, as successive storms pound away at New York. While the summer heat was among the worst on record here, the winter snowfall is certifiably *the* worst. Through these weeks I putter around as best I can, mostly at night in the bedroom, bending over my Putting Track, diddling with my grip.

A couple of days ago I trekked over to the Chelsea Piers on the Hudson River in Manhattan, where the cruise ships are moored. Still under construction, the piers will eventually house a sports and recreation complex that is to a include a golf school under the aegis, if not the active presence, of Jim McLean. A driving range has already opened there, jutting into the river and featuring high-tech ball dispensers in lieu of low-tech wire buckets. You buy an encoded card out front, slip it into one of these electronic dispensers, which one by one automatically coughs up however many balls you're entitled to. Each pops up out of the ground on a rubber tee, so a hacker never has to bend over. This great sport marches on. We no longer have to walk to experience its many pleasures, and now we no longer have to bend. Now, if we can only get rid of the obligation to swing.

When the streets are judged to be slick but passable, I drive over to a covered driving range not far from Gawnrentin. The day is miserable, with temperatures in the thirties, and a freezing rain whips across the range. I have risked this trip because the facility has heated stalls, but I refrain from hitting any of my metal woods for fear they will crack in the Arctic air that swirls around this concrete bunker. I wear thermal golf gloves, a woolen ski cap, three layers of shirts, and long underwear.

February, at last. The Big Shooter and I finally snap. We decide we have lived life without golf long enough, so we steal away to North Carolina for a weekend. We are under no illusions. The weather, we assume, will be chilly but cooperative. It snows the first day we arrive, a sprinkling that dusts the course like a layer of confectioner's sugar.

By midday, though, the powder suddenly disappears, and we tee off in warm sunshine. Neither of us plays very well.

Because he's writing a piece about the place, the Shooter is staying at the Mid-Pines Resort, while I am just across the street at Pine Needles. Both of these resorts are operated by Peggy Kirk Bell, the reigning doyenne of women's golf in America. In just six months, Pine Needles will host the Women's Open, and there's already a buzz of activity here.

Over drinks the first night, the Shooter points out that I'm getting very little turn in my swing. My shots were uniformly weak, and most of them faded to the left. Cutting this not so happy hour short, I wander out onto the deserted, ball-littered range with an eight-iron. I am followed by a friendly husky, who romps after my shots. I concentrate on lengthening the arc of my swing. I am entirely relaxed and content. My hands are soft and pliant. Every shot I hit is crisp. Why can't I take this onto the course?

The next evening I have a drink with Peggy Bell, who's already sporting a spiffy 1996 Women's Open windbreaker. Well into her seventies, Bell still oversees a full schedule of golf schools at Pine Needles, most of them for women only. She tells me that women are much easier to teach than men, more open to drills and exercises. "Men don't even want to admit that they *need* lessons," she says. "They hate to confess that they don't know something."

I ask Bell how she starts a session with a new student.

"First, I take a long look at her swing. Then I try to figure out who she is as a person, whether she's patient or not, whether she'll practice methodically. Most women will. Most men won't. Then I like to make 'em dance." She asks her students to shift their weight from leg to leg, over and over, getting the feel of a proper rhythm. Then she and her staff make sure everyone has a proper grip. But the emphasis remains on footwork. "Footwork is to a swing what the foundation is to a house," she states.

Mustering the courage, I ask Bell if she'd give me a once-over. Delighted, she says. We walk outside to the range. She asks me to hit a few shots with a six-iron. I hit them decently, but all of them too short. I tell her this is symptomatic of my game.

"Let me show you a drill," she says.

Bell instructs me to assume the impact position, with my hands well ahead of the ball and my left wrist flat. She tells me to bring all of my weight onto my left foot, as it properly should be at impact. "Keep your shoulders square to the target line," she advises. "Now, rock back and forth, shifting your weight, swinging the club, always keeping the left wrist in the impact position." After having me rock back and forth for a minute or two, Bell tells me to set up to hit a range ball, again assuming the impact position. This time, though, she says to make a full swing and hit the ball. Club and ball make clean contact. The shot sails about 150 yards. But the best part is when I look back down at the ground at the divot. The divot is a shallow, perfect rectangle, aimed squarely at the target. It is a world-class divot, the kind the Shooter would admire. The Shooter contends that divots tell all about a golfer, and has written that they reveal that "pros are to hackers what a brain surgeon is to a hog butcher." The next day, before we tee off, I show the Shooter the new drill. We then go out and play. I shoot a 104. The divots I leave behind are nasty. For Peggy Bell's sake, I pray they will heal by summer, when the Women's Open comes to town.

Discovery

Do you dare believe
in the simplicity of the swing?
—**Vivien Saunders,** *The Golfing Mind,* 1988

LETTING GO

About ten years ago, a group of us flew down to Pinehurst for a three-day golf orgy. This was back in our manic-obsessive period, when a long weekend was considered a bust if we weren't able to cram in over 100 holes, plus a couple of additional hours on the range each day. At Pinehurst, we were midway through such a marathon when, late one afternoon, I decided to treat myself to a massage. My muscles ached, my hands were covered with blisters, my feet were sore. I needed to be refreshed in preparation for the following morning, when an early-morning tee time would set off another long day of self-flagellation.

The massage therapist, I was pleased to discover, was a pretty brunette in her mid-twenties. Not too suprisingly, there was something whole-grainy about her. She led me into a candlelit room scented with oils and creams and filled with the gentle musical breezes of Windham Hill. She told me to lie on my stomach, so I flipped over and inserted my nose into the hole in the table. She began by working some warm oil into my throbbing shoulders and back. The pleasure was immediate. Her knowing hands were drawn as if by a mystical compass to the considerable number of knots formed by the day's collection of perps, worm burners, skulls, and shanks.

"Gee, you're kinda tight," she said. By now she had worked her way to my spine and lower back.

"Lotsa golf," I phumphered into the table.

I drifted into a state of semiconsciousness. The therapist was now down around my calves, lengthening, cajoling, soothing them. After all, it's not easy climbing in and out of a golf cart for the better part of ten hours. "You're really, really tight," she said again, warily.

Then, with a sudden jerk, the woman pulled her hands away. She had gotten to the soles of my feet, but it was if she had touched a hot iron. The music stopped, and the lights came on. The massage therapist took a step back from the table and told me that she had no choice: She just couldn't go on. "Your vibes are too heavy," she sputtered, adding that she had never had a client who was as "really incredibly tight" as I was, and it was too late in the day for her to deal with it.

"What do you mean, 'my vibes are too heavy'?" I asked, flabbergasted. "And if I am as tight as you say, I probably would have been dead five years ago."

"I don't know what I mean," she replied. "But I just can't go on, that's all. I'm feeling this really negative energy flow."

With that she was gone. I pulled on my clothes and walked back to my room.

What was that *all about?* I wondered. To be sure, the woman was more than a little tightly wrapped herself. And, yes, it *was* late in the day, and maybe she just needed to get home to her cat and a warm bowl of couscous. But I also accepted her point: Thanks to a whole lot of bad golf, I was tighter than a steel drum.

But that was then. Now is now. I'm not nearly that tight anymore, not remotely.

Something big has happened. I am now loose as a goose—and here's why:

I believe I have discovered the golf swing.

Or, the golf swing has discovered me.

I believe I can now put the face of the blade on the nose of the golf ball, if not exactly every time, then often enough. I know that the flight of the ball will almost certainly be straighter and longer than it ever was before.

Or, as the Shooter said when he first spied my born-again swing, "It's amazing how your shots hold their course."

He is right about that. No longer do my shots swoop and swerve, perish midflight like wounded ducks. Now they push gamely ahead, holding their line.

It is late May, some fifteen months after I first set eyes on Brad Redding. I have been in the possession of this new swing, or it has been in the possession of me, for several weeks now. I have tested and retested it over and over at the driving range and have played a fair number of rounds with it. Playing partners who knew me before tell me that I'm much improved. Naturally, I affect false modesty when they observe this, muttering, "We'll see." I am secretly jubilant. When the Big Shooter said what he said my heart leaped—what better testament than one from the Big Shooter himself, who more than any other luckless soul has watched me whiff, slice, and top for more golf seasons than anyone else?

Your shots hold their course. His exact words.

Knowing that I can count on this new swing, I step up to each shot with the confidence that I will hit the ball on its dimpled hooter. When I take my address position, my body feels capable and strong, my feet well planted.

Here's how it happened:

After North Carolina and the meeting with Peggy Bell, I returned to New York, where golf was still in hibernation. I visited the range when the weather was decent, but didn't play at all for over a month. Then, in April, I was invited out to Southampton, Long Island, to play a round at the National Golf Links of America. The National, as aficionados of the game are well aware, is one of the nation's most glorious golf courses. It sits hard by Long Island Sound, right next door to the equally magnificent Shinnecock Hills. A colleague and friend—call him Jack—is a member out at National. Jack is a heck of a guy, a hale and hearty magazine publisher, a great enthusiast, and a talented, if highly unconventional, golfer. Jack had arranged an outing at the club with one of his clients, and was nice enough to invite me along. As it was early in the spring, the storied club was barely open for business, and we had the course pretty much to ourselves. The weather was great, brilliantly sunny, though the conditions were a challenge, thanks to the usual healthy breezes that blow there.

Of the three of us, I was by far the weakest player. Jack's client, just in from L.A., was a tall and powerfully built man, with slicked-back hair and hip sunglasses. He took evident pleasure in playing the round with a succession of Cuban cigars in his mouth. He had an admirable swing, with good tempo and a huge arc, more than sufficient to launch impressively long shots, most of which shrugged off the blustery wind and found their targets.

Jack, too, played better than creditably, but then again he always does. Jack's handicap is in the single digits. His excellent play is in spite of, or because of, the most bizarre-looking golf swing I have ever seen. Everybody likes to kid Jack about his peculiar technique, though no one underestimates his ability to use it to great advantage.

When Jack addresses the ball, he spreads his legs very wide apart, about as far apart as they can go, way beyond the width of his shoulders. Most golf teachers would regard this as a serious offense and would encourage Jack to narrow his stance so that he might gain the benefit of a fuller pivot.

Having so arranged his feet, Jack reaches out to the ball with his arms and club extended out to their full length. Most golf teachers would say Jack was overreaching, running the risk of swinging from the outside in. When Jack places the club on the ground, he resembles a bizarre human tripod, its appendages stretched to their limits.

Jack's grip is also strange. He curls his right hand way, *way* under the club—supination city—with the palm of his hand facing the sky. He neither interlocks nor overlaps, but holds the handle with all ten fingers, baseball style, which is how he learned it as a boy. Most golf teachers would say this grip couldn't possibly allow Jack the freedom to cock and uncock. They are wrong, judging from how hard Jack is able to hit the ball.

Once settled and firmly locked in this spread-eagled position, and holding on firmly with his weird grip, Jack freezes for a good few seconds. Most golf teachers would advise Jack to get things going a lot faster. Time breeds tension, they say. But this lock-in period doesn't seem to tighten Jack up, it actually seems to focus him.

Locked and loaded, Jack now commits the most serious transgression of all, the ultimate violation, something no golf teacher in his right mind could ever condone. Jack's hands and wrists go into a kind of spasm: a furious, herky-jerky waggle, a convulsion, really. It looks as if Jack has been zapped by a bolt of electricity that has somehow snaked up from the ground. This jolt is instantly conducted through the steel shaft of the club directly into Jack's palms. Jack's hands are actually moving, moving spastically, even as he *begins* his swing. For Jack, this spasm seems to serve as a kind of highly unorthodox forward press. No matter. The action almost always precedes a fine, accurate golf shot.

People who kid Jack about his swing have hung a nickname on him: Spare Parts. The name fits. His golf swing *does* look as if it has been assembled from a box of discarded swing parts, cobbled together, held in place with spit. Jack doesn't give a damn about the nickname. Why should he? The swing works. That swing is Jack, and Jack is that swing.

While Jack and the client rocketed long tee shots and fired precise approaches one right after the other, I hacked around as if I hadn't taken a golf lesson in my life. I was sorely outgunned and outclassed by these two. Despite the fabulous weather and spectacular surroundings, all I could manage was to stumble along like a third, creaky wheel.

STORMIN' NORMAN

That night and the next day I kept thinking about Jack and how he defied golf's orthodoxy with his spare-parts swing. About how he had stuck with his oddball style and made it work for him. Then I remembered something I'd read months earlier. It was an article about the eccentric Canadian, Moe Norman, whom many consider to be among the best ball-strikers of all time. I rifled through a stack of old golf magazines, and finally found the piece I wanted in the December 1995 issue of *Golf Digest*. On the cover was a midswing picture of the bulky, white-haired Norman, accompanied by the headline MOE KNOWS WHAT NOBODY ELSE KNOWS. Inside, eighteen pages were devoted to Norman's singular genius and to the mechanics of his unusual swing. In his profile of the golfer, now pushing seventy, David Owen recounted many of the tales, true and apocryphal, that have made Norman a larger-than-life character among golf's cognoscenti.

On Moe's astonishing accuracy: Once, while playing with Sam Snead, Norman announced that he would neither lay up in front of, nor attempt to carry, a creek that crossed a fairway some 240 yards out from the tee. "I'm playing for the bridge," Norman declared, gesturing to a modest walkway that traversed the brook. And this was *precisely* where he landed his ball, which dutifully rolled over to the far side, setting Norman up for an easy second shot.

On Moe's astonishing consistency: Once, during an exhibition years ago, Norman hit 1,540 drives in under seven hours. None traveled less than 225 yards, and all landed inside a designated landing zone just 30 yards wide.

On Moe's astonishing control: When Owen asked Norman about the last time he'd hit a bad shot, the golfer answered, "Thirty years ago." Owen recounted that once on a practice range Moe hit 131 consecutive drives without having to straighten or otherwise adjust his tee.

In the profile, Moe was portrayed as an introverted and lonely man. As a child, Norman was diagnosed with autism, a condition compounded by serious head injuries he'd suffered in a boyhood sledding accident. Moe's early and obsessive interest in golf was greeted by taunts that golf was a game for sissies. Undaunted, Norman devoted his life to the art of hitting a golf ball. It was the purest, possibly the only, joy he knew. He practiced interminably, pursuing the ideal swing (for him) with a determination "verging on mania."

What Moe wound up with was a swing that, like Jack's, and in many of the same ways, grossly violated traditional form:

Norman takes a much wider than usual stance.

He places his club head well behind the ball—at least a foot behind when using his driver, and four inches or more for irons.

He takes a relatively short backswing, using less shoulder and hip turn than the so-called traditional swing calls for. Despite this limited pivot, Moe generates enormous power and drop-dead accuracy. Tour pros can only gape when Norman puts on a show.

Moe's disciples, whose numbers seem to be growing, offer convincing explanations for how and why Norman's swing works—for him and potentially for many of the rest of us. A key reason, they say, is that Norman doesn't hold the club in the fingers of his right hand, as most teachers advise, but in his palm, which most teachers will tell you is a death move. Yet this is the way we do most of life's hitting, whether holding a hammer to drive a nail, a fishing rod to cast a line, or a tennis racket to return a shot. Holding the club in the palm enables the shaft of the club to travel along the same plane as our right arm. Holding it in the fingers puts the shaft on a slightly different plane, which is much more difficult to control. Holding it in the palm also encourages and empowers the golfer to hit and hit hard with his strong right hand and arm, instead of using the weaker left hand and arm to pull the club through (as so many traditionalists urge us to learn). By cutting down on the requirement to turn, Norman's believers argue, we can simplify the swing, reducing the number of rotating planes that must be in sync.

WHAT IF?

I pored over *Golf Digest's* pictures of Moe Norman with the same intensity that I studied Ravielli's pen-and-ink renderings of Ben Hogan decades earlier.

Was this the answer?

I would hold the golf club the way I hold a hammer, or a fly rod—implements I know I can use passably well.

I would stop all this futzing, trying to play with other people's notions and body parts and resolve to hit the ball as hard as I could, using the only side of my body, the only arm, the only hand, that I have ever, and will ever, know how to do anything with—be it brushing my teeth, or spooling spaghetti onto a fork.

I would try to bust out of the thinking man's golf prison, spring myself from what Vivien Saunders calls "the overlearning trap." Saunders is a former British amateur champion, a psychologist, and, something of a golfing tycoon in England, where she runs very successful golf schools at the Abbotsley Golf and Squash Club. Her book, *The Golfing Mind*, published in the late 1980s, strikes me as one of the best in the field: It doesn't try to con us into believing that golf is an easy game— to play, teach, or learn. It acknowledges, rather, that the golf swing is hard enough to begin with, and argues that hackers and teachers have made it harder still by their misguided attempts to analyze its mechanics. This analysis is the bait that leads us into the overlearning trap. Saunders takes mighty issue with the way golf is usually taught. She suggests that we'd teach the golf swing more effectively by encouraging students to learn to hit with a larger than usual ball and a larger than usual club head. The smallness of the regular ball, along with the smallness of the club head, demand unusual powers of accuracy and concentration, qualities in short supply in weekend hackers. Morever, Saunders says that adults have no choice but to try to learn a new thing with what skills they've already acquired, which is why we depend so much on verbal analysis. ("Ye try too hard and ye think too much," in the words of Shivas Irons.) We try to talk and think a new skill into our systems—in contrast to the wondrous ways children learn, through direct observation and mimicry. Adults, Saunders writes, operate under a highly cultivated fear of failure. Kids don't care whether they skull or top a shot, they merely revel in the whack. But as we eventually become all too aware of our inadequacies (at work, at love, at family, at golf), we can no longer step up and deliver that unrestrained and joyful *whack*, but temper our shots, hold back, try to hit with a club of reason and hope. We seek guidance about the exact placement of this limb or that digit. We prattle on about pace and tempo.

Vivien Saunders issues a warning, self-evident perhaps, but one so simple, universal, and essential to our golfing health that it ought to be stamped on every box of new golf balls and on the sole plate of every driver:

The use of language for the learning of physical skills can . . . be detrimental to success.

Saunders also sets down what may be the most plainly intelligent sentence I have ever read about golf instruction: "The golfer must be made aware that analyzing what happens in the golf swing and learning the golf swing are two entirely different things."

MR. NATURAL

The last few pages of *Golf Digest*'s coverage of Moe Norman were devoted to explaining his technique to golf's great unwashed. These pages were written by Jack Kuykendall, yet another engineer/physicist type, who has made it his mission to parlay Norman's swing into a marketable commodity known as "Natural Golf." Kuykendall's GLUT has to with the "scientific principles" that explain, and may even *prove*, why an extrawide stance, outstretched arms, a compact backswing, and a powerful, palm-based grip make it infinitely easier for a hacker to play decent golf than does the traditional golf swing that is taught by nearly all of the game's instructors.

There was, naturally, a book and video on offer, which I promptly obtained. The video consisted of an interminable lecture by Kuykendall on how the Natural Golf method conforms—we've heard this one before—to the irrefutable laws of physics. Moe Norman costars on the tape, his bulky physique festooned with the Natural Golf logo. The enclosed materials proclaimed Natural Golf to be "a new, truly revolutionary system of learning and playing. A system that in theory and in application sweepingly and categorically contradicts the traditional finger-grip system. [It] would be unforgivable and presumptuous if we made even the slightest implication that this discovery was in any way the equivalent of Pasteur's, Roentgen's, Salk's, or even those of Edison, Bell, or Ford. Yet there is one basic similarity: Millions of people benefit."

Hyperbole aside, the materials were logical and persuasive. Traditional instruction was overly based on observations of professional players. Traditional instruction assumed that everybody could learn to do things the way these master professionals do. But the "unnatural" finger-based grip that these great players use was notoriously difficult for amateurs to master.

Having watched the tape and read the book, I went to the driving range. I took the six-iron out of my bag and put a ball on the rubber nipple. I spread my legs far apart, in the manner of Jack and Moe. I took hold of the club with the palm of my right hand, nestling the thumb along the lifeline of my left hand. Standing over the ball this way, I was struck by how much further behind it my head seemed to be. I tried to imagine myself holding a sledgehammer, not a golf club, with the intent of smashing it through an imaginary wall.

Then I swung.

And topped the ball.

It squiggled pathetically a few yards off the tee.

I tried again, with the same result.

I stepped back, relaxed my hands. Once again I spread myself out, this time playing the ball even farther forward in my gigantic stance. I was now doing a pretty fair impersonation of Spare Parts.

This time the ball rocketed off the club. It was not a perfect shot by any means—it was pulled pretty far right—but the impact was solid and satisfying. The shot just kept rising and rising, without a hint of a fade. It roared toward the power alley in left-center field. Most amazingly, I'd kept my balance throughout this smash. My feet remained just where they were at my initial setup.

My life in golf took a new turn in that instant. More boomers rang out, nearly every one struck with a force that I'd known only rarely before this day. Most of these shots also went left. But not one of them was a slice.

I took Jack and Moe's swing out on the course whenever I could. Playing with newfound confidence, I shot a series of nine-hole rounds in the mid- to high forties. My drives sailed down the middle, almost without exception. Not quite knowing yet how to apply the new swing to my short game, I lost a large number of strokes around the green.

Who cared that the swing wasn't pretty?

That swing was *me*.

BE THE MAN!

I resolved that I would not take another golf lesson. For the indefinite future, I vowed that I would hit every shot in the manner of Moe and Jack. If this new swing needed to be fine-tuned, further adapted to the particulars of my height, weight, age, and state of mind, I would make whatever adjustments I felt were in order. No more teachers, no more books. From here on out, I'd be a self-sufficient, golfing hermaphrodite, student and teacher both.

It is a perfect afternoon in early summer. I am standing on a tee box in upstate New York. I am playing, hermaphroditically, by myself. Whenever I play alone like this I wonder whether it really counts, whether it's really "legal." I don't mean because there's a powerful desire to cheat—well, not cheat exactly, but play best-ball with myself, taking the lowest score obtained from both balls and putting that number down on the card. After all, it's not that I haven't hit these shots, so it's not as though I'm incapable of playing a hole in this manner. Right? And there's another reason that a score achieved when playing alone may not be strictly kosher: Such a round is free of distractions, and competitive pressure, friendly, formal, or otherwise. Distractions and pressures are what make golf, so when a hacker plays without them he's playing another game entirely. I am much better at this game than I am at golf. Aren't we all?

But back to the swing. The swing is working great. I'm now playing bogey golf, consistently. I'm comfortable and relaxed. On this particular day, even as I drove up here, I don't even think about breaking eighty, for I know I'm not close to doing that, not today, not yet. With this new swing, I'm at least playing at what I believe is a reasonable level of competence, no longer below same.

I tee up and hit a good drive. Most of my drives are good these days. The sledgehammer grip works especially well off the tee. Walking up the middle of the fairway, I tell myself again that while this new swing is exciting, it is no breakthrough. I don't do breakthroughs any more. Breakthroughs are illusions. That day at Lee-Jane when I discovered what a correct pivot felt like; that run of three perfect holes at Egwani Farms; those five minutes of perfect pitching at the Pelz school—they weren't breakthroughs, they were just memorable steps. Just as the calamities, the horrendous holes, the embarrassing perps, the flubs, the cries of anguish weren't setbacks. They, too, were just memorable steps. With hindsight, I can say with some satisfaction that even on the darkest days I was probably moving forward. Progress is tricky to measure. Often I believed I was going nowhere, but I was probably making some sort of advancement. It's a question of perspective. If anyone had been watching me from a great distance, looking down on me from a gallery on the moon, say, he would have observed that my progress was steady, if slow, but always forward. Yet to me, earthbound, it didn't feel like that at all. It felt, it feels, jagged, jerky, a trip that proceeds in the smallest steps, but one that our impatience magnifies into triumphs or disasters. Until recently, I didn't appreciate how small the steps were, and how many of them, good and bad, would be needed to take me to where I am today, to here, to right now, to walking alone on this summer afternoon, to bogey golf.

I have a pretty clear shot to the green, about 170 yards with a slight wind at my back. Having more confidence in the idiot-proof Heaven Wood than in a four-iron, I pull out the trusty Callaway and survey the shot. I take a reading of the slight breeze, determine the target line, spread my feet far apart, grasp the club firmly in the palm of my right hand. The shot is a bit fat—too little shoulder turn—but it's decent and it'll do. The ball lands on the right-side fringe. I can get down in two if I'm lucky, certainly three. Another bogey is in the bag.

I amble down the middle of the fairway.

Bogey golf is good enough. Bogey golf ain't shabby. All it is is missing a putt. It's not quite reaching the green in two. Bogey golf is what I have always been willing to settle for, ever since I first went out with my father's mixed-and-matched set of clubs. Till now, though, bogey golf was a nine-iron beyond my reach. Now I am only a four-foot putt away.

Breaking eighty—what about that? Have I not achieved it because I failed to learn, or because golf instruction failed me? It is tempting to grumble at how ill-conceived golf teaching is. It's too fragmented. It's contradictory. It's doctrinaire. It doesn't recognize, anticipate, or adapt itself to the peculiarities and idiosyncrasies of the tight, the uptight, the chubby, the anxious, the frail, the tall, the shy, the short, the impatient, the gullible, the obsessive, the stubby-fingered. Golf instruction is too much of the cowlicked, by the cowlicked, for the cowlicked.

But this new swing. If it didn't come from instruction, where did it come from? True, nobody "taught" it to me. It goes down in the book as self-discovery. But without this year of living instructionally, without watching, listening, and reading, the swing never would have presented itself. This suggests that golf instruction didn't fail me at all. Golf instruction was the *enabler*. (There, I said it!) All those lessons and books induced me to pay attention to Jack's swing, to read about Moe, to link Jack to Moe, Moe to Jack.

So I'll say it again: Nobody's to blame here, okay? Not Redding, Patri, Latella, Mazziotti. Not Bobby Jones, Hogan, Armour, Pelz.

Nor me. I'm no failure, either; I simply misjudged. I never should have set out to be better than better. I should have just set out to be better. I knew going in that golf was impossible, but I underestimated it anyway. They all told me I could do it: Hogan, Jones, Palmer, and Redding all agreed—remember?—that breaking eighty was a reasonable goal for a hacker like me. It certainly sounded reasonable. *Breaking eighty.* A throwaway phrase. *Breaking eighty.* A phrase that trips off the tongue, like "walking barefoot," or "going nuts." Often, when I'd return home from a round, Linda would look up and ask, "Hi, dear, did you do it? Did you break eighty?" She did this partly to needle me, partly out of genuine curiosity as in, "Hi, is it still raining?"

Breaking eighty is a bear. I think of it now the way I should have back then: To break eighty you have to go around in just seven over par. The scorecard would have to look something like this, without benefit of a mulligan or a gimme:

Par

Par

Birdie

Bogey

Par

Double bogey

Par

Bogey

Par

Bogey

Par

Bogey

Par

Bogey

Par

Bogey

Par

Par

New swing or no, a round like that is no walk in the woods. To play between par and bogey golf, according to the Golf Research Association, you've got to be able to drive 233 yards on average, hit at least ten fairways, and make it to at least eight greens in regulation. Your average par-four approach club should be a seven-iron, and your average par-five approach club a nine. You need to average around thirty-two putts, and five one-putt greens a round. The average distance of your first putt ought not to exceed sixteen feet. As I say, that kind of round is no joke. It would be as difficult to achieve as, well—what if the assigned task had been to learn to play the piano instead of master the golf swing? What would be the musical equivalent of breaking eighty? A guess: I would have had to be able to sit down before a packed house of strangers and critics and whiz through a credible performance of Bach's *Well-Tempered Clavier*, Books I *and* II, without stopping and without sheet music.

Hah!

Why, then, did I, why do so many hackers, labor under the illusion that we can make shots stop on a dime with a well-tempered wedge? Why does the prospect of hitting a golf ball nearly perfectly, again and again and again over the course of four hours, without gimmes and mulligans, in the wind, while others are watching, over greens the consistency of lumpy doughnuts, strike us as an achievable skill to master? Why do the rhythm and dexterity required to attain a sub-eighty round strike us as more learnable and achievable than sitting down and adroitly executing a composition by Bach?

Why do we labor under the illusion that it's easier to make like Nick Faldo than it is to make like Glenn Gould?

KIAWAH

It is the beginning of August.

Linda, the kids, and I have arrived on Kiawah Island, where we are to spend the next three weeks. This seaside resort in South Carolina has been a favorite vacation place for the last several years. Starting back when we lived in Knoxville, we'd drive down at least a couple of times a year, always in the summer, usually again in the late fall or winter. We come to Kiawah because it's laid back, not overly developed, and because there's something for each of us here. Linda loves being by the sea and having the chance to explore nearby Charleston. The kids love to ride bikes, watch for alligators, net crabs. I've been known to play the occasional round of golf, occasional as in at least once every day.

At Kiawah, there are four good golf courses open to the public, including the Ocean Course, where the 1991 Ryder Cup was played. Just a few months ago, another gem was added, Tom Fazio's private River Course. With these to choose from I am as happy as a marsh clam.

But I am also as twitchy as a Kiawah crab. For these three weeks loom as considerably more than a summer vacation. They will be the test, the crucible. I have a chance to play some serious golf. I will refine the new swing, and broker the long-awaited reconciliation between Selves 1 and 2.

And maybe even break eighty.

Exercising a measure of mature responsibility, I don't so much as unzip my golf bag on the first day. There's too much to do to settle in. But on the second day I am out on the River Course and loving every minute of it. It's truly a beautiful layout, with tee boxes set at tricky angles; curving fairways, generously wide and in great condition; and accommodating greens, immaculate in every respect. I wind my way solo through an empty front nine until I run into a group of players that includes, I'm pretty sure, Fran Tarkenton. There are foursomes just ahead of Fran's, too, so I scoot back over to the first tee and play the front nine again. To this point I have no idea what my score is because I've been simply knocking around a couple of balls.

This second time around, however, I put one of the balls in my pocket and keep count. I shoot a forty-three for these nine holes, thanks to several exquisite shots off the tee, the best being a 235-yard drive on the short but sinewy fifth hole (labeled Double Vision on the score-card because of its twin greens). The new swing has much to do with these shots, no question. But, in the interest of full disclosure, there's something else at work here. Before leaving for Kiawah, I bought myself an eleven-degree, Great Big Bertha titanium driver. I'd been skeptical about the claims I'd heard about these blasters. Harvey Penick, for one, believed that the sweet spot on these clubs was actually *smaller* than those on normal-sized woods. He used the analogy of driving a nail with an oversized hammer; sure, the tool has a larger striking area, but it increases one's chances of hitting a nail off-center. I broke down and bought this baby anyway, unable to resist its advertised results. Now, watching the big dog hunt, I congratulate myself on the best $400 I have ever lavished on this game. Almost every drive is stunning. The sound this club makes on a golf ball is otherworldly.

But there are other shots, too, that in their concentrated frequency get me thinking, *It's going to happen this trip*—if not today, or tomorrow, or next week, then at some point while I am here. I am going to walk off one of these splendid Kiawah courses with a seventy-nine in my back pocket. There are omens, even now. I hole a forty-five-foot chip, clipping the ball just so with an eight-iron. I hit an explosive five-wood off the fairway. I play a masterful, blind sand shot from a deep bunker. When I clamber up to the green, I find the ball sitting just three feet from the cup.

The days tick off, each one offering a round of satisfying and plea-surable golf. I am still a very happy man. But I haven't broken eighty yet, haven't gotten close. Well, that's not true. On most of these rounds, one or the other of the nines promises an imminent rendezvous with destiny. Almost every day brings a nine in which I get down into the lowish forties: 42, 44, 43, 41, 43. Good going, Self 2! The other nine, however, ends up in the hands of Mr. Bluster. He stomps and storms and staggers to his usual 51, 49, 55, 52. Some rounds he plays the front, some rounds the back. I just can't get rid of him, even for a day. Go to Charleston, I tell him. Check out the shops. Buy yourself a *tchotchke*. Have dinner and a good bottle of wine.

The sucker doesn't bite.

It is mid-August. We have been here thirteen days, with a week to go before we head back to New York. Linda and I drop the kids off for a couple of hours at Kamp Kiawah, then get into a golf cart and drive out onto the River Course.

Linda is not a golfer, has never played a round in her life. In fact, the last time we were out on a course together was six years ago, on the eve of that assignment in London. We'd rented a house for a week in Scotland, not far from Inverness. Ned was barely one at the time; Katherine hadn't been born. Knowing that we'd have to travel back and forth to London to look for a place to live, we decided to spring for a nanny to help out with Ned. An agency sent us a packet of C.V.'s, one of which was beyond category. How's this for a candidate—Mary Poppins, Julia Child, and Joyce Wethered rolled into one?

Her name was Maggie Hutchinson. According to her résumé, she was a nanny of the first rank, until recently in the employ of a prominent British family. In addition, she held a culinary degree from the Cordon Bleu in London. And—get this—she was *also* a scratch golfer. In fact, she was captain of her county's amateur team in Wales, where she currently lived. We'd hit the trifecta: A baby-sitter for Ned. A four-star chef for Linda. A golf buddy for me.

The agency's file included a picture of Maggie. It showed a correct and dignified woman of a certain age, properly dressed in a long raincoat and sensible shoes, a prim bow tie knotted at her throat. We instantly signed her up.

In Scotland, Maggie was waiting for us when we pulled up to the house. Turns out she had motored over from Wales—in a racy, black, top-down Lancia, which was parked in the drive. Before we had a chance to reconcile the flashy, two-seated convertible with the lady we'd seen in the picture, the lady we'd seen in the picture came bounding outside, a huge smile on her face. Gone was the proper raincoat, the boxy shoes, the bow tie. Maggie was decked out in a satiny Ellesse warm-up suit. Otherwise, though, she proved to be as advertised, tending to Ned with brisk efficiency, and whipping up in short order an incomparable leg of lamb in a homemade pastry crust.

Every morning for the next few days, after the breakfast dishes had been cleared, Maggie would look outside, take a reading of the steel-gray clouds, sniff the cool highland air, then announce, "Appears to be a fine day for golf."

I resisted these overtures, believing it would be selfish to leave Linda at home with Ned while the nanny and I roared off to the links in her spiffy sportscar. One day, though, Linda suggested that all four of us could use a good long walk—Maggie's home-baked scones and cream-based everything had started to take their toll—and proposed that we check out the nearby golf course. Before I could even find the keys to our car, Maggie had slipped into her links togs and was cooling her heels outside, taking a few practice swings with a wedge.

The next few hours revealed much about the dynamics of marriage, the disintegration of the class system, and the inequities of golf. Hole after hole, Maggie—who had spotted me a laughably meager six strokes—wiped the bloody sod with me, hitting every shot bang up the middle, displaying a short game as razor-sharp as the cutlery at the Cordon Bleu. Her rapid and precise play left her plenty of free time to help me root about for the countless balls I skulled into the heather. And while Maggie was making shepherd's pie out of me, Linda endured the most back-breaking and infuriating workout of her life, trailing us, doing her best to keep up, pushing Ned (strapped into his stroller) across the rugged and rocky Scottish terrain, up and over crags and outcroppings, over tens of thousands of ovine chips, through pesky brambles and prickly thistles.

Afterwards, we all went for a beer, where I settled my debt to Maggie, who sat there beaming, radiant with bliss.

That morning in Scotland may explain why, until today in Kiawah, Linda has chosen not to set foot on a golf course—though on a few occasions, she has hit practice balls and allowed me to pass on a few pointers. (Those who can, do, those who can't, etc.)

But today we are actually playing golf together. Between my own strokes, I am teaching her the Spare Parts swing, which she finds quite comfortable. And she is hitting the ball really well, getting most of her shots aloft. A few of them even carry a smart draw.

Perhaps because I am only half paying attention to my own game, I am striking the ball better than ever. We play four holes. I par two and bogey two. We realize that it's time to go back and get the kids. Linda, having had enough for the day, offers to perform this duty, while I stay out on the course. We return to the clubhouse, where she hops out, then I head back to resume play where I'd left off. But a foursome has by now arrived at the fifth tee, so I wave myself through and drive on to the sixth, a 161-yard par-three with an elevated tee and water on the left. I par it. I bogey the next hole, a 432-yard par-four, the number-one handicap. I then bogey the eighth, but par the ninth. Having skipped one hole on this front nine—that short par-four with the twin greens—I make the turn in thirty-six. If today's the day I'm to break eighty, I tell myself, I will obviously have to go back and play that hole.

I make the turn. There's nobody up ahead, so I tee off without delay. Dense clouds have formed in the distance, out over the ocean, and they're coming my way. Can't worry about them. I make a scrambling five for a bogey. Then I par the eleventh, hitting a fine fairway wood. I par the next hole, hitting the green with a 170-yard Heaven

Wood. I bogey the thirteenth. I have now played twelve holes and I am six over par. My score is fifty-six. Thanks to Jack and Moe, thanks to the Spare Parts swing, thanks to being out here day after day, I have played this round as well as I can play the game of golf. Par for the six holes remaining is twenty-four. To break eighty I will have to finish them in one under.

Only the most certifiably deluded would even remotely regard this as possible. Good old Self 2 is apparently one of them, for there he is, raring to go, already holding the Great Big Bertha as he waits for the rest of us to join him on the fourteenth tee. Self 1, just back from Charleston, can't stop laughing at him for this cockeyed optimism. Then the heavens open up, and the two of them, and the round, are washed away.

STARTING OVER

I suppose the story, the search, the journey should end right here—in the rain that erased all traces of the round that might have been. But it doesn't. There's more.

It is the following day and I'm on the practice range. I've decided to take the day off, at least from playing. I plan to spend an hour or so hitting balls, then join Linda and the kids at the beach.

The man immediately to my right has a beautiful swing, though he doesn't have a cowlick. He's neither sun-bleached nor rail-thin. He looks European. If I had to guess I'd say he was northern Italian, a man in his fifties, intelligent-looking. He is the only man on the range not in shorts. He has on soft cotton slacks and a white golf shirt. He wears neither a hat nor a golf glove.

His golf swing is compelling, classic, beautiful to watch. He holds the club down in the fingers, gripping it lightly. At no point, from the time he gently places the club head down behind the ball, through the time he brings the club back over his shoulder, through the downswing, through impact, does he rush, even slightly. After he strikes the ball, his head, his eyes, linger on the spot where the ball has been sitting. He betrays no immediate curiosity about the direction of any of his shots. His head, his eyes, rest for a moment, looking down, seeing a ball there, then not seeing it there, just a shallow, exquisitely neat patch of dirt where the ball had been. Only now do his eyes come up, as slowly as the sun lifts on the horizon. He practices this wonderful swing over and over, without a wobble. His tempo is calm, relaxing to those who are just watching. Just before this accomplished swing draws to a close, the man's hands and arms slow as if gently braked by some kind of silent gear mechanism.

It is at this moment that I break my vow, shatter my resolve. The temptation is just too great. It wells up, then overcomes me: the need to fiddle, tinker, experiment, futz. I take a step back and relax my grip on the six-iron I am holding. I replace it, gently. Now the instrument is cradled down in my fingers, not in my palms. I step up to a ball. Instead of placing the club head a few inches behind it, I rest it directly behind the ball, almost touching. I open my elbows slightly to the sky, keeping my back straight and my chin up. I inform myself that I am no longer holding a sledgehammer, but something more like a string, a taut one, with something like a pocket knife attached to the end. *Keep the string taut*, I remind myself, and remember what Ben Doyle said on that grainy old tape Brad Redding lent me. *The hands don't move*, he insisted in his mumbly way. *The hands are moved.*

Tem-po. Tem-po.

The club head whooshes loudly. The ball takes off as if powered by its own little jets. To produce this startling shot, which burns cleaner, zooms higher, and flies farther than any six-iron I have hit on this trip, I've done little more than allow my arms to swing freely.

I have dared to believe in the simplicity of the swing.

The next day I take this newer-than-new swing out onto the challenging Ocean Course. Unlike so many other times that I've fiddled and futzed, my game doesn't get worse today, it gets even better. I play the front nine in forty-two, all pars and bogeys. The back nine is five strokes messier, but still respectable. On the thirteenth hole, I size up a sixty-six-foot putt. It drops into the center of the cup.

I play out the rest of our time in Kiawah. At no time do I come even close to breaking eighty. But I am almost always in the high eighties, or very close to that, day after day.

It is shortly after our return, and the Big Shooter and I are trying to arrange a golf date at his upstate club. I mention to him that I have given up natural golf and the Spare Parts swing. I have returned to the fold, the palm grip is history. Even though he has heard this song before, he's incredulous. Why, if it was working so well?

At first, I can't really answer his question. I try to explain that the palm-grip swing never really felt right. Sure, it worked okay, harvested a slew of bogeys, a good number of pars, but wielding that sledgehammer never felt, what—graceful? smooth? accomplished?

Later I thought of some other reasons, too.

I gave up the new swing for a newer swing (even though the newer swing was older), because to do so was risky and interesting. The impulse to continue training, John Jerome said in one of his books, "contains the foolish hope that it will open up other mysteries." That's why we fiddle and futz. That's how we learn. And how we get better. Why should I spend the rest of my golfing existence on a plateau, holding a sledgehammer, when I could be staggering on, clutching a live bird?

According to followers of Zen, golf's official religion, it's the journey that matters, not the destination. It's getting better that counts, not breaking eighty. Enlightened men (not necessarily golfers) have been saying that for thousands of years. George Leonard tells the story of the aikido master who, when asked how long it would take to master the art, replied, "How long do you expect to live?"

And there was Buddha himself who, at the end of his own final round, said that if each of us is to live a satisfying life, enriched and enlightened, we must be a lamp unto ourself—illuminating our time on earth by the light of self-discovery.

An eloquent thought, words to live by.

But then, Buddha never tried to hit a two-iron.

Acknowledgments

Sally Field began by thanking her piano teacher. I'd like to end by issuing a general pardon—to that valiant corps of golf instructors who so courageously tried to instruct me in the many mysteries of The Swing: Joel Aptaker, Peggy Kirk Bell, Jackie Bertram, Jim Chorniewy, Jim Flick, Dick Hall, Martin Hall, Pat MacGowan, Joe Mazziotti, Larry Miller, John Mills, Tom Patri, and, most of all, Brad Redding.

Guys, it wasn't your fault.

I'd also like to thank Tom Doak for his invaluable insights into the architecture of golf courses, and Skip Latella for his insights into the anatomy of those who try to hack their way through them.

Thank you, too, to Bill Longley for his generous hospitality and for affording me numerous chances to break eighty on his home course in Bedford, New York. I am also grateful to John Alderman, Sean Driscoll, Ken Godshall, David Goodson, Jack Haire, Tom Jones, Mike Mulhearn, Dick Raskopf, Cynthia Romaker, Barry Seaman, and Bruce Seide for their kind invitations as well.

For their assistance in arranging play at the River Course, I'd like to thank Pat McKinney and Dan Dickison of Kiawah Island Real Estate, as well as Greg French, the head pro there. I am likewise grateful for the efforts of Ashley Truluck of the Kiawah Island Resort, for her help at Osprey Point, Turtle Point, and the Ocean Course.

More personally, I want to issue a hearty thank-you to the trio of hackers who bore witness to the immortal Wedding Round, who watched the O-fer disappear forever into the dank woods, and who in spite of it all remained true and lasting friends: Michael Pollet, Dan Okrent, and Glen Waggoner, whose delightful account of golf's many miseries, *Divots, Shanks, Gimmes, Mulligans, and Chili Dips*, should be required reading for every hacker who ever had the urge to throw his clubs into a lake.

As for this book, I am indebted to three wise men—how wise? well, none is a golfer—who helped launch and shape this project: Rick Kot, executive editor of Hyperion, who is nothing less than every writer's dream editor—astute, funny, supportive; Bob Miller, publisher of Hyperion, who offered immediate enthusiasm and wise counsel when this idea was hatched back in early 1995; and Jay Lovinger, a friend whose presence on a golf course is utterly unimaginable, but who was nonetheless savvy enough about the game to suggest the subtitle.

Liz Darhansoff, my agent, *is* a golfer, as solid a ball-striker as she is a friend, as determined a hacker as she is an agent. On my card she's close to scratch.

I would be remiss if I didn't own up to the fact that my mother, Eve Greenfield, was right all along about this project. (Isn't that what mothers are for?) In fact, this book *wasn't* about work, it *was* just a fancy excuse to play golf. Mom, I love you even though you can see right through me.

To my beloved children, Ned and Katherine, please know that you two are the best teachers I have ever had. You have helped me understand more about more things than I ever could have imagined—which probably means you won't grow up to be golf instructors. But even if you did, I would still love you from the bottom of my heart.

Finally, I want to thank Linda, without whose patience, grace, and intelligence this life, let alone this book, would have turned out to be just one enormous duck hook.

Playing Partners
and Courses

The following men, women, and occasional kid collectively played along just about every step of the way. Many were strangers I'll never see again; the rest are friends and colleagues who kept a straight face when I told them the title of this book. Thanks to each of you for your fellowship and forebearance out on the course, qualities without which golf would be tennis.

John Alderman   Gary Bentley
Harvey Appelle   Lisa Bentley
Rick Bennett   Brian Bishop

Phil Boren	Joel Lulla
Connie Bousquet	Karen Maikisch-Markle
Peter Britton	Randy Mallicote
Cliff Bryant	Kyle McCoy
Larry Byers	Peggy McMichael
Dianna Doak	Irv Miller
Tom Doak	Dick Morris
Jim Dunning	Mike Mulhearn
Ed and Roy	Dan Okrent
Lee Gatewood	John Okrent
Peter Gethers	Harry Plautin
Ken Godshall	Robert Pondiscio
David Goodson	Tony Randazzo
Arthur Gosnell	Dick Raskopf
Alan Greenberg	Cynthia Romaker
Leo Groenings	Bill Saar
Fred Gruber	Barry Seaman
Jack Haire	Bruce Seide
Bruce Hallett	Geoffrey Symonds
Elise Harman	Frank Travis
Gary Hoenig	Brian Vergin
Gib Ingram	Doc Vinson
Tom Ingram	Glen Waggoner
Clarke Langlall	Jack Walklet
Paul Lieber	Georgette Walsh
Bill Longley	

In 1963, a golfer named Floyd Rood hacked his way into the *Guinness Book of Records* by playing golf clear across the United States, 3,397 miles coast-to-coast. In so doing, he shot a 114,737 and lost 3,511 balls. I can relate to that. The following courses are where *this* journey played out, and where eighty escaped unharmed:

Ardsley Country Club, Ardsley, New York
Bedford Golf and Tennis Club, Bedford, New York
Boca Raton Resort Course, Boca Raton, Florida

Doral Country Club, Miami, Florida

Egwani Farms Golf Course, Rockford, Tennessee

The Governor's Club, Chapel Hill, North Carolina

The Harbour Course, Ocean Reef Club, Key Largo, Florida

High Pointe Golf Club, Traverse City, Michigan

Holston Hills Country Club, Knoxville, Tennessee

Mid Pines Resort, Southern Pines, North Carolina

Mount Kisco Country Club, Mt. Kisco, New York

National Golf Links of America, Southampton, New York

Oak Harbor Golf Course, New Orleans, Louisiana

The Ocean Course, Kiawah Island, South Carolina

Osprey Point Golf Club, Kiawah Island, South Carolina

Patterson Club, Fairfield, Connecticut

Pine Needles Resort, Southern Pines, North Carolina

Pound Ridge Golf Club, Pound Ridge, New York

Red Hook Golf Club, Red Hook, New York

The River Course, Kiawah Island, South Carolina

Royal Westmoreland, Barbados

The Sagamore, Bolton Landing, New York

Sandy Lane Golf Club, Barbados

Sea Island Golf Club, Sea Island, Georgia

Siwanoy Country Club, Bronxville, New York

Stanwich Country Club, Greenwich, Connecticut

Tom Carvel Golf Club, Pine Plains, New York

Turtle Point, Kiawah Island, South Carolina

Westchester Country Club, Harrison, New York

Willow Creek Golf Club, Knoxville, Tennessee

Selected Reading List

The following titles were of particular value as source material for this book. Golfers, read them at your own peril.

Alexander, Jules, et al., *The Hogan Mystique* (Greenwich, CT: The American Golfer, Inc., 1995).

Armour, Tommy, *How to Play Your Best Golf All the Time* (New York: Simon & Schuster, 1953).

Aultman, Dick, and the editors of *Golf Digest, The Square-to-Square Golf Swing* (New York: Simon & Schuster, 1970).

Ballard, Jimmy, *How to Perfect Your Golf Swing* (Norwalk, CT: Golf Digest Books, 1981).

Barlow, Al, *Gettin' to the Dance Floor* (New York: Atheneum, 1986).

Barnes, James M., *Picture Analysis of Golf Strokes* (Philadelphia: J. B. Lippincott, 1919).

Beck, Charlotte Joko, *Everyday Zen* (San Francisco: Harper Collins, 1989).

Cochran, A. J., and M. R. Farrally, eds., *Science and Golf II: Proceedings of the 1994 World Scientific Congress of Golf* (London: E & FN Spon, 1994).

Cochran, Alistair, and John Stobbs, *The Search for the Perfect Swing* (Philadelphia: Lippincott, 1968).

Davies, Peter, *The Historical Dictionary of Golfing Terms* (New York: Michael Kesend, Ltd., 1992).

Doak, Tom, *The Anatomy of a Golf Course* (New York: Lyons & Burford, 1992).

Gallwey, W. Timothy, *The Inner Game of Golf* (New York: Random House, 1979).

Gardner, Howard, *Frames of Mind* (New York: Basic Books, 1983).

Hendricks, Gay, and Jon Carlson, *The Centered Athlete* (Englewood Cliffs, NJ: Prentice-Hall, 1982).

Hogan, Ben, *Five Lessons: The Modern Fundamentals of Golf* (Trumbull, CT: Golf Digest Books, 1957).

Jerome, John, *Staying with It* (New York: Viking Press, 1982).

———, *The Sweet Spot in Time* (New York: Summit Books, 1980).

Jobe, Frank W., M.D., and Diane R. Moynes, *30 Exercises for Better Golf* (Inglewood, CA: Champion Press, 1986).

Jones, Robert Trent, Jr., *Golf by Design* (New York: Little, Brown, 1993).

Jones, Robert Tyre (Bobby), *Bobby Jones on Golf* (New York: Doubleday, 1966).

Kelly, Homer, *The Golfing Machine* (Seattle: Star System Press, 1969).

Lasch, Christopher, *The Culture of Narcissism* (New York: W. W. Norton, 1978).

Leonard, George, *Mastery* (New York: Plume, 1991).

————, *The Ultimate Athlete* (New York: Viking Press, 1974).

Longhurst, Henry, *The Best of Henry Longhurst* (Norwalk, CT: Golf Digest Books, 1978).

MacKenzie, Alister, *The Spirit of St. Andrews* (Chelsea, MI: Sleeping Bear Press, 1995).

McLean, Jim, *The Eight-Step Swing* (New York: HarperCollins, 1994).

McMillan, Robin, *365 One-Minute Golf Lessons* (New York: HarperCollins, 1994).

McMillan, Robin, and John Andrisani, *The Golf Doctor* (New York: Villard Books, 1990).

Miller, Larry, *Holographic Golf* (New York: HarperCollins, 1993).

Morrison, Alec, *The Impossible Art of Golf* (New York: Oxford University Press, 1994).

Murphy, Michael, *Golf in the Kingdom* (New York: Viking Press, 1972).

Nicklaus, Jack, with Ken Bowden, *Golf My Way* (New York: Simon & Schuster, 1974).

Olman, John M. and Morton W., *Olman's Guide to Golf Antiques* (Cincinnati: Market Street Press, 1991).

Owen, David, *My Usual Game* (New York: Villard Books, 1995).

Palmer, Arnold, *My Game and Yours* (New York: Simon & Schuster, 1983).

Pelz, Dave, with Nick Mastroni, *Putt Like the Pros* (New York: Harper & Row, 1989).

Penick, Harvey, with Bud Shrake, *Harvey Penick's Little Red Book* (New York: Simon & Schuster, 1992).

————, *And If You Play Golf, You're My Friend* (New York: Simon & Schuster, 1993).

Peper, George, ed., *Golf in America* (New York: Harry N. Abrams, 1987).

Player, Gary, *Golf Begins at Fifty* (New York: Simon & Schuster, 1988).

Raines, Howell, *Fly Fishing Through the Midlife Crisis* (New York: Doubleday, 1994).

Rotella, Dr. Bob, *Golf Is Not a Game of Perfect* (New York: Simon & Schuster, 1995).

Rotella, Robert J., and Linda K. Bunker, *Mind Mastery for Winning Golf* (Englewood Cliffs, NJ: Prentice-Hall, 1981).

Ryde, Peter, ed., *Mostly Golf: A Bernard Darwin Anthology* (London: Adam and Charles Black, 1976).

Saunders, Vivien, *The Golfing Mind* (New York: Atheneum, 1988).

Sheehy, Gail, *Passages* (New York: E. P. Dutton, 1974).

Snead, Sam, *The Education of a Golfer* (New York: Simon & Schuster, 1961).

Thompson, Kenneth R., *The Mental Side of Golf* (New York: Funk & Wagnalls, 1939).

Toski, Bob, *Bob Toski's Complete Guide to Better Golf* (New York: Atheneum, 1984).

Tutko, Thomas, and Umberto Tosi, *Sports Psyching* (New York: G. P. Putnam's, 1976).

Waggoner, Glen, *Divots, Shanks, Gimmes, Mulligans, and Chili Dips* (New York: Villard Books, 1993).

Watson, Tom, with Nick Seitz, *Getting Up and Down* (New York: Random House, 1983).